FLASHPOINT!

Above: Mujahideen in Nangrahar, Afghanistan, in 1981, move up for a night attack.

At the Front Line of Today's Wars

ARMS AND ARMOUR

ANTHONY ROGERS

KEN GUEST

JIM HOOPER

FLASHPOINT!

Below: A regular PLO fighter, in his green fatigues, throws a hand grenade in Beirut. The satchel over his shoulder contains more grenades.

Contents

Arms and Armour Press
A Cassell Imprint
Villiers House, 41-47 Strand,
London WC2N 5JE.

Distributed in the USA by
Sterling Publishing Co. Inc.,
387 Park Avenue South, New York,
NY 10016-8810.

Distributed in Australia by
Capricorn Link (Australia) Pty. Ltd,
2/13 Carrington Road, Castle Hill,
NSW 2154.

British Library Cataloguing-in-Publication
Data: a catalogue record for this book is
available from the British Library

ISBN 1-85409-247-2

Designed and edited by
DAG Publications Ltd.
Designed by David Gibbons;
layout by Anthony A. Evans.
Printed in Spain

Below: A twisted logistics vehicle and its cargo of Soviet-made 100mm tank shells, 122mm MBRL rockets, 82mm mortar bombs and RPG boosters litter the battlefield near the Cunzumbia River in Angola.

Introduction

I f we have any feelings for our world it behoves us all to know it better, to understand it more deeply, to acknowledge its faults as well as its benefits. However unsavoury we might find it, no harm can come to us by our obtaining a greater knowledge of the dire scenes of conflict which afflict regions far removed from our daily lives. And we should not satisfy ourselves with the necessarily brief information offered to us by television news programmes.

This book seeks to give a greater insight into seven of the 'hot spots' which have seen war over recent years. The photographs were taken to record and inform; the circumstances were seldom exhilarating but, more often, frightening and upsetting. You do not work closely with people, even in a front-line war, without sharing their traumas. The words come from the knowledge of the region which can be gained from study, but are enhanced by the authors' closeness to the subject, which has come from first-hand experience. The information is provided by those they met, lived with, travelled alongside and watched fight for their cause.

Whilst all hope for a day when there will be no warfare to discuss or illustrate, we should all have an understanding of why, how and where wars are currently being fought so as to contribute to the debate which, with political wisdom, might bring them to an end.

KEN GUEST

Afghanistan

A fghanistan is one of the least accessible and poorest countries on earth. It is roughly the size of Texas, and the harsh landscape is riven by great mountain ranges and perilous deserts. The scarcity of good, arable ground has fostered warlike habits among the Afghan tribes: for centuries they swept down from their barren hills, to carry out cross-border raids on the fertile Indian subcontinent. It is difficult to see why anyone should wish to invade such a place. Yet the Russians are only the latest in a long line of protagonists to enter the Afghan arena. The history of Afghanistan is a brutal litany of incursion by greater regional powers – Greeks heading north, Mongols heading south, Persians heading east and Indians heading west. Afghanistan itself has not been the prize, but the highway to conquest.

Alexander the Great, who campaigned in the region between 329 and 327 BC, was one of the first invaders to appreciate the Afghans' robust devotion to their rugged land. He is reputed to have observed that Afghanistan could be occupied, but not vanquished. History was to prove him right. In the eighth century a new kind of conqueror arrived – Islam.[1] The Islamic reformation ignited Central Asia and changed the nature of Afghan society for ever. Henceforth Afghan resistance against the pagan invaders would be a matter of *Jihad* (Holy War). In the centuries that followed, many great armies passed through Afghanistan's unforgiving mountains to subdue the fierce tribes, but few remained for long to hold the tiger by the tail.

The Golden Horde of Ghengis Khan laid waste to the land in the thirteenth century. They were followed, in 1398, by Tamerlane's Mongol horsemen, who galloped in from the Steppes to destroy anything missed by the earlier invasion. People living in central Afghanistan today, who retain a Mongol appearance, maintain that they are the direct descendants of Tamerlane's men. The Mongol forces operated in units each comprising a thousand horsemen and known as a *Hazara*. According to local belief, some of them were trapped when the main force withdrew. The Afghans attribute the regional name of *Hazara Jut* (Land of the Thousand) to that event. Similarly, Afghans from the remote mountains of *Nuristan* (Kingdom of Light) believe themselves to be descendants from the earlier invasion of Alexander the Great.[2] In the sixteenth century another Mongol king, Babur the Tiger, set off from the Afghan capital,

Left: One of the central pillars of Afghan society was their devout belief in Islam. A Mujahid on the plain of Khost, in Paktia, performs one of the five daily prayers demanded by the faith.

1. Previously the dominant religion had been Buddhism, although earlier, pagan culture endured in some regions.

2. This legend is fuelled by the fact that, unusally among Afghans, many Nuristanis are fair-haired.

9

Kabul, to found the great Mohgul dynasty in India. However, when the Mohguls returned later to conduct war against the Afghans, they suffered accordingly. The Yusufzai tribe of eastern Afghanistan destroyed 8,000 Mohgul soldiers in 1587; the Afridis killed 10,000 more in 1672 and decimated an entire army in 1673.

The Afghan nation which evolved from the comings and goings of these passing conquerors was one divided by ethnic origin, language, social mores and political persuasion. Among all of this wide diversity there were only three things that the Afghans agreed upon. The first, and most deeply rooted, was that the land, bleak as it was, belonged to them and no others. The second and third were the cornerstones of their Islamic belief – that there was but one God (Allah), and that Mohammed was his prophet. Any attempt either to wrest their land from them or to interfere with their religion would be fiercely resisted. The mountains of Afghanistan are littered with the bones of foreign invaders who have failed to appreciate this.

In 1747 a Pathan, Ahmad Shah Abdali, rose from the ashes of another collapsing dynasty and forged a new nation, known for the first time as Afghanistan. As the king of this new nation, Ahmad Shah Abdali became better known as *Durran Durrani* (Pearl of Pearls). His southern Pathan tribe adopted the Durrani name and have been major players in Afghan power struggles ever since.

By the nineteenth century, Afghanistan was coming under increasing pressure from the 'gunboat diplomacy' of her new colonial neighbours. In 1839, Britain dispatched an army into Afghanistan, sparking off the first Anglo-Afghan War. Initial British successes, including the occupation of Kabul, were outweighed by later humiliating defeats. Looming large among these was the near-total destruction of the British force compelled to evacuate Kabul in January 1842. The shipwrecked honour of the British Army was rescued by a brief reoccupation of the capital before withdrawal from the country in December of the same year.

In 1878 the touchpaper was lit again when a Russian mission arrived in Kabul. This struck a raw nerve among Russophobic officers in the British Indian Army, who feared it was a prelude to Russian armies marching down the Khyber Pass towards India. They demanded that the Afghans expel the delegation. The Afghans refused, and in the eyes of the British there was thus only one solution – invasion. Events in this second Anglo-Afghan War bore an unhealthy similarity to the first. Initial successes (including the obligatory occupation of Kabul) were soon followed by costly defeats.

During the Battle of Maiwand in 1880 over a thousand British troops were killed. Once again, suitable face-saving revenge was exacted before the British finally left.

The roles were reversed in 1919, when a small Afghan invasion force occupied the Indian border village of Bagh. This sparked off the Third Anglo-Afghan War. Lasting only a month, it was most notable for a new feature of such conflicts – aerial bombing. On 24 May 1919, a British Handley Page biplane bomber flew 140 miles to reach Kabul and released twenty bombs. Of these, four hit the Palace, one hit the tomb of Amir Abdur Rahman and a third destroyed Kabul's only ammunition factory. Honour satisfied, peace followed soon afterwards.

Afghanistan's last king, Zahir Shah, was ousted from power in a bloodless coup on 17 July 1973 while he was away on a diplomatic mission to Italy. The perpetrator was his cousin, Mohammed Daoud, who immediately declared Afghanistan a

Above: The invading Mongols left a permanent reminder of their invasion in the form of Buzkashi, the national sport of Afghanistan. Two teams, mounted on fast horses, compete to score by placing the dead carcase of a goat in the scoring circle of the opposing team. It is said that, when the sport was first introduced, prisoners were used instead of goats! When teams of up to 100 horsemen gather for a really big game, it looks for all the world as though the invading Mongols are back. It is not so much a sport as all-out medieval warfare.

Above left: A Buzkashi player in the Panjshir valley.

Above: Additional merit is earned if prayers are performed communally. These Mujahideen in Nangraha in 1981 are being led in prayer by their commander, Doctor Hamid. The title of Doctor, like that of Engineer, is often applied in Afghanistan as an honorific, and does not necessarily mean that the man is qualified in these fields. Doctor Hamid had been a first-year medical student before he abandoned his studies to join the Mujahideen.

Right: A Pathan Mujahid from Paktia in 1981, regionally identifiable by the way he wears his *patkhy* (turban).

republic. Five years later, in 1978, President Daoud was in turn deposed and killed in what became known as the *Saur* (April) Revolution. The new President was Mohammed Taraki, who strengthened links with communist Russia by signing a Soviet-Afghan Friendship Treaty in December 1978. Less than a year later he was killed in yet another coup. This time the victor was former Prime Minister Haffizullah Amin, but, like his predecessors, Amin was destined not to wear the mantle of the Presidency for long.

When Britain had ruled India many of her officers had been firmly convinced that one day the Russians would come. Thirty-two years after the last British sentry guarding the Khyber Pass had packed up his kit bag and gone home, they were finally proved correct: on 24 December 1979 President Amin was assassinated by Soviet Special Forces spearheading the Russian invasion. The Russians hastily recalled the exiled Afghan communist Barbrak Karmal to step into Amin's still-

warm shoes as the next President, and Afghanistan slid into all-out guerrilla warfare against the Russian presence.

In 1979 the Cold War was still a reality. The consensus of Western opinion in the wake of the Christmas Eve invasion was that Kabul was not the ultimate objective: observers feared that it was but a stepping stone in the old Russian dream of warm-water ports on the Indian Ocean. In 1919 Leon Trotsky had told the Central Committee of the Russian Communist Party , 'The road to Paris and London lies through the towns of Afghanistan, the Punjab and Bengal.' However, Trotsky was long dead and the world had changed beyond all recognition. Whether the ultimate Soviet goal was Kabul or further afield must be left for the historians to debate.

WEAPONS

Reports of Mujahideen fighting the Russians with antiquated black-powder jezzails can be dismissed as romantic fiction. While there *were* many old weapons around, including an assortment of black-powder weapons, few contemplated using them except while posing for photographs. When the war got under way antique weapons were more than offset by the huge volume of modern arms, and no self-respecting Mujahid would dream of confronting the conventionally armed Russian infantry with a black-powder musket. However, this did not impinge on the flow of heroic, contemporary folklore describing such uneven contests.

Even before the war, the possession of a weapon was a prerequisite to the Afghan sense of machismo. This was particularly true among the Pathans in the lands bordering Pakistan. Among these tribes honour demanded the participation in armed feuds, some of which dated back generations. Although the Afghan Mujahideen made no weapons of their own, enterprising village gunsmiths in the adjoining Pakistani tribal lands turned out a ready supply of arms. Most of these locally produced weapons were inferior imitations of the originals. Nevertheless, when the war broke out in 1979 this region was already a well-stocked gun bazaar.

Armed resistance to the communist government in Kabul began before the Russian invasion as most Afghans considered communism 'un-Islamic'. Although it was partly sponsored by Pakistan, which supplied both limited training and some arms, the largest single source of modern weaponry for the Mujahideen in this phase was the Afghan Army itself. Sometimes arms were seized by force, but far more came from deserting Afghan

Far left: It is the duty of all Muslims to defend their faith, particularly against pagan invaders. Haji Khan, with his First World War-vintage No.4 Lee Enfield, volunteered to serve with local Mujahideen in the Safed Khoh range of mountains in 1980. Like many Afghans, his head has been shaved to counter the summer heat. Haji is an honorific term used for anyone who has fulfilled his Islamic obligation to go on *Haj* (pilgrimage) to Mecca at least once in his life. Many Muslims save all their lives to perform this duty. However, most Afghans were simply too poor and, when age began to frost their beards, were granted the title Haji out of respect, with no one enquiring too closely whether they had actually made the pilgrimage.

Above right: Rauf Attullah was 14 years old when he was orphaned by the war in 1981. He left his village near Jalalabad and went to join his uncle with the Mujahideen in the Safed Koh mountains of Nangraha. He is armed with an Iranian G-3 assault rifle, a large number of which entered Afghanistan on the black market after the Shah of Iran had been deposed. Rauf wears Chinese green canvas chest webbing manufactured to complement the Chinese Type 56, a carbine copy of the Soviet SKS. Tucked into one pocket of the webbing is a small Chinese hand grenade.

soldiers, who abandoned the government cause in their thousands. The Mujahideen were even able to obtain limited numbers of weapons from the Soviet forces. The Russians made the mistake of sending Islamic troops (conscripted from Soviet Central Asia) to Afghanistan, in the belief that they would be more acceptable to the Afghans. Most of the black market trading that took place with these troops occurred before the fighting became widespread. Soviet soldiers who indulged in this profiteering had not yet had cause to feel threatened by the sale of a few weapons here and there. Despite these factors, weapons were not always available to the Afghans in sufficient quantities and at the right time. The speed with which the conflict escalated, from low-key, localised clashes into a war of nation-wide proportions, caught everyone off guard, including the Mujahideen.

The first consignments of Western-supplied arms appeared as early as 1980. Initially these were mostly old, stockpiled weapons no longer in service with Western forces. Rifles such as the tried and tested Mks IV and V .303 Lee Enfield were dated but mechanically sound. They were also rugged, easy to maintain and accurate up to 1,000 metres. Moreover, as bolt-action weapons with ten-round magazines, they imposed a degree of fire discipline absent among the Mujahideen, who were largely untrained.

The AK-47 Assault Rifle

As Afghan resistance to the Soviet occupation increased, the West began to improve the supply of weapons. Ideally the Mujahideen required small-arms that utilized the most readily available ammunition – Russian 7.62mm rimless rounds. The AK-47 and its many variants formed the natural choice, the most prolific types being Chinese Type 56 copies (Chinese copies of the Soviet SKS carbine were also common). These well made, sturdy weapons were immensely popular. By 1986 the AK-47 was by far the most dominant weapon among the Mujahideen. Surprisingly, despite the rifle's increased rate of fire in fully automatic mode (favoured by the Afghans), few Mujahids carried more than one or two 30-round magazines, relying instead on Providence to supply their needs. Many were to be fatally disappointed in time of crisis.

With the decline of the Lee-Enfield came a corresponding drop in marksmanship. Only small numbers of Mujahideen, mostly older tribesmen, had truly mastered their weapons. Among the younger generation, volume of fire was more important than accuracy.

The AK-74

It was not long, before another weapon was to lead the Mujahideen wish-list – the new Soviet 5.45mm AK-74, known locally as the *Kalikov*. When these

Above: A silhouette of a Mujahid with a Czechoslova-kian ZB30 light machine gun. These weapons were supplied to Afghanistan in the Second World War as part of an arms package from the Germans.

Above right: The 12.7mm Dshk was occasionally used for direct ground action, and this one is seen in use at Gandamack in Nangraha. Gandamack was the scene of the last stand of the British army retreating from Kabul in 1842, and the site where a treaty was signed in 1879 during the Second Anglo-Afghan War.

Right: Nassrullah arming 60mm mortar bombs with fuses, Tamai 1981. (See overleaf.)

3. The 5.45mm round had a much greater muzzle velocity (900 metres per second, compared to the 7.62mm AK-47's 600 metres per second) and tumbled on entry into the body, causing catastrophic tissue damage. Serious infection followed and this, due to the Mujahideen's ignorance of even basic first aid, often proved fatal.

first appeared in small numbers in 1981 the Afghans reported that they fired 'poison' bullets owing to the high fatality rate among men hit by the new, smaller rounds.[3] Later, as more Soviet troops were equipped with the weapon, larger numbers of AK-74s appeared in Mujahideen hands, though the supply of ammunition remained a problem.

Light Machine Guns (LMGs)

Supplementing the firepower of the assault rifles were light machine guns. The most prolific among these was the 7.62mm belt-fed RPD, dubbed *Schul Daz* by the Mujahideen after its belt of 100 bullets. There were also old Goryunon SG43s, mostly used for air defence, and a few examples of the Czech 7.92mm ZB30 (from which the British had developed the more famous and almost identical Bren Gun).

Heavy Machine Guns (HMGs)

By 1981 the Mujahideen had also received consignments of the DShKM 12.7mm HMG, known to them as the *Dashaka*. These were deployed in large numbers and were most often used for air defence, although occasionally also in direct support of ground attacks against enemy posts. About the same time 14.5mm ZPU-1 and ZGU-1 HMGs (or *Zirgriot*s) were appearing. Difficult to portage, these were used exclusively for the air defence of fixed bases. The Mujahideen were extremely proud of these weapons and keen to fire them, and any base which possessed one had a tendency to echo to the sound of constant 'test' firing at nearby ridges.

Rocket-Propelled Grenades (RPGs)

Among a range of support weapons, the mainstay of the Mujahideen anti-armour arsenal was the RPG-7. While this lightweight weapon gave them some close protection against Soviet armour, it was not popular as a personal weapon. Operators had to get close and rarely had the opportunity to fire more than one or two shots. Nevertheless, it was an essential weapon and was responsible for the destruction of hundreds of Soviet tanks, armoured cars and trucks. The Mujahideen also used it extensively against fixed positions.

With ever greater numbers of RPG-7s (and Type 69 Chinese copies) reaching Mujahideen hands, modifications were introduced to Soviet armour to limit the effects of any hits. Skirt armour and turret blocks were added, although the rear doors of BMP armoured personnel carriers remained vulnerable, not least because they doubled as fuel tanks!

Recoilless Rifles

Both the 75mm recoilless rifle and, later, the smaller, more portable 82mm, were used by the Mujahideen. They were deployed more frequently as direct-fire weapons against fixed enemy positions than against moving armour. Alternatively, they were sometimes used at extreme range as a mobile light artillery.

If the Mujahideen were hard-pressed, heavy weapons were abandoned in favour of a rapid retreat into the hills. The 75mm recoilless rifle, being large and heavy, was often lost by its owners during Afghan Army and Soviet ground offensives.

Mines

The Mujahideen made much use of mines. These might be laid individually, on roads linking Soviet positions, or en masse, to blunt Soviet offensives. While they undeniably caused many Soviet casualties during the war, there were also a lot of 'own goals' among the Mujahideen: local commanders operated independently and were invariably oblivious to the whereabouts of mines laid by other Mujahideen factions, often with fatal consequences.

Mortars

The most useful support weapon possessed by the Mujahideen was the Russian M1937 82mm mortar. It was man-portable and could be transported over precipitous mountains and easily assembled. The high trajectory of the weapon enabled it to be sited in a gully, protected from direct return fire by tanks, heavy machine guns or small-arms. Its main disadvantage was that it required a trained crew. While the Mujahideen were enthusiastic bombardiers, they did not generally have the skill to use the full

potential of the weapon, although, with plenty of opportunity for practice, some did become proficient. Chinese 60mm mortars were also used. While these were light and mobile, they lacked hitting power, particularly against fixed or entrenched positions.

The Soviets used their greater range of mortars (82mm to 160mm) to far greater effect. Trained Soviet mortar crews brought their weapons into action much faster than *ad hoc* Mujahideen crews although, against widely dispersed guerrillas on precipitous terrain, the damage might still be surprisingly slight. Nonetheless, Soviet teams worked in coordination with one another, increasing the effectiveness of the barrage. Around fixed bases they used predesignated Defensive Fire Zones (DFZs). To be caught in a Soviet DFZ was no laughing matter.

Artillery

Most Soviet strategic and tactical philosophy was derived from the savage battles of the Second World War. Consequently the Soviet war machine had a devout respect for artillery (Stalin had referred to it as 'Russia's god of war'). In

Above: Some of Jalaluddin Haqani's Mujahideen admire a recent additon to his arsenal, an 82mm recoilless rifle.

Below left: For many years, the backbone of Mujahideen stand-off strike capability was the 82mm mortar. It had to be carefully sited at night, as the flash when firing could reveal its location. Here one is seen in action against Tamai, in Zurmat, in 1982.

Below: Mujahideen with a 60mm mortar at Memakh Khiel, Nangraha, in 1981.

Right: A 76mm gun captured by the Mujahideen. The problems of manoeuvring artillery pieces, and keeping them supplied, restricted their employment by the Mujahideen. A few saw limited use close to the Pakistan border.

Afghanistan the Soviet forces were firm supporters of the use of artillery barrages. Typical tactical deployment involved a rolling barrage in advance of mechanized armour and infantry. While ideal for the flat steppes of the Soviet Republic or in western Europe, this technique was less effective against a widely dispersed guerrilla resistance in mountainous terrain. When the Afghan resistance refused to lie down and die, the Soviets experimented with an American approach to the thorny problem of counter-insurgency operations – 'area denial by fire' to keep the guerrillas at bay.

As was to be expected among a guerrilla force operating in difficult terrain, the Mujahideen lacked artillery. A few smaller pieces, mostly 76mm howitzers, were located in bases close to (and even inside) Pakistan, and occasionally these were dusted down and used in larger operations close to the border. Only after the Soviet withdrawal did a significant number of artillery pieces fall into Mujahideen hands – in time for the civil war that followed.

Multi-Barrel Rocket Launchers (MBRLs)
From the mid-1980s the multi-barrel rocket launcher began to overtake the mortar as the Mujahideen's most favoured offensive weapon. Its greater range helped to offset their loss of ground to increasingly effective Soviet counter-insurgency operations. The standard Mujahideen rocket was the Chinese Type 63 107mm. These were supplemented by the 122mm, which had an even greater

16

Below: The terrain made target acquisition difficult, as the Mujahideen were often well sheltered by multiple ridge lines such as these, 20km east of Kabul.

Above: These two Mi-34s (an export version of the Mi-24) flew into the Panjshir valley and surrendered to Ahmad Shah Massoud after the Russians pulled out of Afghanistan in 1989.

Right: Mujahid carries a Stinger up a mountain in Paktia during 1986. He was one of NIFA's two-man Stinger teams, trained in Pakistan and known as 'The Sacrificers'.

4. Standard 250/50kg bombs or RBK-250 cluster bomb dispensers (each containing sixty AO-2-5-2 high-explosive bomblets).

5. Four UV-32-57 rocket pods, with 128 S-5.57mm rockets.

6. Replaced on later 'Hind-Fs' with a twin-barrel 23mm GSh cannon.

7. They dropped pods which opened during descent, showering hundreds of PFM-1 anti-personnel mines (known as 'butterfly mines') over a wide area.

range. The Soviet and Afghan Army arsenals also included larger calibre MBRLs – 122mm, 140mm and 240mm.

Tanks

The Soviets and their Afghan Army allies deployed hundreds of tanks during the war. The standard workhorse of Soviet armoured divisions was the T-62. Older T-54s and T-55s were used by the Afghan Army, which also possessed a few T-34s of Second World War vintage. Later in the war, when the Soviets upgraded their arsenal, T-72s and T-80s (with reactive armour) arrived. However, lacking an armoured enemy to engage, Soviet tanks were used as static or mobile artillery in support of infantry operations.

The Mujahideen did not have the resources to crew and maintain captured tanks, nor could they obtain ammunition. Even if this had not been the case, the usefulness of these vehicles was somewhat limited to a guerrilla force operating predominantly in mountainous terrain and most armour captured by the Mujahideen was simply set alight. In 1982 Commander Jalaluddin Haqani captured two intact T-54s in Zurmat. Despite the best efforts of his men to spirit them away, they had to be abandoned in the mountains with the onset of winter. The following spring a second attempt was made to convey them to Pakistan but this also failed. In the end the only casualty caused by these particular T-54s was an Italian journalist, Raffaele Favero: a Mujahideen tank driver reversed over him while he was filming their attempts to retrieve the tanks from the mountains.

After the Soviet withdrawal in 1989 the *modus operandi* of the Mujahideen changed. As the forces

of the Communist Afghan government teetered, the resistance captured more tanks. In their 1991 attack on Gardez, shortly before the final collapse of Kabul, the Mujahideen used as many as fifty tanks. However, for the majority of the war, the most significant mechanised item deployed by the Mujahideen was not the tank but the Toyota pick-up truck! This improved their mobility and was hardwearing, versatile and capable of withstanding severe punishment over rough terrain.

AIR DEFENCE

One of the deadliest weapons deployed by Soviet forces against the Mujahideen was the helicopter gunship. The Mi-24 'Hind-D' could fly at 156 knots carrying a fully equipped section of eight men in the back and deliver a formidable payload. Its armaments were bombs,[4] rocket-pods[5] and a chin-mounted, four-barrel gatling gun capable of firing 3,400 rounds a minute.[6] In addition, the air-delivery of mines[7] meant that the Afghans had to remain alert to danger even in inaccessible areas.

In the Mi-24 the Soviets possessed the perfect weapon for the task confronting them. At first they squandered this advantage through a combination of inexperience and over-caution: they were slow to capitalise on the tactical advantages of the surprise air-delivery of combat troops and to explore the possibilities of close air/ground co-ordination in support of such troops.

In Vietnam, a decade earlier, American heli-

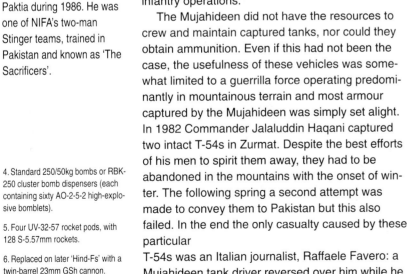

Left: Engineer Abdul Rahman had been a major in the Egyptian Army, and had gone to Afghanistan for his vacation. Although he had no training to fire the SAM-7, he insisted that he be allowed to fire one of the few with which Commander Jalaluddin Haqani had been supplied.

Above: A quad-barrelled 12.7mm HMG being used for the air defence of a Mujahideen base in Paktia Province in 1981.

8. The effectiveness of the RPG decreases dramatically after the first 200 metres. By the maximum range of 500 metres, the probability of a hit is around 5 per cent.

copters had been vulnerable to small-arms fire. Consequently, at the beginning of the war Russian pilots tended to attack from an altitude which rendered both gunship attacking fire and Mujahideen defensive fire inaccurate and ineffectual. In fact, the superior design and armament of the Mi-24 made it almost impervious to small-arms. Such oversights allowed the Mujahideen a breathing space in which to gain experience of air-attack strategy. It was immediately obvious that there was no comparison between a hit on an Mi-24 with an assault rifle and a hit on a Mujahid by a 1,000lb bomb! The Afghans began to hate the Mi-24 with a vengeance and treat it with respect.

The first standard defensive measure universally adopted by the Mujahideen involved the use of a blanket! At that stage – before American and Saudi aid projects distributed sleeping bags – every Afghan carried a blanket, called a *petou*. These came, almost exclusively, in varying shades of natural brown or grey. If caught in the open by approaching gunships, the Mujahideen would immediately lie on the ground and cover themselves with their *petous*. Against a background of earth, scrub and rock, this simple procedure rendered them invisible from the air. However, although the blanket was an effective and cheap defence during most encounters with gunships, it was of little use if the latter were flying an area-denial mission, bombing, rocketing and strafing irrespective of ground activity. Survival under these

circumstances was reliant upon another essential ingredient for the guerrilla fighter — luck.

Although, in the early years, the Mujahideen possessed few weapons capable of inflicting significant damage to an Mi-24, the Soviets did suffer losses. Afghan spokesmen claimed that some low-flying gunships had been downed with RPG-7 anti-tank rockets. With a maximum range of 500 metres,[8] the RPG would have to be very close to a hovering helicopter to score a hit; furthermore, the flash of a rocket discharge would reveal the location of the gunner. Helicopters hovering to land troops were closely supported by other helicopters circling above, and it would take a very brave, or very desperate, Mujahid to launch an RPG in such circumstances. Nonetheless, given the quantity of the RPGs possessed by the Mujahideen, and the opportunities to target helicopters as they landed or took off, it is possible that a few helicopters were destroyed in this manner.

When consignments of 12.7mm heavy machine guns began to reach the Afghans they were deployed in large numbers, but, unless several were able to achieve a concentration of fire, they were limited in effectiveness against the helicopter gunships. More effective were the larger calibre 14.5mm HMGs: with armour-piercing ammunition, these could inflict serious damage on an Mi-24. Unfortunately for the Afghans, the heavy 14.5mm guns were difficult to portage by mule or camel and were generally restricted to air-defence duties at base camps.

At the end of 1985 a new weapon appeared – the Oerlikon-Buhrle GA1-B01, a single-barrel, 20mm anti-aircraft gun. This had an effective range of 12,000-18,000 metres and was by far the largest piece of ordnance that the Mujahideen acquired from the West, but it was unsuited to mobile guerrilla warfare as it was bulky and weighed 1,500lb. The Oerlikon's presence in Afghanistan owed more to Western 'feel-good' propaganda than to a sound military justification for its deployment and probably fewer than 40 were delivered.

The West had not been slow to recognise the need for surface-to-air missile technology to counter the Russian air threat. Soviet 9M32 'Strela-2' missiles (known in the West as SAM-7s) had been purchased from Egypt and supplied as early as 1980. A few Mujahideen had been trained in secret camps in Pakistan to operate the new weapon. The SAM-7's effective deployment was hindered by several factors. First, the weapon system had been designed to be used in concentrated numbers as part of a co-ordinated defence plan. Under such conditions, an attacking aircraft would

find it difficult to evade the many missiles homing in simultaneously from different directions. However, used on a 'one-off' basis, as they were in Afghanistan, the weapons performed poorly. Secondly, the social hierarchy of the Afghans meant that the Mujahid trained to operate the system in Pakistan was often not the one to fire the missile back in Afghanistan. Commander Jalaluddin Haqani was supplied with seven SAM-7s in early 1981. Of these, he allowed five to be used by various (untrained) neighbouring commanders in goodwill gestures and one by a former Egyptian Army major enjoying a vacation on *Jihad* in Afghanistan, leaving only one for Malim Shakoor, the man actually trained to use it. A further problem was that the missiles supplied were often defective. Of the same seven missiles, two barely left the launcher, falling to the ground a few feet away; three ground-looped (hitting a boulder, a stretch of water and the building being used by the Mujahideen as a base); and two flew an erratic flight path before falling back to earth as the Mujahideen ran for cover.

Initial supplies of SAM-7s were quickly exhausted, but the Mujahideen had in any case lost all confidence in them. Nevertheless, their appearance had led the Soviets to introduce anti-SAM magnesium flare dispensers on aircraft and heli-

Far left: A 14.5mm single-barrelled anti-aircraft gun in Paktia. The usual practice in a conventional army would be to use a round of tracer every five rounds, interspersed with normal shot and armour-piercing. The Mujahideen have loaded this belt almost totally with tracer rounds (red-tipped), which would have limited stopping power. The woolly hat was typical Mujahideen wear in Paktia in the early 1980s, often being worn under the turban, even in summer!

Near left: A single-barrelled 20mm Oerlikon-Buhrle GA1-B01 anti-aircraft gun.

Lower left: Mohammed Gallani, the son of Pir Gallani, leader of the NIFA Mujahideen faction, stands next to a 12.7mm gun in Paktia. The hand-held walkie-talkies were not usual, only used here to enable the members of Mohammed Gallani's personal escort to chat with each other.

9. 'Hisbe-i-Islami' means Party of Islam. Confusingly, there were two Hisbe-i-Islami parties among the Mujahideen; the more fundamentalist of the two was led by Gulbadin Hekmatyr (see also footnote 30). The second party was known as 'Hisbe-i-Islami Khalis' after its leader, Yunis Khalis (see under 'Abdul Haq...').

10. The Iranians' possession of American Stingers was dramatically confirmed on 8 October 1987 when an American helicopter survived a hit by a Stinger (the warhead failed to detonate) fired by Iranian Revolutionary Guards in the Straits of Hormuz in the Gulf.

11. Afghan name: Mahaz-i-Milli-i-Islami. A moderate, pro-Western, but ineffective faction commonly known as 'the Gucchi Guerrillas'.

copters and generally to behave in a more cautious manner when approaching ground targets. SAM-7s may also have been a factor in the disappearance of the lone patrol. After they were deployed, Soviet gunships always flew in twos or threes, normally flying at staggered altitudes with the lead helicopter lowest.

The mid-1980s saw the Soviets developing more effective and aggressive air tactics. In the beginning, poor air/ground co-ordination had left their convoys vulnerable to ambush on the narrow mountain roads. However, the Russian military machine learned its lessons and implemented improved tactical deployment to good effect. Mi-24 helicopters were increasingly used for routine patrols and convoy security, the supply of isolated garrisons, bombing and ground attack. On occasion, predatory hunter-killer packs of 16 to 24 gunships attacked without warning. Afterwards, élite Airborne or Spetsnaz troops were sometimes landed to conduct mopping-up operations.

Traditional caravan routes, utilised by the Afghans for thousands of years, began to stink from the hundreds of camels and horses killed in air attacks. Soviet ground ambushes along Afghan supply lines also badly disrupted the Mujahideen war effort. The plains of Loghar and the deserts of Khandahar became littered with the fire-blackened hulks of Afghan pick-up trucks. As the Russians began to dominate the daylight hours, the Mujahideen were correspondingly forced to conduct most of their movements under cover of darkness. Morale plummeted as they became ever more nervous and increasingly enraged by their inability to deliver an effective counter-strike. Having gained the initiative, the Russians had started to win the war.

While the Mujahideen badly needed a weapon capable of tipping the balance in their favour, the political 'deniability' policy of the United States precluded the direct supply of lethal US ordnance. This unwillingness to back the Mujahideen openly was to last until 1986. However, in 1985 the Americans persuaded the British government to send about 300 Blowpipe surface-to-air missiles to Afghanistan. Although more sophisticated than the SAM-7, the Blowpipe also required a skilled operator, which reduced its effectiveness in Mujahideen hands. Nonetheless, it was valued by the Afghans as the first state-of-the-art Western weapon they had received. In 1987 one of Abdul Haq's local commanders in Maidan Shah received a Blowpipe. Unable to bring himself to use this symbolic piece of ordnance in case it could not be replaced, he wrapped it carefully in

blankets and buried it. Two years later it was still interred – by which time the Russians had left!

Blowpipe did cause a small increase in Soviet air losses (but not nearly equating to the number of missiles supplied), and, once again, the result was improvements in Soviet air strategies. These were already taking effect when, in mid-1986, the United States changed its policy and began to supply the Mujahideen with US-manufactured Stinger missiles. The simple 'fire-and-forget' technology of Stinger was ideal for the Mujahideen. The first Soviet air losses credited to the weapon were attributed to Engineer Ghafar, one of Gulbadin Hekmatyr's fundamentalist Hisbe-i-Islami[9] commanders. Ghafar claimed to have downed three Soviet helicopters in Nangrahar in a single day, 26 September 1986. Although Soviet air losses showed a marked increase with Stinger deployment, US Army sources claiming a 79 per cent kill rate for the missile were excessively generous. This was possibly to justify the danger of Stingers supplied for use in Afghanistan leaking clandestinely onto the world arms market.[10]

Despite high hopes, the Afghans failed for the most part to maximise on the potential of Stinger. While they mastered the mechanics of launching the missile, its tactical deployment proved problematic. Operation 'Avalanche', mounted by NIFA (National Islamic Front of Afghanistan[11]) and commanded by Abdul Rahim Wardak in December 1987, was a typical example. Supplied with two Stingers for this operation, Wardak sited them not in close support of the 107mm multi-barrel rocket launchers which they had been intended to protect, but next to his own position, a discreet twenty miles away! Consequently, when Soviet jets bombed the rocket launchers, the Stingers were of no use at all.

The West also minimised the potential impact of Stinger by not releasing the weapons en masse to the Mujahideen. Instead, they adopted a cautious 'trickle-feeding' system which allowed the Soviets time to develop counter-measures. After a peak in early 1987, Soviet air losses decreased as these defensive strategies took effect. In the latter years of the war the average attack altitude of Russian Su-25 jet fighters was 20,000ft. While the aircraft remained safely beyond the range of Stinger, bombing from this height was also less effective. The helicopter gunships, on the other hand, unable to outrange Stinger by altitude, were forced to fly lower. By contour flying, they could remain below the 20-degree minimum angle required by Stinger teams for the effective launch of their missiles. However, while this tactic rendered the gunships almost immune to Stinger, they were correspondingly more

21

vulnerable to normal ground-fire, even RPG rockets. Nonetheless, the Mi-24 remained a feature on the forward edge of the Afghan battlefield.

The deployment of Stinger also coincided with an increasing Soviet desire to be rid of its costly problems in Afghanistan. By the end of 1986 this combination of factors had led to a dramatic decrease in the number of Soviet air strikes. Inevitably, the Afghans attributed this directly to Stinger. Massoud Khalili, a spokesmen for one of the leading factions, gave the helicopter gunship a dramatic epitaph: 'For seven years the Dragon has ruled the skies. Now the Dragon is dead.' After years of ferocious air attack, it was a desperately needed reprieve, and Afghan morale soared as the Mujahideen regained the use of the daylight hours.

Of course, whether the gunship-dragon had indeed been slain by Stinger or whether it could still be considered, in the words of one Soviet pilot, 'a good, dependable killing machine' was debatable. The statistics are illuminating. The total Soviet air losses in Afghanistan are estimated at between one and two thousand. While 80 per cent of these are thought to have been helicopters, the figures must be compared with those for Vietnam, where the United States lost over 5,000 helicopters alone. In fact, it was not sophisticated Western missiles systems but fragmentation injuries from mortars and mines which accounted for most Soviet casualties in Afghanistan. When the Afghans tell their own, oral histories of the war however, this detail is unlikely to figure. In any good story, the heroic underdog requires a weapon of special potency to redress the balance. As David, to the Soviet Goliath, the Mujahideen had teetered on the brink of effective military defeat. For them, Stinger *was* the magic sword which had dramatically transformed their tactical environment.

THE IMPACT OF PAKISTANI POLICY ON THE WAR IN AFGHANISTAN

The West was reluctant to back the Mujahideen openly and implemented a 'deniability' policy, allowing Pakistan to control the distribution of arms. However, the Pakistan end of the arms conduit was subject to a high volume of leakage and manipulation. Large numbers of weapons ended up on the black market in Pakistani tribal lands and more were simply not distributed.

The control of the covert Western arms supply was also a heaven-sent opportunity for the Pakistani Inter-Service Intelligence bureau (ISI) to manipulate the shape of a future Afghan government. They consequently opted to filter arms through their favoured Mujahideen political lead-

Above: Afghan Air Force Mi-8 shot down in the Panjshir valley.

ers, based in Pakistan, rather than deal directly with commanders who were effective in the field. The rival political factions began stockpiling against the likelihood of a civil war following the Soviet withdrawal. Some sources estimate that as little as 30 per cent of the billions of dollars' worth of weapons sent actually reached the Mujahideen in the field.

The ISI's other, fundamental error was in consistently over-emphasising the need for more advanced technology at the expense of basic training. Scant effort was invested in helping the resistance develop even elementary tactical or weapon-handling skills: indeed, very few Mujahideen engaged in the fighting received any training at all.

These policies were not vindicated by the performance of the Mujahideen. As the war ground on, Pakistan longed for a significant propaganda victory. To this end, it began to infiltrate military observers into Afghan border provinces, to evaluate what should be done. What followed gave no indication that the Pakistan Army had learned anything from its own repeated military defeats (at the hands of neighbouring India). Lacking experience of guerrilla warfare,[12] the Pakistanis encouraged the lightly armed and disunited Afghan resistance to adopt strategies suited to disciplined, conventional forces. The attempt to impose conventional warfare on the Mujahideen resulted in a series of humiliating and costly military failures which wasted both material resources and human lives – Khost (1985), Zahawar (1986), Khost again (1987 and 1988), Jalalabad (1989), Kabul (1990) and Gardez (1991).

STRATEGY AND TACTICS IN AFGHANISTAN

When the USSR invaded Afghanistan in December

12 Other than an uneven campaign against the Baluchi tribes in the preceding decade.

13 From *Agricola*.

1979 less than ten per cent of the fifteen million Afghans were living in towns of ten thousand or more. The Soviets had not anticipated lengthy problems from the predominantly peasant society, least of all a costly war which was to last for the next ten years.

While the Mujahideen achieved few significant battlefield victories, and were never to achieve the cohesion for anything but a piecemeal war of attrition, the technologically superior Soviet forces were unable to eradicate them. To the Afghans, resistance, even to death, was a matter of honour. In addition, they did possess many attributes suited to guerrilla warfare. Accustomed to wresting a meagre existence from the land, they were hardy, they habitually travelled light and they could exist on a frugal diet. They also enjoyed the advantage of detailed topographical knowledge and commanded widespread support among the local population.

The Soviets vented their initial frustration by decimating wide swathes of the countryside in heavy-handed offensives reminiscent of the campaigns of the Roman Empire (described by Tacitus, who said, 'They make a desert and call it peace.'[13]). The purpose of this was primarily to clear the land of civilians sympathetic to the Mujahideen. A third of the population fled into exile in Pakistan and Iran.

The Mujahideen faced this onslaught with peasant fortitude. In 1981 tribal commander Jalaluddin Haquani commented, with typical stoicism, 'It does not matter if I win today: it only matters that I fight. As long as I fight, I can survive; and if I survive, I will be the victor.' Though such faith inured them to adversity, other characteristics inherent in Afghan society endowed the Mujahideen with problems. They were fragmented into thousands of localised groups, each with differing political and tribal loyalties and often hostile to each other. Within their groups they also suffered from fatalism, poor leadership and a lack of training. Weak strategic planning was compounded by appalling logistical support. Although the unity essential to a truly national resistance effort was never to emerge, there *were* times when this, the greatest failing of the Mujahideen, was also their strongest defence. Reverses suffered by one group did not directly affect the morale of others. In order to defeat them totally, the Soviets needed to defeat every group – clearly an unattainable goal.

The Afghans possessed one further asset — the hostile landscape of their homeland. The Russian forces were ill-prepared for what they encountered in Afghanistan. Despite their technological superiority, the Soviets' system of indoctrinated military thought produced soldiers of rigid habit. Their infantry had been trained and equipped for a rapid, massed style of warfare, appropriate to the flat, central plains of Europe: in Afghanistan they were demoralised by the high mountains and narrow valleys. In this strange environment their formations were unwieldy and ineffective and they were reluctant to deploy far from their armoured personnel carriers. When they did, they lacked the level of fitness required to operate efficiently in mountainous terrain. On incursions into Mujahideen-controlled territory, the Russians often made use of their Afghan Army allies as a casualty sponge at the spearpoint of offensives. Units such as the Afghan Army 38th Commando Brigade made regular battlefield appearances and performed reasonably well. The Russians also utilised the resources of the Kabul government to relieve Soviet units for more important tasks.

Around the major towns, heavily armed Afghan *Sarondoy* (Paramilitary Police) kept much of the urban landscape under control. In addition, many Afghan civilians were recruited into government militias. These were most effective when recruits were enlisted *en masse* under a recognised and respected leader, such as General Abdul Rashid Dostman. For much of the war Dostman com-

23

Below: Pakistan was heavily involved in the covert arms supply. It also sent personnel into Afghanistan to observe and make recommendations. Not all Pakistanis in Afghanistan were working for the ISI. Abdul Rashid, a former corporal in the Pakistan Army, earned a living as a freelance instructor for the Mujahideen. He is seen here with Jalaluddin Haqani's 75mm recoilless rifle in Paktia during 1981.

manded a division of Uzbeck and Tadjik militias, based along the Soviet supply lines from the Salang Pass to the Amu Darya River on the Russian border.[14]

As the war progressed, Western arms began to reach the Mujahideen in larger quantities. Tragically for the Afghans, these were not always used solely against the foreign invaders: inter-tribal violence increased, particularly in the south among the Pathans. The Soviets, in tandem with the communist Afghan government, were able to exploit these rivalries. Mullah Malang, from Khandahar, went over to the Russian side in the early 1980s, as did Sher Agha, of Herat, in 1982. In early 1984 the Afghan Government was able to raise its first regiment of Pathan warriors from the Rud-e-Ahmazadzai tribe of Paktia.

Of course, there were also defections in the opposite direction. Esmat Muslim was from the ruling family of the Acheckazais of Khandahar (a branch of the powerful, southern Durrani tribe). He was a captain in the Afghan Army when, in 1981, he defected to the Mujahideen cause. He became a commander with NIFA but in 1983 fell out with the Pakistan ISI. They dubbed him a troublemaker and cut off his supply of weapons. After struggling on for two years, Esmat finally transferred his allegiance back to the Soviets, taking his Acheckazai

tribe with him. With his knowledge of Mujahideen supply routes and bases, he was able to wreak havoc among the local resistance.

As the Soviets gained experience on the ground, they began to implement changes which enhanced the quality and capabilities of their soldiers at the sharp end of the conflict. They improved the safety of convoys moving up narrow mountain roads. Those venturing into dangerous areas on offensive operations were preceded by a route security unit (Soviet designation: GPZ). These were equipped with platoons of T-62 tanks fitted with bulldozer blades to scrape the road surface clear of mines. Better ground/air co-ordination also increased the effectiveness of Soviet air strikes, and interdiction of Mujahideen supply lines by élite Airborne and Spetsnatz units became a regular feature of the war. The lumbering Russian bear metamorphosed into a far more agile and dangerous animal.

The evident evolutionary process within the Soviet forces was seldom matched by improvements in the Mujahideen. Their habitual use of the same caravan routes to ferry supplies into Afghanistan rendered them vulnerable to air and ground attack. Only the northern commander, Ahmad Shah Massoud, in the Panjshir Valley, developed a truly mobile and effective form of guer-

Above: A shipment of arms from Pakistan crosses a river in the Safed Koh mountains of Nangrahar in 1981. Logistics remained an Achilles' heel for the Mujahideen. Hundreds of thousands of donkeys, mules, horses and camels were used to transport supplies.

14. In April 1992, faced with the approaching collapse of the communist government, General Dostman formed an alliance with Mujahideen commander Ahmad Shah Massoud. Over the following years of civil war he was to switch allegiance with monotonous regularity.

rilla warfare. By and large, other than the fact that they possessed a more sophisticated range of weapons, most Mujahideen of the late 1980s behaved remarkably like the Mujahideen of the early 1980s. This was partially because of the lack of an educated elite among their ranks. Radical social reforms in the 1960s and 1970s had polarized Afghan society between educated town-dwellers and the largely uneducated rural majority. While some of the political leaders of the Mujahideen factions (based in Pakistan) were drawn from the urban elite, it was rare to find educated Afghans serving in the field. Those few who did often emerged as the more competent leaders.[15]

The Mujahideen soon learned, to their cost, that direct confrontation was casualty-heavy. They preferred stand-off attack against local targets such as small enemy posts. For this the 82mm mortar, the backbone of the Mujahideen arsenal, was ideal. When a mortar was deployed, it was inevitably accompanied by more Mujahideen than required to operate it. Within the identity of the group, each Mujahid felt himself to be an essential part of the attack force and equally responsible for the results – even if his sole function had been to keep the mortar crew company.

Right: As the war ground on, mules and horses became harder to find. Many died from maltreatment and overwork. The USA stepped in and flew several hundred mules to Pakistan from Tennessee, and these formed part of Operation *Avalanche* in Kabul Province in 1987.

15. Ahmad Shah Massoud, Abdul Haq and the Islamic scholar Jalaluddin Haqani were examples.

16. Range of 107mm rocket: 8km; range of 122mm rocket: 11km; range of 82mm mortar: 3.47km.

17. Operation 'Magistral', 19 November-29 December 1987.

The timing and method of attack favoured by each group was influenced by the type of terrain in which it operated. For example, those groups based in the foothills of Paktia had less need to cloak themselves under cover of darkness than Mujahideen operating in the dangerous flat lands around Khandahar. Soviet forces stationed in less mountainous regions were better able to exploit their mobility and firepower to trap the Mujahideen in the open. The Soviet 70th Motorised Rifle Regiment, based in Khandahar, was justly renowned for its effectiveness against the Mujahideen of this predominantly flat region.

From 1984 onwards there was a noticeable battlefield improvement in the effectiveness of élite Soviet troops (Spetsnatz and Airborne). This was matched by an equally noticeable decrease in the Mujahideen's ability to strike at Soviet units. Losing ground, and with their supply lines in tatters, the Mujahideen desperately needed longer-range weapons if they were to keep up the pressure. Rocket technology supplied the answer. Vast quantities of 107mm and 122mm rockets were supplied. These had a far greater range than the limited reach of the 82mm mortar.[16] Multi-barrel rocket launchers (MBRLs) were quick to follow, allowing long-range salvos of up to twelve rockets at a time. Stand-off attack by MBRL soon became the standard Mujahideen offensive operation. During the four-month siege of Jalalabad in 1989 (after the Russian withdrawal), the Mujahideen fired over 130,000 rockets into the city.

As late as November 1987, the Soviets were confident enough to launch a major ground offensive to relieve the siege of Khost — Operation *Magistral*.[17] This offensive carved right through the mountain bastion of Mujahideen commander Jalaluddin Haqani, in Paktia. It required the skilful co-ordination of aerial bombing operations, heliborne troop landings and conventional ground forces, in a tactically fluid situation. For over a month the Mujahideen were afforded an opportunity to demonstrate their abilities. They were active in a target-rich environment, on terrain perfectly suited to guerrilla warfare. Furthermore, they enjoyed the additional advantage of short lines of supply to their stockpiles of weapons and munitions just over the Pakistan border. Yet, despite the possession of Stinger missiles and a wide range of weapons not available to them at the beginning of the war, they were unable to stop, or even significantly impede, the Soviet juggernaut. The Russians lifted the siege of Khost with few losses and, in the process, inflicted heavy casualties on the Afghan resistance.

By early 1988 the Soviets were beginning to wind down their involvement and, with rockets, Kabul was once again within striking distance of the Mujahideen. A year later, as the last Soviet aircraft took off from Kabul airport, the balance finally shifted in favour of the resistance. Alone, the Afghan Army was nowhere near as formidable as its powerful allies had been. It was outnumbered and demoralised and there were mass desertions to the Mujahideen. The fall of Kabul was only a matter of time: the only question remaining was, to which of the contending Mujahideen factions would it fall?

MUJAHIDEEN COMMANDERS

There was no single, characterising feature which defined the Mujahideen: they were as varied as the circumstances in which they fought. Those in mountainous terrain had a geographical advantage over those in the wide open plains; those from tribal regions were more restricted by traditional patterns of social hierarchy than those from urban areas. Many of the most able commanders were killed early on, long before wide-scale Western support arrived to help them. Of the remainder, some learned their lessons and went on to make names for themselves which carried far beyond the lofty peaks of their national borders. A closer look at four different commanders serves to illustrate the diverse nature of the war in Afghanistan.

Akbar Khan – Local Tribal Commander

Only in rare circumstances was a man able to lead by force of personality alone: Akbar Kan[18] was such a man. Although tall, with a powerful, Pathan physique, he was softly spoken. His gift for persuasive oratory was honed to perfection by years of trading among the local tribes. In the beginning, as a member of the nomadic Coochi tribe,[19] Khan was more disadvantaged than most local leaders. Other Pathan tribes in Paktia, where he operated, traditionally regarded the Coochi with distrust. Undeterred, Khan proved that he was forged from the right metal: his star shone brightly, if tragically briefly.

In the wake of the Soviet invasion, rather than flee to Pakistan he gathered together a small band of his tribesmen and headed for the hills. The Spartan, nomadic lifestyle of the Coochi had endowed Khan with a hardy constitution and a thorough knowledge of all the secret mountain trails of Paktia. This, and his sharp, trader's mind, was to serve him well in the escalating guerrilla war.

At first the Coochi were ignored by the local tribes, who were suspicious of interlopers operating

in their mountains. Undeterred, Akbar Khan and his handful of men embarked on the typical limited action of most Mujahideen groups. They ambushed likely looking traffic along lonely stretches of the Urgun-Matun road and mounted night attacks against soft targets (isolated militia posts or police stations). Occasionally more daring attacks, against unsuspecting Afghan Army posts,[20] were ventured.

In these small-scale operations Khan enjoyed greater success than many of his contemporaries. Gradually he developed a network of local tribes willing to support more ambitious attacks planned by him. Men from the local valleys went along, in return for a share of the spoils. By carefully choosing his targets, Khan consolidated his reputation. In time, whilst the hard corps of his Coochi supporters rarely numbered more than thirty, he was able, if required, to call upon a force of over a hundred men.

Akbar Khan's style of leadership would have been instantly recognisable to British troops campaigning in Afghanistan a hundred years earlier. Personally courageous, he believed in commanding from the front, by example. In March 1981 he collaborated in an operation with Jalaluddin Haqani, another Paktia commander whose fortunes were on the rise. Some 300 Mujahideen were to attack a post at Taraghry (on the southern tip of the Khost plain, in Paktia). The target was well sited on a steep knoll, protected by an outer cordon of mines and two lines of inner trenches. It was garrisoned by soldiers from the 666th Division of the Afghan Army, who could call upon artillery support from a battery of 130mm guns based a

Left: A wounded Mujahid strapped to the top of a camel on his way to Pakistan; Paktia, 1986.

18. The name *Akbar Khan* means 'Great Leader'.

19. Although this Pathan tribe are also known as the Ghilzai, they are more commonly referred to as the Coochi.

20. There was little Soviet presence in Paktia province at this stage in the war. They were initially cautious of being sucked too far into the mountains.

Above: Commander Akbar Khan (back to camera, with bandolier) organises the unloading of a 75mm recoilless rifle before attacking an enemy post at Taraghry, Paktia, in 1981.

Right: A wounded Mujahid in a Red Cross hospital in Pakistan.

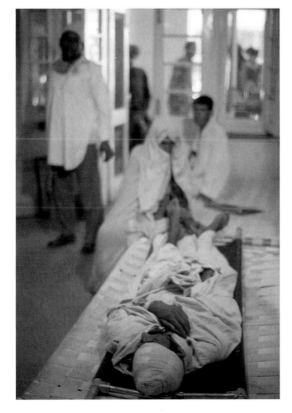

21. Haq's real name was Abdul Rauf; 'Haq' was his *nom de guerre*.

boost morale.

The attack began with rapid salvos from Haqani's recoilless rifle and a heavy barrage of 82mm mortar bombs, from two mortars positioned on the floor of a neighbouring gully. Choosing his moment, Akbar Khan attempted to maximise the element of surprise and, under cover of small-arms fire, he and his assault group of thirty men sprang forward and rushed the enemy position.

The Mujahideen passed safely through the minefield by advancing up the track on which soldiers had been observed, fetching water from the river. But, once among the first line of trenches, they were unable to resist the shower of grenades raining down from the second line on higher ground. Having sustained casualties, the Mujahideen were forced to retire.

It was hard for Khan to persuade them to launch a second attempt. To galvanize them into action, he bounded forward alone, knowing that honour demanded that his men follow him. They had barely regained the empty trenches, when Khan was speared squarely through the chest by a burst of light machine-gun fire. Dragged under cover, behind some boulders, he died a few minutes later.

With the loss of their leader, the attack faltered and the Mujahideen melted away. As they withdrew, 130mm artillery shells from Nadershah Kot began to pound the surrounding ridges. Cloaking Akbar Khan in a blood-sodden blanket, his loyal Coochi cohort hurried him through the night, beneath the star-studded sky, over the mountains he loved. He was laid to rest in Miram Shah, with the green flags of martyrdom fluttering over his grave.

Abdul Haq – Urban Commander

Not all Mujahideen commanders operated exclusively in the mountains. Commander Abdul Haq's[21] special talent lay in urban guerrilla warfare on the fringes of the sprawling metropolis of Kabul. Barely twenty when the Soviets invaded in 1979, Haq already had a long track record in political insurrection. His boyhood tutor had been none other than Yunis Khalis, who was later to form the Hisbe-i-Islami party into which Haq and his brothers were inducted. Whilst still in his teens he had been an inmate of the infamous Poli Chaki prison in Kabul, where he was under sentence of death for political crimes against the Daoud regime. Fortune, and family connections, saved him. During the period of upheaval after the Saur revolution in 1978, his wealthy family bribed the right official and secured his release.

With the arrival of the Russians, Haq became

few kilometres away in, Nadershah Kot. Once the assault was launched, Akbar Khan was reliant on speed to escape retaliatory artillery fire. For the lightly armed Mujahideen, it was a formidable objective. Jalaluddin Haqani's contribution to the operation, other than additional manpower, was a Chinese 75mm recoilless rifle. At the time, in 1981, a weapon of this type was extremely rare among Mujahideen forces, and its presence did much to ever more frustrated with the limited action being conducted by the rural Mujahideen in his native province of Nangrahar: hampered by tribal rivalries, they achieved little more than harassing Afghan Army posts in the mountains. Haq had a larger target in mind – the Russian Army in Kabul. Relying on an elder brother, Abdul Qadir, to supply arms, Haq returned to Kabul and set about organizing his own group within the framework of Yunis Khalis' Hisbe-i-Islami faction.

In 1980–1 the Russians seldom ventured far from the principal towns and main highways. The capital city, Kabul, with its heavy concentration of Soviet forces, was one of the most dangerous environments in which to operate. It was situated on the floor of a wide basin, surrounded by high ridges, and the flat area around the city was ideal for Russian tanks and armoured cars.

Once inside Kabul, Haq and his Mujahideen were surrounded by their enemies. They began a series of attacks, relying on their intimate knowledge of the local streets and terrain to effect their escape. As they were hungry for arms, these attacks were initially aimed at soft targets such as Afghan government police, militia and army posts. However, Haq was principally interested in killing Russians, at which he was to prove adept. It was from them that the best weapons could be captured and most fame won. His growing reputation for daring attacks and personal bravery enabled Haq to attract urban Afghans to his banner. In tandem with increasing military muscle, he developed an effective intelligence network. This served him well as the Soviets began to gain a stranglehold on the capital.

By 1984 it had become too dangerous for armed guerrillas to operate permanently within the capital. Slowly the Soviets pushed the Mujahideen ever further from Kabul. Haq was forced to withdraw his base to the Phagman mountain range just west of the city. This severed his direct control over operatives still within Kabul's perimeter, and, without the dynamism of his presence, they drifted increasingly towards information-gathering and away from active military operations.

Haq's Kabul exploits had by this stage brought him a level of notoriety outside the borders of Afghanistan. To Western military attachés and visiting journalists in neighbouring Pakistan, he also possessed one further appealing attribute – he spoke English. This was a rare asset among Afghan military commanders and it made Abdul Haq a useful man to know. Haq was quick to seize on the potential political benefits to be derived from media exposure. The results which he had achieved early

on, with minimal resources, had demonstrated the inadequacies of other regional commanders and incited envy within Khalis' Hisbe-i-Islami. Consequently, logistical support from the Party was no longer so readily forthcoming. By capitalising on his reputation, Haq hoped to circumvent the political parties and secure direct military aid for himself. He began spending increasing periods of time in the border town of Peshawar, Pakistan, where he could cultivate journalists and important diplomatic connections.

Some Peshawar-based journalists found it expedient to report almost exclusively on Haq's exploits. Interviews in English, and in Peshawar, were undoubtedly preferable to dangerous trips into Afghanistan to interview other commanders.[22] However, as his celebrity increased, the number and duration of Haq's own forays to Afghanistan declined. This was unfortunate, as within the Mujahideen his authority rested on 'hands-on' control. In fact, his hard-won position inside Afghanistan was being eroded almost in inverse proportion to his rising fame.

The zenith of Abdul Haq's influence was in 1986. In one six-week period during July and August he was responsible for two successful, high-profile operations. First, he led an attack on the Sarobi Dam, the main hydro-electric power supply for Kabul. Although his 250kg of explosives were insufficient to blow up the dam itself, he was able to destroy its main control room. Then, in

Left: Abdul Haq was one of the principal Mujahideen commanders around Kabul during the early phase of the war. His specialisation was urban guerrilla warfare, but by the mid-1980s the Soviets had established three 'rings' of defences around Kabul to protect it from the Mujahideen. After this, Abdul Haq's fortunes began to decline.

22. Partially as a result of all the media attention, Haq was selected to meet both President Reagan in the United States and Prime Minister Margaret Thatcher in Britain.

August, he destroyed a large ammunition dump near the Qarga Dam, only a few miles from Kabul. While these operations undoubtedly represented a huge propaganda coup, closer examination reveals Haq's growing tendency to overstate the complexity of his operations in order to conceal his declining influence around Kabul. The attack on the Sarobi Dam illustrated his drift towards targets further from the heavy concentrations of Soviet troops around the capital: the objective was over 24 miles from Kabul and defended principally by the Afghan Army. Furthermore, the destruction of the Qarga ammunition dump (also an Afghan Army target[23]) owed more to wild good fortune than Haq was inclined to admit. It was hit by one of four free-flight 107mm rockets, renowned for their inaccuracy; indeed, it is possible, though not certain, that the Qarga dump was not actually the target!

In any event, these were to be Abdul Haq's last major military successes. On a night march in October 1987 to mount a rocket attack against Kabul airport, he stepped on a mine. The resulting explosion shattered the front of his right foot. His men struggled to carry Haq through snow and mud for 25 miles, to reach an Afghan doctor in Maidan Shah. He was luckier than most Mujahideen. After arrival in Pakistan, a week later, he was evacuated to a hospital in America.

Abdul Haq gamely braved several more trips into Afghanistan after this injury, but his war had ceased to be one of urban guerrilla activity. He had

been forced away from the capital, and the old standbys of mountain guerrilla warfare were back on the agenda – attacks against isolated enemy bases and lonely stretches of the Kabul-Jalalabad highway. Back in the countryside, Haq was once again hindered by the rural inter-tribal rivalries from which he had been so determined to escape.

This was a bitter setback for a man whose war had been waged against not just the cutting edge of the Russian Army but also the entrenched traditionalism of the Mujahideen. Almost alone among the Pathan commanders, he had tried to modernise and adapt their customary tribal methods of warfare. He had established one of the few Mujahideen-controlled training camps in Pakistan. There, and in the field, he had striven to instil in his men a stricter sense of discipline. These measures were not always popular. Many Pathans felt that it impinged on their honour to submit to stricter discipline, or to be told that they needed training. In addition, there was a growing resentment of the media attention Haq commanded. Wary of his ambitions, Yunis Khalis' Hisbe-i-Islami ultimately withdrew support for his training camp and forced its closure.

Despite his waning influence on the ground, Haq's media star was by now in the ascendant. His medical treatment in the United States had generated widespread publicity. Dubbed 'The Lion of Kabul' by various reporters, he was widely tipped as the man most likely to capture the capital when the Soviets pulled out. In fact, when the withdrawal finally came, Abdul Haq was not poised in the mountains above Kabul but besieged by journalists in his Peshawar office.

As the dust of the Russian retreat settled, the media feverishly estimated that Haq had several thousand Mujahideen lurking in the Phagman mountains ready to pounce. In reality, the spearpoint of his forces in Paghman at the time numbered fewer than twenty men and one sick donkey: most of the rest had long since been killed, or had dispersed to refugee camps in Pakistan for the winter. The skeleton staff that remained were scattered among several almost deserted bases. The attrition of war, poor support and Haq's own long absences had been telling.

With no sign of the imminent fall of Kabul, Abdul Haq had a lot of explaining to do. It was but a short step from 'The Lion of Kabul' to yesterday's man. Yunis Khalis cut off his supply of Western arms. Ultimately, the lack of support from his own party was the root cause of Abdul Haq's downfall. The need to win arms and resources had curtailed his effective presence on the ground and propelled him

23. The Qarga Dam ammunition dump was located at the headquarters of the Afghan 8th Army.

into the arms of the media with disastrous results. An able and progressive commander, he deserved better.

Jalaluddin Haqani – Regional Tribal Commander

The pre-eminent guerrilla commander among the eastern Pathan tribes of Paktia was Jalaluddin Haqani, a devout Mullah and Islamic scholar. For many Pathans, Haqani, with his proud bearing, luxuriant black beard and impeccable Islamic credentials, epitomised the ideal Afghan warrior-poet. A member of the powerful Zadran tribe, he commanded a large following, for whom he secured an ample supply of arms by his affiliation with Yunis Khalis. Like many prominent Mujahideen commanders, Haqani's military career predated the Soviet invasion: he had been active in the Paktia mountains since 1978.

As a tribal leader, Haqani found that much of his time was taken up by delicate negotiations, forging alliances with neighbouring tribes, repairing rifts and generally maintaining the political status quo. In addition, members of his own Zadran tribe had every right to expect a personal audience with Haqani to discuss their grievances. Even urgent military business might have to wait while a farmer from Miran Jan discussed, at length, the number of pomegranates that disappeared from his orchard whenever the Mujahideen passed!

On offensive operations Haqani was forced to be very sensitive to casualties. The loss of just one Mujahid could jeopardise an attack – the entire tribe concerned being quite likely to depart, to carry home their dead comrade. Deaths in battle also required that strict social precedents be met. The tribe might indulge in a period of public mourning (according to the social standing of the deceased). Haqani would also pay a small sum of compensation to the relatives, to ensure that no grievance or blood feud developed over the cause of death. Lesser sums were sometimes paid for lesser wounds.[24]

In the beginning Haqani's *modus operandi* (like that of most Mujahideen commanders) was the small, indirect harassing attack, rarely involving more than twenty to thirty men. The general scale of his operations was increased in 1981 by the acquisition of his first recoilless rifle. This important status symbol marked Haqani as an important commander and drew followers to his banner. Word that the *top* (gun) was on its way preceded it through the mountain villages and generated much excitement. Over a period of days Mujahideen would gather to admire the gun and wait for Haqani himself to arrive. Then a few more days would

Left: Jalaluddin Haqani, a member of the powerful Zadran tribe, was the most influential Pathan leader. His powerbase was in Paktia, which bordered Pakistan.

inevitably pass, in planning and delicate negotiations, before the gun crew finally set off for the attack. Although the operation might last several hours and could also involve support from one or more mortars, casualties on both sides tended to be fairly low.

Gradually Haqani began to stage more daring attacks. On 29 January 1981 he targeted a government militia post at Mandouzah, in the middle of the flat Khost plain. The commander of this militia unit had refused to co-operate with Haqani. His intransigence, and Haqani's retaliatory attack, had as much to do with tribal grudges between them as with political differences. Under cover of darkness a raiding party of seventy men slipped down from the hills and made the approach march across the dangerously exposed plain. At 20.30 hours they had reached the outskirts of Mandouzah village when a sentry called out a challenge. Not receiving a reply, he fired the first shot thereby raising the alarm. The Mujahideen raced for cover, but before they could reach the buildings more of the militia began firing. Haqani's men were forced to swerve off to the right, floundering across a muddy field to storm the village from another side. The action began to intensify.

The fire-fight raged through the village for 5

24. In 1981 this author witnessed Haqani in protracted negotiations for a missing thumb!

Right: Jalaluddin Haqani's second-in-command, Fattioullah, handled much of the administration in order to free Haqani for more important work. In 1982 Fattioullah also oversaw the two-month (February-March) siege of Burrai in Paktia. He was killed during the Russian offensive against Haqani's major base in Zahwar.

hours, illuminated by the flickering light of burning buildings. When it was over, half the sixteen-man militia force had been killed, the rest escaping into the darkness. Among the dead was the militia commander and his teenaged daughter, who had snatched up his AK-47 to defend her father's body. During the action the Mujahideen raiders used several hundred rounds of small-arms ammunition, fired eleven RPG rockets and threw over twenty grenades. When they finally withdrew they were loaded down with spoils, including a pair of binoculars, one 1914 Lee Enfield rifle, 2,000 rounds of .303 ammunition, nine sheep, a bicycle, a sewing machine, an alarm clock and a bottle of shampoo!

Later in the war Haqani was encouraged by the Pakistani ISI to organise much larger offensives, numbering from a few hundred to several thousand men. These operations were only made possible by Haqani's skill at uniting different tribes and political factions. Months of planning were required, not only to guarantee that adequate munitions arrived at the right time but also to ensure that everyone turned up. A typical example was the 1985 attack on the town of Khost,[25] in which about 5,000 Mujahideen participated.

The initial success of this attack evaporated as the Mujahideen, after years of enforced exile in the mountains, reached the outer suburbs of Khost

Right: Jalaluddin Haqani and his Zadran Mujahideen pose for a photograph. This was taken in January 1981, and represents the hard core of permanent Mujahideen which he could field at this time. He could call upon far larger numbers on a temporary basis if required. Half of this party were dead by 1984, and even more before the Russians pulled out in 1989.

25. Matun was the principal town in Paktia. The media often incorrectly named Matun as Khost. In the Pushto language of the Pathans, *khost* means plain and describes the geographical location of Matun, not the town itself. To simplify reference with other sources, I have also referred to it as Khost.

and, in time-honoured tribal manner, became more interested in looting than fighting. Having lost their momentum, they began milling around in large numbers seeking plunder. As they came under accurate mortar, artillery and bombing attack, casualties mounted.

The ISI also encouraged Haqani to establish a fixed base near the Pakistan border. They wanted a showcase Mujahideen supply camp to exploit for propaganda purposes. The site chosen was only six kilometres from Pakistan, at Zahawar. In fact, as he enjoyed such short lines of supply to the border anyway, Haqani had no need of such a base. For a guerrilla force it was a major tactical blunder, and one for which the Mujahideen were to pay dearly.

In September 1986 the Soviets finally decided to teach Haqani a lesson and mounted a major ground offensive to destroy the base at Zahawar. During the course of this attack over a thousand Mujahideen were killed. Among them was Haqani's second-in-command, Fatioullah. The base was overrun and huge stockpiles of arms were captured and destroyed before the Soviets pulled out.[26]

Although, encouraged by the ISI, Haqani had attempted to expand his level of warfare, he was never really successful: he was handicapped by the tribal context in which he fought. While he was able to forge alliances and unite rival tribes, such alliances were often unstable and constant levels of manpower could never be relied upon. However, unlike many Mujahideen in other areas, he *did* possess plentiful stocks of arms and the benefits of short supply lines. Despite his dogged persistence, his failure to make significant headway over the course of a long war leads one to conclude that Haqani lacked the necessary military aptitude to exploit his advantages fully .

Ahmad Shah Massoud – Modern Mobile Guerrilla Commander

Among the many Mujahideen commanders, one man stood head and shoulders above all the rest – Ahmad Shah Massoud. The son of a retired army officer, Massoud was a non-tribal Tadjik from northern Afghanistan. He studied engineering at the Russian Polytechnic in Kabul but, as a student activist, was forced to flee Afghanistan in 1973 after the King was toppled from power by Mohammed Daoud.

With his sharp mind and deep political convictions, Massoud began to prepare himself for what, he suspected, would be a long struggle. He underwent military training in Pakistan[27] before infiltrating back to his native Panjshir Valley[28] in 1975 to par-

ticipate in an armed uprising. This was doomed to failure, but, back in the sanctuary of Pakistan, Massoud applied himself to learn from the abortive coup. Alone among future Mujahideen commanders, he studied all the classic texts of guerrilla warfare, including those of Che Guevara, Mao Tse Tung and Van Nguyen Giap, and an American Special Forces manual (which he later described as the most instructive).

In 1978 he was back in Afghanistan, again in the Panjshir valley. A second armed revolt met with initial success but was finally crushed by the Afghan government (now headed by the even more radical Mohammed Taraki, who had assassinated President Daoud). Nevertheless, when the Russians rolled into Afghanistan on Christmas Eve 1979, Massoud was better prepared to face them than any other Mujahideen commander. He had both studied the theory of guerrilla warfare and gained practical experience; more importantly, he had learned from his past mistakes and crystallised plans for future armed resistance.

Over the next decade Massoud was to prove to be a gifted commander. He inspired loyalty and dedication among the Mujahideen who served him. While his hawk-nosed features were gaunt from privation and stress, he exuded a quiet confidence

Left: Ahmad Shah Massoud was the most competent of all Mujahideen commanders, and was the only one to evolve a truly mobile form of guerrilla warfare. The rest mostly operated on a strictly localised basis, close to their own villages and valleys.

26. Haqani had been superficially wounded in the fighting and, incredibly, left in the middle to go on *Haj* (the Islamic pilgrimage to Mecca in Saudi Arabia). He was wounded a second time during Operation 'Magistral', the 1987 Soviet offensive to relieve the siege of Khost.

27. The Pakistanis were already worried about the communist leanings of Afghanistan's new regime.

28. In the *Dari* (Persian dialect) of northern Afghanistan, *Panjshir* means 'Five Lions'.

29. He was affiliated to Professor Rabani's *Jamiat-i-Islami* (Islamic Society) which experienced particular problems with Gulbadin Hekmatyr's faction of Hisbe-i-Islami.

under pressure. Behind the hooded gaze worked an agile intelligence, capable of improvising plans to enable him to adapt to rapidly changing circumstances.

Although Massoud's Tadjiks were not riven by the complex tribal rivalries which divided the Pathans in the south, his long supply lines to Pakistan unavoidably passed through hostile tribal areas, which caused him endless difficulties throughout the war. Nor was he spared the problems of rivalry and interfactional fighting among the Mujahideen political groups.[29] Furthermore, as the most competent Mujahideen commander, Massoud was the most frequent target of major Soviet offensives. By the end of 1981 his Mujahideen had withstood four major Soviet incursions into the Panjshir valley.

However, despite these hindrances, Massoud had forged a formidable fighting force, composed of élite, company-size units known as *Grup-i-Mottahrek* (Mobile Groups). Their special function, in addition to normal, local defence, was to carry the war far beyond the Panjshir . In April 1982 Massoud led several Mottahreks in a daring raid over the high ridges of the Panjshir and down across the wide Shamlai plain. Their objective was Bagram, one of the principal Russian air bases in

Afghanistan. The Mottahreks struck the unsuspecting Russians just after midnight. With covering fire from 82mm mortars, they penetrated the outer defences and destroyed twenty-three helicopters and planes parked in dispersal points along the runway. It was a hard-hitting strike of surgical precision, with the Mottahreks safely back in their Panjshir mountain eyrie before dawn. With few Mujahideen casualties, and with damage to Russian military hardware running into millions of dollars' worth, this was one of the most successful Mujahideen raids of the entire war.

Shocked, the Russians quickly mounted a retaliatory fifth offensive against the Panjshir in May. A battalion of heliborne Russian troops were deployed to take the Mujahideen by surprise while a second column closed in from behind, having entered the Panjshir via the northern Anjuman Pass. Despite air activity from almost a hundred Mi-24 helicopter gunships, to ensure that no Mujahideen escaped, Massoud and his Mottahreks successfully evaded the hammer and anvil trap.

Four months later, in August, a larger and even more punishing Soviet offensive was launched. This time, rather than risk the prospect of serious damage to his Mujahideen, Massoud negotiated a cease-fire. Signed in January 1983, the uneasy

33

Left: The natural colours favoured by the Afghans help this Mujahid from Paktia blend into the background.

Right: Some of Massoud's Tadjik Mujahideen from northern Afghanistan. Unlike other Mujahideen, they had some semblance of a uniform from early on. Here they are dressed in Soviet uniforms purchased on the black market.

truce lasted until March of 1984. Naturally, this was very controversial among other Mujahideen factions, particularly those in areas not so threatened by Soviet forces. The Soviets had envisaged that the resulting furore would neutralise Massoud politically; moreover, with the cessation of hostilities in the region in which they were sustaining the heaviest casualties, they felt that they had secured the upper hand. In fact, they came off with the worst of the deal.

The terms of the cease-fire left Massoud free to continue the armed struggle outside the Panjshir. During this period he was also able to reorganise and resupply his Mujahideen and consolidate wider political gains. By patient and protracted negotiation he created a workable alliance among the Mujahideen factions of northern Afghanistan under a multi-party banner – The Council of the North. In 1984 he returned to the Panjshir to demonstrate the improved capabilities of his Mujahideen. Fresh outbreaks of fighting, particularly along the sensitive Russian Salang supply route, quickly evolved into a vicious tit-for-tat campaign.

More determined than ever to crush Massoud, the Soviets launched their seventh offensive into the Panjshir in April 1984. This included carpet bombing by Tu-16 bombers flying from the Soviet

Union. Several days of this preceded a heavy ground offensive. In the sparsely populated and precipitous mountain terrain of the Panjshir, the bombing had little effect. The psychological value of such tactics against the Mujahideen was minimal; in fact, when Massoud's men saw how ineffectual the bombing was, their morale increased. On 20 April a typical Soviet rolling barrage heralded the advance of the ground forces. Lacking a concentration of opposing forces to target, the barrage achieved little other than to warn the Mujahideen it was time to move out of the way. Massoud's Mottahreks survived intact yet again.

By 1986 Massoud felt sufficiently sure of his Panjshir heartland to spend much of the time away, fighting in other regions. The attack on the Afghan Army position at Kalafaghan, in Takhar province on 14 July 1987, was one of his most ambitious operations, notable for its methodical planning and preparation. It involved some 200 men from his Mottahrek units and 100 drawn from his local *Zabet* (fixed) units. After a heavy bombardment by 107mm rockets, 82mm mortars, and 82mm and 75mm recoilless rifles, the assault went in just after 17.00 hours. All five of Khalafaghan's strongpoints were overrun in less than forty-five minutes. The position was seized and the 500 soldiers defending

Right: The border town of Teri Mangal was one of the jumping-off points for caravans of arms being taken into Afghanistan. The ridge line in the background is the Pewir Kotal pass, the scene of one of Lord Roberts's victory against the Afghans during the Second Anglo-Afghan war in 1879.

it were killed or captured. This success was followed on 29 October 1987 by the seizure of
another battalion-size base at Kiran-o-Monjan, in
the far northern province of Badakshan.

Mikhail Gorbachev's historic 1986 speech at the
Moscow Party Congress, in which he referred to
the 'bleeding wound' of Afghanistan, had been the
first public hint of a Soviet withdrawal. By the end
of 1987 Massoud, unlike most other Mujahideen
commanders, was convinced that the Russians
genuinely wanted to leave. This had a marked
affect on his strategy: he began to avoid major
conflict with Soviet troops. Inevitably there were
still clashes, but gone were the titanic confrontations for which he was justly famous; instead he
began to prepare for the civil war between rival
Mujahideen factions which would inevitably follow
a Soviet withdrawal.

By April 1992 the Russians had gone and the
communist Afghan government was on the verge
of collapse. The race for Kabul was on between the
two principal contenders, Ahmad Shah Massoud
and Gulbadin Hekmatyr. Massoud was the man
who had persistently done the most to ensure that
the price for staying in Afghanistan was too high for
the Soviets. Gulbadin Hekmatyr was an anti-West-
ern Islamic fundamentalist who had exploited the

anomalies of Pakistani arms distribution to receive the lion's share of Western aid. This he had proceeded to use more ruthlessly against his fellow Mujahideen than against the Russians.[30]

Lead elements from both forces entered Kabul on the morning of 25 April 1992. Superior planning by Massoud ensured that his men secured all key points, including the historic Bala Hissar fortress, from which they had a commanding view over the city. Hekmatyr, in a fit of pique, ordered the shelling of the Bala Hissar. Meanwhile Massoud, supported by the former Afghan Air Force,[31] seized Kabul's Qahra International Airport to ferry in the bulk of his forces by Antonov transports. By the end of the second day he was firmly in control of the capital, with the sole exception of the Ministry of the Interior building, held by Hekmatyr. Unlike Hekmatyr, Massoud displayed no self-interest in his prize and held the city on behalf of the Mujahideen Coalition Government, in which (even as he shelled the city) Hekmatyr was Foreign Minister.

Ahmad Shah Massoud was undoubtedly the most outstanding Mujahideen commander to emerge from the war. As the man who ultimately seized Kabul for the Mujahideen, his place in history is assured.

36

BIBLIOGRAPHY
Svetlana Alexievich: *Zinky Boys: Soviet Voices from a Forgotten War*, Chatto & Windus, London, 1992
Michael Barthorp: *The North-West Frontier: A Pictorial History 1839–1947*, Blandford Press, Poole, 1982
Patrick Brogan: *World Conflicts: Why & Where They Happen*, Bloomsbury, London, 1989
Andre Brigot & Olivier Roy: *The War in Afghanistan*, Harvester Wheatsheaf, London, 1988
Gennady Bocharov: *Russian Roulette: The Afghanistan War through Russian Eyes*, Hamish Hamilton, London, 1990
Arthur Bonner: *Among the Afghans*, Duke University Press, US, 1987
Artyom Borovik: *The Hidden War: A Russian Journalist's Account of the Soviet War in Afghanistan*, Faber & Faber, London, 1991
Sir Olaf Caroe: *The Pathans 550 BC – AD 1957*, Oxford University Press, Karachi, Pakistan, 1980
Anthony Cordesman and A. Wagner: *The Lessons of Modern War*, Vol.3, Mansell Publishing, London 1990
Louis Dupree: *Afghanistan*, Princeton University Press, USA, 1980

Left: Living conditions were primitive. Mujahideen huddle round a fire inside their hut in Tizeen, Kabul Province, in 1987.

30. Among innumerable incidents, Gulbadin Hekmatyr's men were involved in the following: the murder of French doctor Thierry Niquet (1986); the hijacking of a 96-horse caravan of medical supplies belonging to the French aid organization Médecins sans Frontières, the death of US journalists Lee Sharpiro and Jim Luindalos and the murder of British cameraman Andy Skrzypowiak (1987); and the ambush and death of seven commanders and 23 Jamiat-i-Islami Mujahideen in Takhar province (9 July 1989).

31. In the weeks leading up to the fall of Kabul, large numbers of Afghan government forces went over to Massoud.

Major-General J. G. Elliot: *The Frontier 1839–1947*, Cassell, London, 1968

John Fullerton: The Soviet Occupation of Afghanistan, *Far Eastern Economic Review*, Hong Kong, 1983

Edward R. Giradet: *Afghanistan: The Soviet War*, Croom Helm, London, 1985

Cyril Glasse: *The Concise Encylopaedia of Islam*, Stacey International, London, 1989

T. A. Heathcote: *The Afghan Wars*, Osprey, London, 1980

Ian Hogg and John Weeks, *Military Small Arms of the 20th Century*, Arms & Armour Press, London, 1991

David Isby: *Russia's War in Afghanistan*, Osprey, London, 1986

David Isby: *War in a Distant Country*, Arms & Armour Press, London, 1989

David Isby: *Weapons & Tactics of the Soviet Army*, Janes, London 1988

Robert Kaplin: *Soldiers of God*, Houghton Mifflin, Boston, USA, 1990

John Keegan & Andrew Wheatcroft: *Zones of Conflict: An Atlas of Future Wars*, Jonathan Cape, London, 1986

John Laffin: *War Annual 1*, Brassey's, London, 1986

John Laffin: *War Annual 2*, Brassey's, London, 1987

John Laffin: *The World in Conflict 1989*, Brassey's, London 1989

Lt. General MacMunn: *Afghanistan*, Abid Bokhari, Quetta, Pakistan, 1979

Charles Miller: *Khyber: British India's North-West Frontier*, Macdonald & Janes, London, 1977

Edgar O'Ballance: *Afghan Wars 1839–1992*, Brassey's, London, 1993

D. S. Richards: *The Savage Frontier, A History of the Anglo-Afghan Wars*, Macmillan, London, 1990

Olivier Roy: *Islam and Resistance in Afghanistan*, Cambridge University Press, 1986

Amin Saikal and William Maley (eds): *The Soviet Withdrawal from Afghanistan*, Cambridge University Press

Maj. Oleg Sarin and Col. Lev Dvoretsky, *The Afghan Syndrome: The Soviet Union's Vietnam*, Presido Press, USA, 1993

Victoria Schofield: *Every Rock, Every Hill*, Buchan & Enright, London, 1984

Rob Schultheis: *Night Letters: Inside Wartime Afghanistan*, Orion Book, New York, 1992

General Sir Andrew Skeen: *Passing It On*, Aziz Publishers, Lahore, Pakistan, 1978

Hans-Heiri Stapfer: *Mi-24 Hind*, Squadron/Signal Publications, 1988

Arthur Swinson: *North-West Frontier*, Hutchinson & Co, 1967

Percy Sykes: *A History of Afghanistan*, 2 vols, Oriental Book Reprint Corporation, New Delhi, 1981

Vladislav Tammarov: *Afghanistan: Soviet Vietnam*, Mercury House, San Francisco, USA, 1992

Mark Urban: *War in Afghanistan* (2nd edition), Macmillan Press, 1990

Mohammad Yousaf and Mark Adkin: *The Bear Trap*, Leo Cooper, 1992

G. J. Younghusband: *Indian Frontier Warfare*, Anmol Publications, Delhi, 1985

Zaloga, Luczak and Beldam: *Armour of the Afghanistan War*, Concord Publications, Hong Kong, 1992

Below: Having just fired his RPG-7 towards retreating FAPLA forces near Cachingues, this camouflaged guerrilla advances under well-coordinated covering fire.

JIM HOOPER

Angola

'The land at the end of the earth', the Portuguese called it before they cut and ran, leaving Angola to be fought over by a confusing cast of players and supporters. And picked and fought over it has been in the two decades since – by the Chinese/US-backed FNLA, the Soviet/Cuban-backed MPLA and the South African/US-backed UNITA.[1] Few countries came to exemplify Cold War politics quite so much as Angola.

The coast of Angola was known to Portuguese explorers for almost 100 years before they established their first fort at Luanda in 1575 for the purpose of slave trading. By the time slavery was outlawed, millions of blacks had been exported to the Americas. Although apartheid in the South African sense was never applied (mixed-race marriages were not uncommon and carried no social stigma), Portuguese administration was severe and led to numerous rebellions that were put down with great brutality by the authorities.

In 1956, Portuguese-educated blacks and mixed-race *mesticos* from Luanda, led by Agostinho Neto and quietly backed by the Soviets, formed the anti-colonial MPLA. Four years later, Holden Roberto, a Bakongo chief, established the anti-colonial and anti-communist FNLA. With the independence of the Belgian Congo, both movements set up headquarters in the newly-named Zaire. In March 1961 Roberto's FNLA crossed into northern Angola in an uprising that killed more than 700 white farmers. Within days, Portuguese paratroopers and combat aircraft began arriving to commit wholesale revenge for the deaths of the colonialists. By October as many as 20,000 black Angolans had died, while another 150,000 had fled to Zaire.

In 1965 Jonas Savimbi, an Ovimbundu chief who alternated between university studies in Switzerland and serving as secretary-general of the FNLA, broke away from the movement to found UNITA. Convinced that neither the FNLA nor MPLA could prevail against the Portuguese by conducting hit-and-run raids from Zaire or Congo-Brazzaville (where the MPLA was already receiving training from Cuban advisers), Savimbi and ten co-revolutionaries travelled to China to learn guerrilla warfare. To the anger of the MPLA and FNLA, within the year UNITA had established itself deep inside Angola and was training new recruits.

1. FNLA – *Frente Nacional de Libertacao de Angola* – National Front for the Liberation of Angola; MPLA – *Movimento Popular de Libertacao de Angola* – Popular Movement for the Liberation of Angola; UNITA – *Uniao Nacional para a Independencia Total de Angola* – National Union for the Total Independence of Angola.

Savimbi's early attacks against Portuguese settlements were disasters of planning and execution, and held out little hope of future success. In spite of his efforts to establish alliances with the MPLA's Neto and the FNLA's Roberto, growing animosity between the three liberation movements resulted in open clashes even as they were each conducting ineffectual guerrilla warfare against the Portuguese. However, as the low-intensity conflict dragged on, it became intensely unpopular among the Portuguese working-class who were providing the bulk of increasingly reluctant conscripts to fight in Angola.

In April 1974 a group of pro-Soviet Portuguese army officers overthrew the Salazar regime in Lisbon and announced that all of Portugal's colonies would be given independence. Neto, Roberto and Savimbi flew to Lisbon to sign the Alvor Agreement, which stipulated the establishment of a coalition government between the three until elections following independence on 11 November 1975. But, even as the Portuguese junta was paying lip service to democratic elections in Angola, it was allowing Soviet surrogates in the form of Cuban advisers to train FAPLA, the MPLA's army. In response to what Peking saw as Soviet hegemony, China began sending arms to Holden Roberto's FNLA. The quirkiness of Cold War politics saw the US join China in supplying covert aid to the staunchly anti-communist FNLA.

The new coalition government took office on 31 January 1975, but within 24 hours fighting had broken out between the MPLA and FNLA. Cuban troops immediately stepped in to blunt the FNLA's advance, while Cuban ships waiting along the coast began offloading tanks, helicopters and more troops. Additional Cuban forces standing by in Congo-Brazzaville were airlifted to Luanda. UNITA, enjoying the largest popular support of the three movements but militarily the weakest, withdrew into the bush. The fifteen-year war of liberation moved directly into a bitterly contested civil war between those who had been fighting for independence.

The stakes were high – not only for the three liberation movements, but for the major Cold War antagonists. The Soviet Union, its long-term geopolitical strategy focused on eventual domination of southern Africa and its immense treasury of natural resources, had everything to gain and little to lose by gambling a few million dollars on the MPLA.

The USA, freshly traumatised by its defeat in Vietnam (for which the USSR could claim much credit), was deeply concerned at the prospect of another geo-strategic Third World country falling under Soviet influence. Washington upped the ante by sending weapons and CIA advisers to the FNLA and UNITA.[2] Unwilling to become directly involved in another foreign conflict so soon after Vietnam, the USA (along with a number of black African states terrified by Soviet expansionism), persuaded the South African Government to intervene.

By late September the first South African Defence Force (SADF) liaison officer arrived at Savimbi's headquarters in Huambo. October saw two hastily assembled and lightly armed battle groups – dubbed *Foxbat* and *Zulu* — crossing into southern Angola in what would enter SADF legend as Operation *Savannah*. Though untested on the battlefield since the Second World War and using obsolescent equipment, the SADF forged northward, their goal to capture as much territory as

> *Although the wars in Angola and South West Africa/Namibia were distinctly separate, they were inextricably entwined owing to the simultaneous involvement of South Africa in both. While the author has attempted to encapsulate each as much as possible, some overlap between the chapters on Angola and Namibia is unavoidable.*

Right: UNITA guerrillas listen to a briefing for a forthcoming attack against an Angolan garrison base in Bié province in central Angola. The central figure in this photograph carries a Soviet-manufactured 7.62mm PKM GPMG, while the others are armed with AK-47s. The guerrilla to the left has mounted a Soviet-manufactured M-60 anti-personnel rifle grenade on his Kalashnikov.

Below: UNITA's leader, Dr Jonas Malheiro Savimba, explains the current military situation in Angola during an interview by the author at his headquarters near Jamba in Cuando Cubango Province.

40

on Independence Day. Instead he sent his soldiers advancing towards the city and into a heavy Cuban artillery and rocket barrage. This broke the back of the FNLA and convinced the South Africans to concentrate their support on UNITA.

On 11 November the Portuguese High Commissioner, who had been tasked with ensuring the peaceful transition to independence and democracy, boarded a warship in Luanda harbour and sailed away. With the arrival of more Cuban troops and equipment, the collapse of the FNLA and the quick recognition of the unelected but *de facto* MPLA government by growing numbers of African states, the South Africans were in an awkward political position. To make matters worse, the CIA advisory and training teams had decamped without a word, and Washington was suffering severe amnesia about its request for intervention.[3] The only solution was a leisurely withdrawal by the SADF, while rendering UNITA what assistance it could. It was in this latter stage that the SADF and UNITA forged close links that would last for the next fifteen years. The last elements of *Savannah* crossed into Namibia on 27 March 1976, having learned lessons that would prove invaluable in the coming years.

THE GUERRILLA WAR BEGINS

The withdrawal of the South Africans left the ill-trained and under-armed UNITA facing the Cubans and the Angolan army alone. Its political headquarters in Huambo soon came under attack by MiG-21 fighter-bombers, 122mm multiple barrel rocket launchers (MBRLs), tanks and mechanised infantry. By late August UNITA was deep in the Angolan bush, from where Savimbi's ill-armed guerrillas began to launch hit-and-run raids against small FAPLA bases.

The South African Government was well aware of the potential benefit of supporting UNITA. If Savimbi controlled areas along the Angolan-Namibian border, insurgents of the South West Africa People's Organization (SWAPO) would be prevented from using them. The SADF's stores of obsolete equipment began to trickle to UNITA. By 1977 King Hassan of Morocco was also providing training bases for selected UNITA officers. Instructors from the French army, augmented by shadowy American 'experts', put them through a rigorous six-month course. At the same time, UNITA was allowed to establish its external headquarters in Rabat, where it was afforded official diplomatic status by Hassan. It was suspected that the training camps and diplomatic mission were financed by Middle Eastern countries at the request of the CIA,

2. In a collateral operation, the CIA funded a white mercenary force for the FNLA. Led by the psychopathic Costas Georgiou, a Greek Cypriot with the *nom de guerre* of 'Colonel Callan' (who executed 14 of his men for cowardice), they were routed by the Cubans. Of the twelve who were captured, Callan, two British and one American were executed after a lengthy show trial.

3. US Secretary of State Dr Henry Kissinger, the chief architect of South African intervention, would later testify before a Senate committee that South African had launched Operation *Savannah* in response to pleas from UNITA 'by sending military equipment and some personnel, without consulting the USA'. This was after pro-MPLA Democratic Senators Dick Clark and John Tunney had pushed the Clark Amendment through Congress, cutting off all aid to UNITA.

possible before the 11 November independence date. The speed of their advance took everyone by surprise as one objective after another fell to them. Numerically superior Cuban and FAPLA units that did not retreat were trampled underfoot.

South African Air Force (SAAF) C-130s carrying ammunition, troops and spare parts for the Eland 90 armoured cars (the South African version of the French Panhard AML 90) began flying deeper and deeper into Angola to resupply the two main battle groups. Their advance was accompanied at different times by either FNLA or UNITA troops. Undisciplined, unaccustomed to conventional warfare and demoralised by Cuban 122mm rockets, they were less concerned with engaging the enemy head-on than with occupying territory in the wake of the South Africans.

By 7 November one battle group was poised with FNLA forces 60km north of Luanda. The South Africans advised Roberto to consolidate the areas he controlled in order to be in a position of strength

as part of a covert operation to get around the Clark Amendment, which had cut off all aid to Savimbi.

The following year, in an equally secret operation, the Chinese (apparently at the behest of the USA) sent a major shipment of arms to UNITA. More than 500 tons of Communist Chinese weapons reached the guerrillas with the help of the vehemently anti-communist South Africans via Namibia.

UNITA GOES ON THE OFFENSIVE

By the end of 1979 the Benguela railway line linking the Angolan coast with Zaire, an important source of revenue for the communist MPLA government, was operating at a much reduced capacity as the result of UNITA sabotage. Long sections of track had been damaged, and most of its bridges destroyed. Up to this time, UNITA's guerrilla forces had conducted relatively insignificant harassing raids and ambushes designed to capture weapons and keep the Cubans and Angolan army off balance. With the return of officers from Morocco, however, Savimbi decided it was time to incorporate semi-conventional operations against his enemies. The first strategic objective was to take and hold Cuando Cubango Province in south-east

Angola. If successful, this would seal much of the border between Angola and Namibia, provide regular land routes for equipment supplied by the South Africans and give UNITA greater international political credibility.

In a carefully planned attack, a superior UNITA force overran the 600-man FAPLA garrison at Mavinga, a former Portuguese administrative centre 250km north of the Namibian border in Cuando Cubango Province. Stripping the town of everything usable, they then abandoned it. In mid-April 1980 a semi-conventional force using accurate rocket and mortar fire ahead of a classic infantry assault overwhelmed a 900-man garrison at Cuangar on the Namibian border. Other posts near the border also fell permanently to UNITA. A Cuban-led FAPLA motorised brigade attempting to retake the town of Savate was thrown back with heavy losses. Five months later, Mavinga was retaken and held.

With much of Cuando Cubango Province now secured, and his permanent headquarters developing in Jamba in the far south-east corner of the province, Savimbi began extending his operations to the west and north. Often operating in conjunction with the South African Defence Force 32 Battalion or the Reconnaissance Commandos, UNITA took and held more and more territory. An attempt

Above: Following an attack on a government base in central Angola, a dead government soldier is briefly examined by the victorious guerrillas. UNITA followed the classic guerrilla tactic of always attacking with overwhelming strength, destroying the enemy's infrastructure and then withdrawing before the arrival of reinforcements.

Below: Under examination by UNITA guerrillas, the remains of this Soviet-manufactured MiG-23 'Flogger' lie near the Cunzumbia River 100km north-west of UNITA's base at Mavinga. Towards the latter part of the war the use of US-supplied Stinger surface-to-air missiles almost completely neutralised the Angolan air force. Many Angolan pilots flatly refused to fly over areas where UNITA forces were known to operate, while those who did fly generally stayed above 6,000m, well out of range of the deadly missile.

by communist Angolan forces advancing from Cuito Cuanvale to retake Mavinga was badly beaten by UNITA. Accusations by the Angolan government that the South Africans had been directly involved in the fighting were probably correct, but were denied by both Savimbi and the SADF. Guerrilla operations continued as well, extending into the cities of Lobito, Benguela and the capital of Luanda itself, where bombs regularly disrupted power and water supplies.

Although the Carter Administration in Washington had maintained a cautious line of communication with UNITA, Savimbi's fortunes received an immeasurable boost with the 1980 election of Ronald Reagan. An avowed opponent of Soviet expansionism, Reagan set about persuading Congress to repeal the Clark Amendment, and sent a US military team to Angola to determine what UNITA needed in terms of military hardware.

In a politically delicate move, a group of South African military intelligence officers was invited to Washington to brief the CIA and Pentagon officials. Within weeks, the White House leaked its intention of linking elections in South African-controlled Namibia with a Cuban withdrawal from Angola.

The counterinsurgency (COIN) war between the South Africans and SWAPO along the central Namibia-Angola border was sharply escalated by the SADF with Operation *Protea* in August 1981, aimed at SWAPO bases in Angola. The FAPLA, Cuban and Soviet forces supporting SWAPO were hit hard by the SADF attack. Much of the 4,000 tons of Soviet-built military equipment captured by the SADF was passed to a grateful Savimbi.

To make clear its support for UNITA, the Reagan Administration invited Savimbi to Washington at the end of 1981. Well-publicised meetings with General Alexander Haig, the US Secretary of State, and Chester Crocker, the Deputy Undersecretary of State for African Affairs and the prime mover behind Reagan's southern African policy, produced promises of military aid. The visit effectively legitimised UNITA and provided the movement with an unprecedented propaganda coup. As though to emphasise UNITA's effectiveness, the Belgian-owned Petrofina oil refinery in Luanda was destroyed while Savimbi was in Washington. Although UNITA claimed credit for the attack, the possibility of it being a submarine-delivered South African special forces raid was high.

By late 1982 UNITA was expanding its semi-conventional operations north of the Benguela railway line. Important Cuban and Angolan army communications and logistics centres were successfully attacked, looted, and then abandoned. With the Cubans' advantage in fighter-bombers, helicopter gunships and armour, UNITA doctrine dictated retreat rather than a confrontation that could only end in defeat. Additionally, during an attack, clear avenues of escape were left open for the FAPLA soldiers, the rationale being that, if surrounded, they would fight more desperately and inflict greater casualties on the UNITA attackers. Being allowed to escape, they also spread stories of UNITA's military capabilities, further adding to the demoralisation of the government soldiers.

In mid-July 1983 Savimbi's forces captured Cangonga, Munhango and Cangumbe, all towns on the railway line. These would be repeatedly relinquished to Cuban-led FAPLA forces and retaken again in the course of the war. The few engines and little rolling stock that still ventured along the regularly damaged and repaired Benguela railway line continued to be reduced by guerrilla

ambushes.

Cangamba, a 3,000-man Cuban-commanded Angolan army garrison 200km south of the railway line in Moxico Province, became the focus of UNITA's largest semi-conventional attack up to that time. Setting aside much of the doctrine that had worked so well, Savimbi's forces brought in captured artillery pieces and surrounded the base with more than 6,000 troops; the first the garrison knew of their presence was the start of the pre-dawn artillery barrage on 4 August. Massed infantry attacks followed, during which UNITA suffered badly from anti-personnel mines. Cuban MiG-21 fighter-bombers and Mi-17 helicopter gunships made repeated bombing and strafing runs on the attackers, inflicting heavy casualties, but failed to stop them. The 200-man Cuban contingent, carrying its dead and wounded, was evacuated by helicopter when it became clear that Cangamba would fall. Eleven days after the attack opened, UNITA overwhelmed the last positions. The escaping defenders left behind almost 900 dead and over 300 prisoners. It was a stunning victory for the one-time rag-tag guerrilla army.

With UNITA morale at an all-time high, Savimbi launched a widespread guerrilla and semi-conventional offensive. Two garrisons within 200km of

Luanda were taken, but the Cubans struck back hard, recapturing both towns and inflicting heavy losses. Undeterred, UNITA overran the Angolan government's district capital of Cazombo, near the Zairean border, on 15 November. On 24 November Andulo, 100km north of the railway line in Bié Province, fell. Five days later Alto Chicapa, 150km north of Luena in Lunda Province, was captured. On 18 December Cacolo, another 100km north of Alto Chicapa, shared the same fate. Even farther north, the Chifufo diamond mine, guarded by former British SAS security guards and crucial to the Angolan economy, was seized on 23 February 1983, looted of millions of dollars' worth of diamonds, and abandoned.

None of these actions approached the scale of Cangamba, but Savimbi and his military commanders were content to concentrate on small posts in the countryside. Although they were individually insignificant, collectively they knitted together areas of growing UNITA control, forcing FAPLA and the Cubans to concentrate within the larger towns. The advantages were clear: domination of the countryside meant influence over the local peasantry, control of food production and greater freedom of movement; isolating the enemy allowed UNITA to predict their movements more accurately, and forced them to

Right: Using the old laterite road constructed by the Portuguese before independence in 1975, a column of UNITA guerrillas marches from Chicala towards Cachingues in western Bie province. The heavily loaded machine-gunner takes a short break as the others move steadily past him.

Below: Protected by South African supplied ponchos, a column of UNITA guerrillas halts under driving rain somewhere in the central highlands of Bie Province.

44

4. These offensives were faced with three major environmental obstacles: the terrain, which was often both sandy – wearing out tank track pins very quickly - and heavily forested; the heat, which played havoc with engines designed for European conditions; and the summer rains, which made the ground entirely too soft to support armour. Major offensives took place during the cool July-October dry season.

5. Almost a year later, Savimbi and the South African Government were deeply embarrassed when Captain Wynand du Toit of the Reconnaissance Commandos was wounded and captured by the Angolans in Cabinda. Two other special forces soldiers were killed, while the balance of the nine-man team escaped in rubber boats, presumably to a waiting submarine. Under interrogation Du Toit admitted his mission had been to destroy Gulf Oil storage tanks, pipelines and fire-fighting equipment. UNITA propaganda leaflets in his possession would have been left at the scene to give credit to Savimbi's guerrillas.

6. However intimidating these figures may have seemed, they were never an indication of actual aircraft availability. Inadequate maintenance kept a large percentage on the ground, while non-operational mishaps among the Angolan units caused more losses than combat. Of the eight SU-22s delivered, for example, within two months only one remained, the rest having been destroyed in training accidents. It was estimated by South African Military Intelligence that barely 50% of the Angolan Air Force was airworthy at any given time.

rely on airlifted supplies or easily ambushed convoys.

Following UNITA's success at Cangamba, the Angolan government sent a delegation to Moscow to plead for more sophisticated weapons systems. By early 1984 the shipments began to arrive. Among them were MiG-23 fighter-bombers and Mil Mi-25 helicopter gunships (the export version of the Mi-24). Up to then, UNITA had made reasonably good use of its captured, though unreliable, SAM-7 missiles and anti-aircraft guns, shooting down over 40 fixed-wing aircraft and helicopters. The Mi-25, however, had sophisticated anti-missile defences and a titanium hull that was almost impervious to weapons of less than 14.5mm. Its first employment came after UNITA forces had overrun Sumbe on the Atlantic coast and were withdrawing, when they were caught in the open by Cuban-flown Mi-25s and badly mauled.

OFFENSIVES AGAINST UNITA

Emboldened by its new weapons and the arrival of another 4,000 Cuban troops, the MPLA launched a dry-season[4] offensive from Luena against UNITA in May 1984. The objective was the recovery of towns in the Cazombo salient, which juts into Zambia and Zaire on Angola's easternmost border. Although UNITA suffered heavy casualties, it stopped the advance and forced a retreat. In August, a second FAPLA/Cuban offensive advanced towards Mavinga from Cuito Cuanavale and simultaneously from Luena towards Munhango, Savimbi's birthplace. This, too, was beaten back.

UNITA's guerrilla war continued apace with the semi-conventional one. In April 1984 a truck bomb containing more than 300kg of TNT exploded out-

side a barrack used by Cuban and Soviet officers in Huambo. Up to 200 people died, including almost 40 Cubans and three senior Soviet officers. Two months later more than 130 FAPLA troops were killed less than 200km from Luanda when their train was attacked and destroyed. In July guerrillas struck the US Gulf Oil complex in Cabinda, killing two dozen Angolan workers and destroying sections of pipeline. The following month UNITA claimed credit for sinking two East German ships in Luanda harbour, though the amphibious attack had all the hallmarks of a South African Reconnaissance Commando operation.[5]

By now, both UNITA and the South African Government openly acknowledged the links between each other. The delivery of arms and ammunition, much of it from stocks captured by the SADF on cross-border operations against SWAPO and its communist allies, had increased dramatically. Equipment that was difficult to replace, such as barrels and ammunition for the Chinese Type 63 107mm MBRLs received in 1977, was manufactured for UNITA by small engineering firms in South Africa. One company installed a complete machine shop and assembly plant at UNITA's main logistics base at Likuwa for the production of the rockets. Diesel to fuel UNITA's hundreds of captured and South African-built trucks arrived weekly. Tactical field radios, medical supplies, rations, boots, chest webbing and hundreds of other items arrived in convoys from SADF bases in the Caprivi Strip or by air.

The arms deliveries to Angola from the Soviet Union that had begun in early 1984 continued through most of 1985. By the end of August Western intelligence agencies estimated that the communist forces now had 30 MiG-23s, 8 Sukhoi Su-22s and 50 MiG-21 fighter-bombers, plus 34 Mi-25 helicopter gunships and 68 Mi-8/17 helicopter transports/gunships. Aircraft bought from Western countries included some 30 Alouette III and 22 Wasp helicopters, 25 Pilatus PC-7s and a wide variety of light and medium transport aircraft.[6] Ground forces were supported by at least 30 T-62 main battle tanks, 250 T-54/55s, 160 ageing T-34/85s and 50-odd PT-76 light amphibious tanks. Added to those numbers were numerous BRDM and BTR armoured personnel carriers (APCs) and BMP armoured fighting infantry vehicles (AFIVs). But the heat and the often sandy or heavily forested terrain, coupled with slipshod maintenance, substantially reduced their combat readiness.

Troop build-ups kept pace with arms deliveries, and by late 1985 at least 30,000 Cuban troops were in Angola, together with over 3,000 Soviet and East German staff officers, intelligence analysts and specialist technicians. These figures were used by the pro-UNITA lobby in Washington to effect the repeal of the Clark Amendment in mid-July, opening the door for overt aid to Savimbi. The MPLA, anticipating the dangers of such aid — which would begin the following year — reacted swiftly by planning and launching Operation *Congress II*, the biggest offensive yet against UNITA. To bolster Angolan army ranks, SWAPO and the African National Congress (ANC) were ordered by the Angolan government to contribute heavily to the operation as a *quid pro quo* for using Angola to base and train their forces.

Late July saw four motorised infantry brigades set off from Luena for Cazombo, and five more strike eastward from Cuito Cuanvale for Mavinga. Another nine brigades were held in reserve. Led by Soviet and Cuban advisers, it was a two-pronged advance designed to split Savimbi's semi-conventional army and force him to fight on two fronts simultaneously, without hope of reinforcements or adequate logistic support. Under constant daylight air cover, *Congress II* steam-rollered towards its objectives. Desperate UNITA ambushes and harrying attacks wounded the advancing columns, but failed to cripple them. By early September the communist forces had reached the outer defensive perimeters of both objectives through sheer weight of numbers. The situation for Savimbi was critical. He could fight on both fronts and possibly lose both, or concentrate on one. The decision was made to abandon Cazombo and redeploy those forces to Mavinga; should the enemy take the strategically located town and all-weather airstrip, it would give them a springboard towards UNITA's headquarters in Jamba.

Pretoria, equally concerned, rushed 32 Bn and G-5 155mm artillery to Mavinga and ordered air strikes in support of the defenders. Reinforcements, South African intervention and the Angolan army's Achilles' heel – a long and difficult logistics line under constant attack by UNITA and elements of 32 Bn – combined to halt the offensive and send it retreating on 7 October. It was the closest Savimbi had come to a strategic defeat since the beginning of the war, and caused great concern in Washington. Before the end of the year, the first shipments of Stinger shoulder-launched surface-to-air missiles and TOW anti-tank missiles were arriving in Jamba.[7]

At the same time, Soviet General Konstantin Shagnovitch, who had made his name in Afghanistan, arrived in Luanda as the new com-

mander of all forces aligned against UNITA. Planning for the next dry-season offensive was soon under way, with heavy emphasis on logistics. Troop build-ups began at Cuito Cuanvale, where the main thrust would be launched. Stockpiles of ammunition and diesel were amassed at the main logistic centre at Menongue, to where supplies would be flown or carried by rail directly from the port of Namibe, and then convoyed to Cuito Cuanavale.

In January 1986 Savimbi's international profile was boosted by another invitation to Washington. Meetings with President Reagan and State Department and Pentagon officials produced promises of yet more aid. On his return to Jamba, Savimbi ordered an escalation of guerrilla operations across the length and breadth of Angola in an attempt to draw some of Luanda's forces away from the coming offensive and divert some logistic support. Shagnovitch was not to be deterred, and on 27 May 1986 his forces set off from Luena towards Munhango, and from Cuito Cuanvale for Mavinga.

UNITA responded by hitting the lumbering enemy's flanks hard while reinforcing Mavinga. The

Above: After a successful attack against a government base, this exhausted UNITA officer poses in front of a faded MPLA flag painted on a building in the former Portuguese town. He is armed with a US-supplied M-79 40mm grenade launcher and carries a South African-supplied tactical radio.

7. It was one of the ironies of the war that while Gulf Oil was paying taxes to the US government on the profits from its Angolan oil concessions (granted by the MPLA government), the US was, at least theoretically, using those taxes to provide UNITA with advanced weapons systems to defeat the MPLA.

Right: The entrance to UNITA's well-maintained headquarters at Jamba in the far south-eastern corner of Cuando Cubango Province.

SADF deployed artillery to the Mavinga front, along with elements of 32 Bn and the Reconnaissance Commandos. Other 32 Bn companies were sent north in support of UNITA units harassing the columns advancing on Munhango. On 4 June a South African Navy *Minister*-class fast strike craft entered Namibe harbour under cover of night and fired Skerpioen missiles that destroyed two storage tanks containing fuel crucial to Shagnovitch's operational plans. In the confusion that followed, divers from the Reconnaissance Commandos' amphibious warfare section placed underwater charges that sank one Cuban freighter and severely damaged two Soviet cargo ships loaded with arms and ammunition. It was a brilliantly executed action that severely disrupted the logistic tail extending from Namibe to Menongue to Cuito Cuanavale.

UNITA's escalation of guerrilla operations in the far north finally had its intended effect of drawing off part of the communist forces advancing toward Munhango. This reduction of manpower, coupled with determined UNITA attacks on logistics lines, caused the communists to bog down far short of their objective. Farther south, attacks on the supply route between Menongue and Cuito Cuanavale, plus heavy UNITA resistance, halted the Soviet-led advance less than 20km after it started. Unexpectedly, UNITA launched a counterattack with the help of SADF long-range artillery and air strikes. To the dismay of the Soviets and Cubans, at the end of July the Angolan troops followed their SWAPO and ANC allies in a panicked retreat back to Cuito Cuanavale, abandoning weapons, tanks and vehicles on the way. The Soviet general's first offensive in Angola had been an ignominious failure.

THE LAST HURRAH

Making the same basic mistakes that their US counterparts had made in Vietnam 25 years earlier, Shagnovitch and his staff officers concluded that UNITA could be beaten if a still larger force with more advanced weapons could be put into the field. Sophisticated equipment was soon arriving from the USSR, some so new that Western military experts had never seen it. The inclusion of SA-6, SA-8 and SA-9 surface-to-air missile systems suggested that South African air strikes had played a major role in blunting the Mavinga axis of the last offensive. Overall, it was a quantum leap in men and *matériel*. As the 1987 dry season approached, preparations went forward for the most powerful thrust yet into UNITA-controlled Angola.

Late July saw the beginning of the offensive. The northern axis aimed for Cangamba, while a two-pronged attack from Cuito Cuanavale headed for Mavinga. By the middle of August the northern axis had been forced to retreat after debilitating losses to UNITA. The heavier advance from Cuito Cuanavale was not so easily thwarted, though the terrain and constant attacks by UNITA and SADF armoured vehicles slowed them to barely 4km a day. The Reconnaissance Commandos had also been at work: the bridge from Cuito Cuanavale across the Cuito River had been so badly damaged by a special forces team that it could not support vehicles. As a result, long delays occurred as supplies were ferried across by boats or lifted over by helicopters. But the mere weight of the advance drove it forward. Two FAPLA brigades, the 16th and 21st, struck due east, with the intention of swinging right to hit Mavinga from the north. Another two, the 47th and 59th, were clawing their way to the south-east to attack Mavinga from the south.

Unwilling to accept the threat to the Namibian border if UNITA were defeated, the South Africans had already committed themselves to battle in what was named Operation *Modular*. With 32 Bn already supporting UNITA in attacking convoys along the Menongue-Cuito Cuanavale supply route, batteries of 127mm MBRLs supported by 120mm mortars were rushed into place south of the Lomba River. They were soon followed by long-range G-5 155mm artillery and elements from the South West Africa Territory Force (SWATF) 101 Bn.

By 8 September FAPLA's 21 Brigade had reached the River Lomba. Two days later it was crossing the wide savannah bordering the river when salvos of South African 127mm rockets, 155mm shells and 120mm mortar bombs virtually wiped it out. Six Soviet specialists manning an SA-8 mobile missile launcher also died. On 11 September elements of 59 Brigade attempting to cross at another point were surprised by combined 101 Bn and UNITA forces. The survivors hastily withdrew, leaving 300 FAPLA dead. The South Africans next struck 47 Brigade, killing almost 400 before FAPLA disengaged. As the remnants of 47 Brigade were moving north to link up with 59 Brigade, they were hit again by the SADF and effectively destroyed. The terrified survivors fled, abandoning T-55 tanks, BM-21 122mm MBRLs, BMP armoured vehicles, logistics vehicles, anti-aircraft cannon and SA-8 missile batteries.

Although the battle had now been decided, the opportunity to administer a *coup de grâce* to the three remaining FAPLA brigades was too good to miss. More 127mm MBRL batteries were deployed from South Africa, along with a squadron of Olifant tanks and a number of G-6 155mm guns (the self-propelled version of the G-5). The G-5s and G-6s dropped tons of high explosives on the already badly damaged Angolan forces, pinning them in place. At the same time, Cuito Cuanavale received the attention of the South Africans' extremely accurate long-range artillery. South African Air Force Mirage fighter-bombers added to the carnage by streaking in under Angolan radar cover and pulling up to toss their bombs on to the target from a range of 8 to 10km before racing back south.[8]

The overwhelming defeat suffered by FAPLA and its Soviet and Cuban leaders occurred under a complete SADF news blackout. As a result, the Angolan propaganda campaign claimed that exactly the opposite was happening, leading the international media to report that it was the South Africans and UNITA who were being beaten. Fidel Castro, his Latin *machismo* severely bruised, began deploying 50 Brigade, Cuba's most professional unit, to Angola in November, while new tanks and thousands of raw FAPLA recruits were sent to

Menongue. It was clear that another offensive was imminent, and the South African G-5s and G-6s continued to pound Cuito Cuanavale and the supply corridor from Menongue.

Operation *Modular* blended into Operation *Hooper* as the rains came and the SADF prepared itself to meet an unprecedented wet-season offensive. In a surprise move, 21 Brigade broke through UNITA resistance in late January 1988, but failed to exploit its advantage before being driven back by South African forces two weeks later. In mid-February an SADF mechanised battalion hit the reconstituted 59 Brigade 20km east of Cuito Cuanavale. The Cuban-led brigade fell back, regrouped and counterattacked. It was a brave but fruitless effort. Badly mauled, they were forced to retreat, leaving the battlefield littered with more high-tech equipment.

More spoiling actions took place through February as Operation *Hooper* was replaced by *Packer*,

8. Faced with SA-3, SA-6, SA-8 and SA-9 missile batteries linked to six different radar systems and manned by Soviet technicians, the SAAF were, according to one pilot, 'operating within a very narrow survivability envelope'.

Left: A UNITA crew load South African-manufactured 107mm rockets into a Chinese-manufactured Type 63 MBRL 30km south of Munhango on the Bengula railway line. Easily transportable via Unimog or oxcart, this weapon was employed extensively by UNITA throughout Angola.

Right: This veteran UNITA guerrilla will remain hidden while the rest of his comrades continue their advance into central Angola, waiting to see if enemy forces are following. Once he and others of the trail element are convinced their presence has not been detected, they will rejoin the main force. Tucked behind his chest webbing are two 60mm mortar bombs.

Left: With a fierce battle raging for the town of Cuemba on the Benguela railway line a few kilometres to the east, these UNITA semi-conventional forces rush toward the front carrying 120mm mortar bombs.

Left: Near the town of Munhango on the Benguela railway line, these UNITA guerrillas examine a Mil Mi-17 helicopter gunship destroyed by mortar fire.

Left: The Kwanza River was the demarcation line between what UNITA termed 'Free Angola' and the 'Disputed Territories'. Here UNITA guerrillas cross the Kwanza at the beginning of an operation to attack and destroy the Angolan garrison base at Cachingues.

Above: A highly detailed 'mud map' of Cachingues is surrounded by the UNITA guerrillas who will lead the assault. It faithfully duplicates defensive trenchworks and locations of support weapons, as well as dead ground to be used during the assault. Each building is represented by stones marked with small flags to denote its use – HQ, communications centre, barracks, dispensary, lecture hall and mess. An intelligence officer briefs them on the enemy's strength, state of readiness and morale.

Right: After attacking and occupying Angolan army positions, UNITA guerrillas resupply themselves with captured ammunition. These men will each take what they can comfortably carry from the pile of 60mm and 82mm mortar bombs found in a hastily abandoned bunker.

which dug in with its G-5s in range of Cuito Cuanavale as insurance against the communist forces launching another attack. But the Soviet-commanded battle groups were no longer capable of offensive action. Almost 5,000 combatants were confirmed dead and thousands more were wounded, many of whom would subsequently die or be permanently disabled. Equipment losses of 14 fighter-bombers, 23 helicopters, 103 tanks, 19 complete missile systems, and more than 450 armoured and logistic vehicles and ancillary supplies, either destroyed or captured, were conservatively valued at over a billion dollars.

The beating at the hands of the South Africans and UNITA had exhausted and demoralised the survivors. New officers and NCOs would have to be trained to replace those who had been killed or seriously wounded. Many vehicles which had escaped direct battle damage required extensive maintenance, and depleted stockpiles of crucial supplies were in need of replenishment. To compound the humiliation, two Cuban air force pilots – one of them Lieutenant Colonel Manuel Rojas Garcia, the air force commander for southern Angola – had been shot down and captured while flying a photo-reconnaissance mission east of Cuito Cuanavale. (When asked by his UNITA interrogators why he was flying the mission himself, Rojas admitted that all of the Angolan pilots under his command had refused.)

On the other side, 31 South Africans had died, and two aircraft, three tanks and four Ratel-90 armoured fighting infantry vehicles had been destroyed. UNITA's losses, never revealed, probably lay in the region of 2,000 men. It was, all in all, a stunning victory for the UNITA-South African alliance, leaving Savimbi's forces in a stronger military and political position than before the series of offensives against him. A disgraced Shagnovitch was recalled to Moscow, and Soviet Premier Mikhail Gorbachev began to look at the pros and cons of continuing to gamble a billion dollars a year on a war that was clearly unwinnable.

But the South Africans were equally tired of the war. Pretoria's support of Savimbi was purely pragmatic: UNITA protected much of the Namibian border from SWAPO infiltration. That counter-insurgency war was already costing the South African Government upwards of a million dollars a day, on top of what it had invested in building up and sup-

Above: The men who will lead an assault against an Angolan army base listen intently to a briefing by an intelligence officer whose information has been received from a guerrilla reconnaissance team that has been watching the base for over a week. The weapon in the right foreground is a captured Soviet-manufactured AGS-17 30mm automatic grenade launcher, flanked by a 7.62mm PKM GPMG. In the right background one guerrilla holds an RPG-7 with an anti-personnel warhead, while next to him another man has plugged the end of his US-supplied 40mm M-79 grenade launcher by inserting a round into the muzzle.

Above: Without the support of the local population to provide shelter, food, intelligence and logistical help, no guerrilla movement can survive. These Angolan civilians serve as ammunition bearers for UNITA. The man in the foreground carries a 107mm rocket, followed by women with 82mm mortar bombs.

9. The SAAF was ill-equipped to counter the air threat. Although the superior quality of its pilots in their ageing Mirages gave them better odds in close-in dogfights, they were hopelessly outclassed by the Soviet longer ranging, head-on shoot-down air-to-air missiles carried by the MiG-23s.

10. When the CIA operation was in full swing, three US Air Force C-141 flights a week delivered supplies to Kamina in Zaire, while daily C-130 flights ferried the stockpiles – including diesel – to UNITA logistics bases in Angola.

porting UNITA. Until the Marxist SWAPO renounced the armed struggle and the Cubans agreed to withdraw from Angola, however, the South Africans could not afford to allow elections in Namibia. A pro-Soviet government in Windhoek, supported by Cuban and Soviet troops on South Africa's border, was completely unacceptable. Discreet approaches were made to Moscow: send the Cubans home and we will implement United Nations Security Council Resolution 435, calling for UN-supervised elections in Namibia. The response was positive. With the USA and the Soviet Union acting as mediators, negotiations opened between South Africa, Angola and Cuba.

In the meantime, his enemies spent and staggering, Savimbi confidently stepped up operations across the country. With the support of captured T-55 tanks, UNITA overran the FAPLA defenders at Munhango in a morning. Other towns along the Benguela railway line were quickly retaken, and sabotage attacks increased in and around Luanda and other major towns and cities. By the time Cazombo fell to UNITA again, the Angolan army and its Soviet and Cuban advisers were once again confined to easily defended population centres. Savimbi was rid-

ing a crest, while for the communist government the security situation had never been worse.

But the war had achieved its own dynamics, the most unpredictable element of which was Fidel Castro. His internationalist Holy Grail remained a Marxist Angola, and he began deploying yet more troops even as negotiations were progressing. This gave spine to the Angolan government, which still had delusions of a military solution to its political impasse with UNITA. Concerned by this development, Washington let it be known that, in order to keep the South Africans at the table and protect UNITA, it was planning to treble its military aid to Savimbi. What other inducements and secret agreements were reached with the South Africans is unknown, but the SADF began a staged withdrawal from Angola in March after a last clash near Cuito Cuanavale.

Yet, even as the SADF moved south from bases in south-central Cunene Province, the vacuum was being filled by Cuban and FAPLA troops accompanied by SWAPO insurgents. By 23 May Cuban troop levels in Angola had risen to almost 50,000, of which more than 10,000, supported by tanks, anti-aircraft guns and missile batteries, artillery and 122mm MBRLs, had advanced to within 60km of the Namibian border. The airfield at Xangongo was improved to accept MiG-23s, which began violating Namibian airspace.[9] To those who had studied Castro, it seemed that the threatening move might be no more than a propaganda exercise that would allow the Cuban leader to claim he had chased the South Africans out of Angola. On the other hand, it could be a prelude to the Cubans invading Namibia and installing a SWAPO government – as they had done for the MPLA in Angola in 1975.

The inevitable confrontation finally took place. An armoured and mechanised South African force near Calueque was waiting to cross the Cunene River into Namibia on 26 June when it was attacked by elements of the Cuban 70 Armoured Division supported by mechanised infantry. The veteran South African commander, supported by a company from 32 Bn and G-5 artillery, immediately engaged the over-confident, newly-arrived Cubans. When the attackers retreated they had lost three tanks, three BTR-60 armoured vehicles and more than 300 men. South African losses amounted to one dead, two wounded and two Ratel AFIVs destroyed. It was the last action the SADF would fight on Angolan soil.

But the war was far from over. Although part of the negotiations stipulated an end to South African military aid to UNITA, the CIA was already stepping in to provide Savimbi with whatever he needed.[10]

Far left: This young Angolan soldier, forced into the army by government press gangs and given the most rudimentary training, never stood a chance against the seasoned guerrilla force that overwhelmed his position. Still wrapped in the blanket in which he was sleeping when the pre-dawn attack came, he was left behind by his panic-stricken comrades, who fled their poorly prepared defensive positions.

Near left: An exhausted UNITA officer pauses after an ambush against an Angolan army unit, which quickly disengaged and retreated to the town of Cangonga on the Benguela railway line. Soon afterwards, a battery of Soviet-commanded D-30 122mm howitzers raked the area.

Far left: This French-trained UNITA officer carries a well-maintained AK-47, a Browning 9mm pistol and South African chest webbing for his Kalashnikov magazines.

Near left: Operating somewhere in Moxico Province, this UNITA officer pauses until a reconnaissance unit ahead of the column confirms that there are no enemy troops in the area. He carries a South African-supplied tactical field radio.

Right: With a heavy contact occuring between UNITA and FAPLA troops two kilometres to the east and Angolan-flown Mi-8 helicopters attempting to land at Cangonga six kilometres to the north, General Arlindo 'Ben-Ben' Pena, UNITA's deputy chief of staff (far right) calls for pre-registered 120mm mortar and 127mm fire to prevent the helicopters landing with supplies and to pick up wounded.

Right: The charred body of a FAPLA or Cuban tank commander lies next to his T-55 after it was hit by South African tank fire. The biggest tank battle on the African continent since the Second World War took place during the attempted FAPLA offensive against UNITA in 1987. In the tank-to-tank encounters FAPLA lost 73 tanks, while failing to destroy any SADF tanks. (Tim Rudman)

Right: UNITA engineers adapted this Russian-made KPV 14.5mm heavy machine-gun to a British Land Rover. As heavy as it is reliable, the KPV was originally designed for use against aircraft, but is excellent for long-range supporting fire. This crew was waiting for an advancing Cuban-advised MPLA brigade near Cuemba on the Benguela railway line.

By now UNITA effectively controlled 65 per cent of the country and was operating throughout the rest. The Angolan government, however, believing that the cessation of direct South African intervention would now tip the balance in its favour, refused Savimbi's offer of negotiations and began preparations for another push. In late October 1988 a half-hearted Soviet- and Cuban-led offensive retook Cuemba, Munhango and Cangonga on the railway line. Savimbi scored a strategic victory by returning the two Cuban pilots and promising not to attack Cuban forces so long as they were not directly involved in combat operations. The war would now be a slugging match between UNITA and FAPLA. A year later, with the Soviets and Cubans providing only logistical and technical support, a two-pronged push set off from Cuito Cuanavale for Mavinga again, but was stopped by UNITA near the Cunzumbia River and forced to retreat after advancing less than 40km.

THE LAST CHAPTER?

With the final withdrawal of the Cubans, a number of peace initiatives were brokered between the two forces. Each fell apart as a muscular UNITA took more territory in anticipation of a straightforward military victory – or elections, whichever came first – and an obdurate communist government refused to prune its Marxist roots by acceding to multi-party elections. The communist hardliners also clung

desperately to the belief that one more offensive could take Mavinga, drive on to Jamba and win the war. In consequence of that belief, another massive build-up took place at Cuito Cuanavale, and UNITA reinforced Mavinga. This last determined attempt by FAPLA, with front-line leadership by Portuguese mercenaries, almost proved them right, reaching the outskirts of the town before it was stopped by an equally determined UNITA. The fighting lasted for weeks, but in the end FAPLA was driven back.

A truce was finally called, and negotiations led to elections on 30 September 1992. It is generally reported by the international media that when Savimbi saw that UNITA had lost he attacked the MPLA. According to a senior South African diplomat who was in Luanda at the time, however, on the day after the elections FAPLA tanks surrounded the UNITA party headquarters and opened fire. The truth of who fired the first shots may never be known, but the war exploded once more. Within weeks, UNITA had taken Huambo after the biggest battle to be fought on the African Continent since the Second World War, although the fighting was ignored by the international media because of what was happening in the former Yugoslavia. More than 10,000 lives were lost.

In the meantime, the communist government began hiring more mercenaries: Russians to fly their few remaining MiGs and Israelis to service them; Portuguese and Spanish to protect Luanda

Right: Senior UNITA field commanders inspect a position in part of an L-shaped ambush position along the route of an expected Angolan armour and mechanised infantry advance. The weapon in the foreground is a captured Soviet AGS-17 30mm automatic grenade launcher.

Centre right: After the storming of the Angolan garrison post at Cachingues, UNITA destroyed what remained of the former Portuguese town. These men glance back at a barracks being blown up.

Below: This South African-supplied Unimog command vehicle operating near the Cunzumbia River east of Cuito Cuanavale carries a Soviet-made KPV 14.5mm heavy machine-gun.

56

and South Africans to retake crucial oil-storage and pumping stations captured by UNITA. One of the few such actions of which anything is known occurred after UNITA captured the petroleum complex at Soyo. Under the auspices of 'Heritage Oil', a former officer of 32 Bn was contracted to raise a 100-man mercenary force. Composed of former members of 32 Bn, the Reconnaissance Commandos and Koevoet, it was flown first to Namibia and then on to Luanda. After a sharp fight, the mercenaries took and secured Soyo before handing it over to FAPLA forces, which one hardened South African veteran of the Angolan war described to the author as 'worthless'. Within weeks, UNITA had driven out FAPLA and reoccupied the coastal town.

By late 1993 the communist Angolan government again agreed to talks. At the time of writing, both sides are in Lusaka, seeking a solution. They talk, and the war continues.

Below right: A BMP-2 armoured fighting infantry vehicle lies in pieces after being hit by a US-supplied TOW missile during an offensive in October 1989.

Like the Americans in South East Asia, the Cubans and Russians in Angola fought a conventional war against an increasingly sophisticated will-o'-the-wisp guerrilla army enjoying two decades' worth of bush warfare experience. And the Angolan troops they supported were every bit as moribund as the South Vietnamese soldiers the Americans – with equal frustration – supported two decades earlier with massive quantities of arms and *matériel*, yet forever failed to forge into a viable army. While UNITA lived off the land *à la* Viet Cong, their enemies relied on food ferried through hostile territory, where mines and ambushes took a heavy toll. Air deliveries were equally risky. In October 1988 the author watched Angolan-piloted Mi-8 helicopters attempting to land at Cangonga on the Benguela railway line. Heavy mortar and rocket fire from UNITA positions drove them away. In response to their radio calls for help, MiGs scrambled from Luena reported that they were approaching the target at 3,000m. The threat of Stingers, however, sent them another 3,000m higher, from where their bombs were scattered harmlessly across the thick forest. From UNITA's side, supplies moved steadily, albeit laboriously, along its version of the Ho Chi Minh Trail – thousands of kilometres of torturous dirt tracks that were never successfully interdicted. By the mid-1980s UNITA was conducting operations throughout 90 per cent of Angola. That the Cubans, having trained insurgent forces in Central America, and the Soviets, with their own COIN experience against the Mujahideen in Afghanistan, never developed tactics to counter Savimbi's guerrilla forces was a case of professional incompetence and undoubtedly a major factor in UNITA's military success.

Below left: A narrow bridge of saplings crosses one of the many small rivers in Bié Province. When UNITA semi-conventional forces moved into a new area, long-emplaced guerrillas acted as guides and performed reconnaissance for them.

Below: Waiting for the order to continue, these UNITA semi-conventional soldiers pause in the thick bush of Bié Province near the Benguela railway line.

Above: To the victors... A UNITA staff officer inspects a Soviet-built BMP-2 destroyed by indirect fire during an attempted offensive against Mavinga.

Above right: Hardened UNITA guerrillas, veterans of 15 years of war, take a short break west of the Kwanza River in Bié Province.

KEN GUEST

Cambodia

T he original Cambodians, or *Khmers,* called their land *Kok Thlok,* loosely meaning 'Land of Trees'. This description is no less accurate today than when it was carved into the stonework of a temple over a thousand years ago. Situated between modern Thailand and Vietnam on the flat, fertile plains of a prehistoric sea bed, this small country was to grow into the dominant regional power.

At its height, between the ninth and fifteenth centuries, the Khmer Empire stretched westwards from the coast of what is now Vietnam, across Thailand, to Burma in the east. From its southern extremities, in the Malayan peninsula, it extended north almost to China. During their six hundred years of power and prosperity, the Khmer kings undertook massive building projects. The forests and jungles of Cambodia bloomed with huge, stone temple complexes, exquisite carvings and artificial lakes. The greatest of the temples was Angkor Wat, the largest religious building in the world.

The glory years of Cambodian power began with King Jayavarman II in the ninth century. It was he who liberated Cambodia from Javanese domination and was responsible for the first great expansion of the Khmer Empire through military conquest. His martial successes are reflected in his name, which roughly translates from the Sanskrit as 'Protected by Victory'. Jayavarman also borrowed the principle of divine kingship from the Hindu religion: from his reign forward Cambodia was ruled by god-kings.

It was not until the fifteenth century that cracks began to appear in the Empire. In the late 1460s the Khmers were preoccupied with internal conflict between two rival kings and concerned about the direct threat posed by Siam (Thailand) to their west. When the small country of Champa, on their north-eastern border, appealed for aid against incursions by the Annamite Kingdom (Vietnam), they failed to respond. Champa fell in 1471, thus removing an important buffer state between the Khmer Empire and the ambitious Annamites. The subsequent innumerable campaigns between them began to erode the dominance of the Khmers.

In 1556, when the Burmese captured the neighbouring Siamese capital of Auyutthia, the Khmers seized the opportunity to grab back border regions previously lost to the Siamese. By 1587 Siam had recovered sufficiently to counter-attack with a vengeance and capture the capital of Cambodia, then

Left: Recruitment was open to all who wanted to join. Some guerrillas were very young.

located at Lovek. The combined pressure exerted by these deadly neighbours eventually proved too much. It is small wonder that, even today, the Khmers refer to their ancient enemies, Thailand and Vietnam, as 'The Tiger and the Crocodile'. With this relentlessly nibbling at its borders, the once great Khmer Empire slipped into decline.

The nineteenth century was the great empire-building era of the Western powers. The map of South-East Asia was to be transformed by the arrival of the Dutch, the British and the French. Cambodia and Vietnam, along with Laos, were swallowed whole and reconstituted into parts of French Indochina. The region became a distant colonial backwater, enlivened by occasional bloody rebellions. A century later, in the 1950s, resistance to the French presence finally erupted into bitter war in Vietnam, while, over the border in Cambodia, communist guerrillas also agitated for independence. By 1952 the Cambodian commu-nists occupied approximately one-sixth of Cambo-dia's sparsely populated countryside. They received limited support from both the Viet Minh (Vietnamese communists) and the government of Thailand (which feared the colonial ambitions of the French). Although this enabled the commu-nists in Cambodia to tie down thousands of French troops, the scale of fighting was nothing like that in Vietnam.

Eventually, endless warring having undermined her morale, France bowed out and granted inde-pendence to her colonies in Indochina. In Decem-ber 1953 Cambodia was declared an independent

Above: Prince Ranariddh at the Thai border in 1986, sending off a column of men and supplies to Cambodia.

monarchy. The communists, who had been such a thorn in the sides of the French, now campaigned for constitutional reform in order to gain political power. The internal guerrilla war continued. Within a year the communists claimed to control 50 per cent of the countryside, although most of the terri-tory under their domination was uncontested forest and jungle.

The inevitable slide towards all-out civil war in Cambodia was accelerated by the intervention of the United States in neighbouring Vietnam. The supply lines of the communist North Vietnamese passed through Cambodia along the Ho Chi Minh Trail, and the US brought pressure to bear on the Cambodian government to interdict the Trail in sup-port of South Vietnam. Fearful of their powerful

Far left: The war was a dan-gerous game of cat and mouse, often fought at very close range owing to limited visibility in the forest which covers much of the land-scape. An ANS guerrilla, fin-ger on the trigger of a B-50 (a Chinese copy of the RPG-2), advances as 'point man' through dense vegetation. Hanging from his belt, tightly wrapped up, is his hammock (every soldier carried one of these).

Left: An ANS guerrilla with an RPD light machine gun. He wears a cheap camou-flage outfit made in Thailand. These rarely lasted more than one or two months in the field.

1. Khieu Samphan, one of the leaders of the Khmer Rouge, was at this time a minister in Sihanouk's government.

Above: The Cambodian resistance received far less aid than the Afghan *Mujahidin*. This ANS platoon in 1986 shows how short of supplies they were at that time. Several men lack a uniform of any description, and those that have one are all wearing something different. None have proper boots for the hard walking they did, and not every man is armed. The seventh man carries the only water container the platoon possessed, a large plastic can.

Right: An ANS column on the move. Note the wide assortment of uniforms, before larger aid programmes from the West after 1986. Sometimes the forest was so dense that movement was dangerously slow. The guerrillas would follow dry river beds (depending on the season), which speeded up movement but made them more vulnerable to ambush and plunging fire from the banks.

Far right: As the rains continued, the flooding became worse. An ANS soldier with his AK-47, 1986.

communist neighbours, the Cambodians failed to respond. The clandestine US bombing of Cambodia which followed resulted in massive loss of civilian life and further polarized Cambodian society between the traditional establishment and the supporters of communism.

Although the internal strife continued, Cambodia's head of state, Prince Norodom Sihanouk, attempted to appease Cambodian communists by including some of them in his government.[1] Indeed, it was not the communists who were to topple Sihanouk from power in 1970 but his own former Prime Minister, General Lon Nol, who was secretly favoured by the Americans. Five more years of civil war followed before the Lon Nol Regime was overthrown by the communist Khmer Rouge.

Under their secretive leader Saloth Sar, better known by his *nom de guerre* Pol Pot, the Khmer Rouge immediately embarked upon one of the most radical and merciless social experiments the world has ever seen: the return to 'Year Zero'. This began with the emptying of the cities. Education was considered subversive, and many educated, urban dwellers were systematically exterminated. As in China's Cultural Revolution, Pol Pot's intention was purportedly to return to an imagined agricultural idyll of simple peasants and common ownership.

The new state was to have a new name: Democratic Kampuchea. Henceforth in this 'egalitarian Utopia', there would be no education, no religion, no modern technology, no private ownership, no traditional culture and no individuality. Even the bright sarongs and colourful ikat-weave commonly worn by Cambodians disappeared, to be replaced by the ubiquitous black pyjama-suits of the Khmer Rouge. In addition, all contact with the outside world was severed. For the next three and a half years, Cambodia was plunged into a secret hell of bloodlust and despair.

Estimates of the death toll during this period vary from 20 to 50 per cent of the total population of about 4 million. Many perished as a result of exhaustion, malaria and malnutrition while being forced to work on huge agricultural construction projects entirely reliant on manual labour. Such projects were intended to emulate the great achievements of the ancient Khmer Empire. Unfortunately, the Khmer Rouge's efforts were a cata-

strophic failure, paid for in the lives of hundreds of thousands of Cambodians. Tragically, in a naturally abundant land (Cambodian having previously been known as the 'rice bowl' of south-east Asia), many people starved to death.

The Khmer Rouge leaders were unable to accept that Year Zero had been misconceived and they began a paranoid witch-hunt for the 'traitors' responsible for its collapse. The party fractured into two. Pol Pot and those at the most senior level were ideologically aligned to China. However, many cadres had been trained in Vietnam, which had since switched its allegiance to China's great enemy, Russia. In the search for traitors, where better for the Khmer Rouge élite to lay the blame than on those ancient enemies of Cambodia the Vietnamese? Thousands more Cambodians were butchered in the bloody party purges that followed. With their own lives now at stake from their former colleagues, several hundred Vietnamese-trained Khmer Rouge fled across the border to Vietnam.

These events began to stoke the long-cherished territorial ambitions of the Vietnamese. During 1978 there were several Cambodia/Vietnam border clashes, instigated by an increasingly belligerent Khmer Rouge government. The Vietnamese were not concerned by the genocidal policy of the Khmer Rouge other than in the fact that it presented them with a great opportunity – to fulfil their historical ambition of regional domination. Nguyen Co Thach, Vietnam's Foreign Minister, was later to tell US Congressmen Steven Solarz that 'Human rights were not a question. That was *their* problem – *we* were concerned only with security.'[2]

The Khmer Rouge defectors in Vietnam had formed themselves into the National Union Front for the Salvation of Kampuchea (NUFSK). This force now claimed to be an anti-Khmer Rouge faction and officially requested Vietnamese assistance. On 28 December 1978, approximately 300 NUFSK members invaded Cambodia, 'supported' by an army of 200,000 Vietnamese. Unable to withstand a conventional war against such military might, the Khmer Rouge regime was swiftly crushed, to the universal delight of the Cambodian people.

THE CAMBODIAN RESISTANCE

The general enthusiasm which greeted the fall of Pol Pot was checked when it became clear that the new PRK (People's Republic of Kampuchea) government[3] was composed primarily of ex-Khmer Rouge cadres who had fled to Vietnam. Men such as the new President, Heng Samrin, had held high rank under the Khmer Rouge[4] and had imple-

Above: An ANS soldier in Thmar Pouk with an M-79 grenade launcher.

mented genocidal policies without question, until their own lives were threatened by Party purges. It also became apparent that the Vietnamese Army was settling in for a long stay. The 'liberation' force had become an occupation force.

Those who had once struggled to oppose the Khmer Rouge now began to fear for the survival of an independent Cambodia under the Vietnamese. Scattered groups began to consolidate into a more organised resistance. Even more significantly, though the Khmer Rouge old guard were down, they were not out for the count. The Vietnamese had not seized the opportunity to destroy them as a viable military force when they had the chance; instead, they had allowed them to retreat to their traditional strongholds in the Cardamom Mountains. This expediency enabled Vietnam to justify the continued presence of her troops in Cambodia.

Although the newly installed PRK government was reliant on the Vietnamese Army, a secret, shadow administration of Vietnamese 'advisors' was also set up to ensure that it continued to obey instructions. By the early 1980s resistance to this puppet government and its foreign overlords had coalesced into three factions. Militarily, the most significant were still the Khmer Rouge, which numbered in the region of 30,000 cadres. There were

2. *Documents on the Kampuchean Problem*, 1979-85, p.IV, Ministry of Foreign Affairs, Bangkok, Thailand.

3. Formed in January 1979.

4. Also Hun Sen (later elected Prime Minister), Chea Sim and Math Ly (members of the National Assembly), Kang Sarin, Ney Penna, Nou Beng etc. Some of the worst atrocities under Khmer Rouge rule took place in the Eastern province where Hun Sen was an officer and Heng Samrin a battalion commander.

also two non-communist groups steadily growing in number: the Khmer People's National Liberation Front (KPNLF), which had evolved from the remnants of the old Lon Nol regime; and the Armée Nationale Sihanoukist (ANS), composed of supporters of the ex-monarch, Prince Sihanouk. It was the Sihanoukists who were to really capture the hearts and minds of the people. While the old Prince's regime had been called corrupt in its day, Cambodians looked back on it, in comparison with what followed, as a halcyon time of peace and prosperity.

Internationally, this state of affairs led to some complex diplomatic footwork. Vietnam's presence in Cambodia was regarded as a coup d'état by a foreign power and the United Nations refused to recognise the new Cambodian government. While the Western powers secretly favoured the non-communist resistance, they did not constitute a legal government-in-exile and could not be awarded the UN seat. On the other hand, the Khmer Rouge, who were in fact the legally recognised government of Cambodia, could no longer be countenanced because of the atrocities of their regime. Consequently, despite their ideological incompatibility, the non-communists were persuaded to enter into a political marriage of convenience with the Khmer Rouge. Together they formed a notional 'Coalition Government of Democratic Kampuchea' (CGDK), which was then collectively awarded the UN seat.

This was always an uneasy alliance. The three factions retained separate identities. While there was some military collaboration on the ground between the Khmer Rouge and the non-communists, there were also clashes. Nevertheless, the non-communists were forced to be pragmatic. They could not hope to fight the militarily superior Vietnamese and the Khmer Rouge at the same time. There would be time to deal with the Khmer Rouge when the Vietnamese had gone.

THE K-5 PLAN
Much of the basic administrative structure of Cambodia remained unaltered after the Vietnamese invasion. Local authorities were often the same under the new PRK government as they had been under the Khmer Rouge. There was little evidence that the new leadership had renounced the policies or practices of the previous regime: violation of human rights, arrest without trial, torture and arbitrary execution remained a feature of life for many Cambodians.

From 1982 the population was conscripted to

65

Right: The first tank captured intact by the ANS thunders up the dusty road near Thmar Pouk in 1988.

work on massive communal defence projects. These were very reminiscent of the labour-intensive programmes of the Khmer Rouge, and just as costly in terms of human lives. The PRK government claimed that they implemented these strategies to 'fight the enemies of the revolution'. Even the political rhetoric sounded familiar.

The worst abuse of human rights perpetrated by the PRK was undoubtedly the colossal 'K-5 Plan', also known as the *Tov Kap Prey* (Clearing Plan). The intention was to seal the Thai/Cambodian border by a combination of deforestation, dykes, canals, strategic fences and minefields. This ambition had been brought about by a change in the policy of the Thai government. Apprehensive about Vietnamese territorial expansionism, Thailand had opened her borders[5] to allow the Cambodian resistance secure bases on Thai territory – better that the Vietnamese should be preoccupied with an active Cambodian resistance than at a loose end for new fields to conquer! This new open-door policy meant that the resistance could mount offensive operations in Cambodia and evade retaliation by retreating to safety in Thailand. In order to put a stop to such tactics, the Cambodian PRK government compelled its civilians to labour on the K-5 Plan to close the border. At any one time, the workforce on this project numbered up to 120,000.

Unfortunately, the border regions comprised part of the worst terrain in Cambodia. Some areas already contained dangerous minefields, laid by the Khmer Rouge. Untrained, conscripted civilians laboured to clear the forests and remove enemy mines before planting new ones. As many as 90 per cent of the workforce became infected with malaria. The improvised camps in which the workers were kept had poor sanitation and lacked medical facilities. Armed guards arrested or shot anyone attempting to escape. It has been estimated that 50,000 people died in the first two years of this project alone.[6] The causes of death were primarily poor diet, maltreatment, malaria, dysentery and mines. Although refugees who survived, or had somehow escaped, the K-5 plan described it as 'slow death', the mounting toll went, for the most part, unremarked by the outside world.

In tandem with the K-5 Plan, the Cambodian government implemented a counterpart K-6 Plan, concerned with internal security needs. Under this scheme, villages in disputed areas were designated 'combat villages' (not dissimilar to the American 'strategic hamlets' during the Vietnam War years). This involved building 'strategic fences' around dwellings, bridges and military defences or along roads in order to deny them to the enemy.

The PRK government coined a phrase to describe the massed mobilisation of the civilian population on these large-scale plans – 'Sacrifice for Military Service'. This could not have been more appropriate, for sacrifice they did: tens of thousands of Cambodians perished working on projects which, like those of the Khmer Rouge which preceded them, were destined to fail miserably. Among ordinary Cambodians the lament could often be heard: 'We are in the same car, only with a different driver.'

WEAPONS

As in all conflicts, military matters in Cambodia were shaped by politics. The Vietnamese were dependent on support from their Soviet allies to underwrite the cost of their military adventurism in South-East Asia. Similarly, the Chinese government backed *their* ideological brothers, the Khmer Rouge (although some Chinese arms were also supplied to the non-communist resistance). Consequently the weapons carried by the combatants in the Cambodian guerrilla war were almost identical on both sides: Russian and Chinese versions of the SKS carbine and the ubiquitous AK-47 assault rifle were the norm.

The high volume of fire offered by these

Above: Noumali, a soldier with the ANS at Thmar Pouk in 1988.

5. While the Khmer Rouge had been in power, Cambodia had formed a buffer zone between Thailand and Vietnam. During this period, Thailand had refused to allow either resistance groups, or refugees, egress over her borders. Indeed, on occasions, refugees had been forcibly returned to certain death in Cambodia. As a result of the new open-door policy, Thailand was to become host to more than 300,000 Cambodian refugees over the next decade.

6. The K-5 Plan started in 1985. The statistics quoted were compiled by a French doctor, Esmeralda Luciolli, in the *Indochina Report*, April/June 1988. The doctor was a fluent Khmer speaker who spent the best part of seven years (from 1979) working both inside Cambodia and with Cambodian refugees on the Thai/Cambodian border.

Above: An ANS guerrilla with an M-79, 1986.

Above right: An ANS RPG gunner. His shoulder flash is a small ANS flag. In common with the flags of all other Cambodian factions, the ANS flag features the symbolic towers of Angkor Wat.

weapons was ideal for the short-range clashes fought in Cambodia, where visibility was limited by dense vegetation. The side which could pin down the opposition with a concentration of rapid fire might retain the mobile initiative, outflank the enemy and win the fire-fight. Alternatively, if a smaller unit were hard-pressed and outnumbered by a larger opponent, a high volume of fire could hinder hot pursuit and facilitate escape.

Later in the war the non-communist factions secretly received additional backing from other sources. By the late 1980s those sources were encouraged by developments on the ground to step up their support. In addition to various training programmes, improved Western-type weapons arrived. Although there was speculation that Britain and the United States were among the countries which directly supplied the non-communists, the American-designed M-16 assault rifles which began to proliferate were not manufactured in the United States: the Cambodians were supplied with less controversial Singaporean copies. Lighter than the AK-47, and with a higher rate of fire, the M-16 was immensely popular. Its real value however, was more symbolic than military. For the first time, the ordinary non-communist guerrilla held a weapon which was patently not derived from communist

China. It was a tremendous morale-booster – the first, tangible evidence of support from the Free World. Abdul Gaffar, a spokesman for the non-communist KPNLF faction, was able to sum up what the arrival of the M-16 meant to them: 'It is true that a bullet from an M-16 can kill only one man just as a bullet from an AK-47, but there is a difference as great as sky and earth . . . when the ordinary villagers see us coming, they notice our weapons are not the same as the Khmer Rouge . . . Then the old men say, "My sons are coming, and my sons are free."'

As Western-type weapons and training were only a feature of the latter part of the war, the primary influence on the military thinking of all three resistance factions was China. The central strategy advocated by the Chinese was that the lightly armed guerrilla resistance should get close to the more heavily armed and armoured enemy in order to overcome any relative weakness in the quantity or quality of their equipment. 'Closeness' was therefore a feature of the Cambodian battlefield.

One support weapon particularly reliable at close range was the RPD light machine gun, which China supplied in quantity. With its belt of 100 rounds, its greater firepower supplemented the individual weapons of the ordinary soldier and was particularly useful in ambush situations. Hand grenades were also carried and used extensively in contact, although their use was sometimes limited by thick shrubbery or low overhead branches. Another popular short-range weapon supplied in great numbers was the Type-50 RPG (rocket-pro-pelled grenade) launcher, which was considered to be better than the original Russian RPG-2 upon which it was based. Despite this, operators com-plained of the tendency for the 4lb warhead to bounce off the target![7] The Type 50 RPG was avail-able with either anti-armour HEAT (High Explosive Anti-Tank) rockets or anti-personnel HE (High Explosive). In Cambodia the weapon was most often used in an anti-personnel role despite the fact that the majority of warheads provided by China were anti-armour.

On ambush operations it was common for up to a third of the ambush party to be armed with Type 50 RPGs. The resistance believed, from experi-ence, that the louder the attack the larger it was perceived to be. There was also a sprinkling of the more powerful Type 69 RPG (copied from the Russian RPG-7). These weapons came into their own as 'bunker busters' during attacks against Vietnamese posts. The slightly built Cambodian RPG gunner would routinely carry up to eight rock-ets. One projectile would be kept ready in the launcher at all times, in case of ambush, with seven spares carried on his back in an improvised bamboo frame. When manoeuvring inside Cambo-dia, it was possible to gauge the level of danger by keeping an eye on the RPG operators. If they sus-pected an enemy presence they would prime their spare rockets with propellant charges, ready for use.

Both the Vietnamese and the resistance made use of mortars. The Vietnamese were able to set up permanent 82mm and 120mm mortar positions within the perimeters of their bases. Of these, the 82mm was the most prevalent. When permanently sited, the weapons were assigned to fixed Defen-sive Fire Zones (DFZs). If movement were detected within these DFZs, the mortar crews could react quickly and bring accurate fire to bear on the suspected enemy force.

The resistance were restricted by what they could carry and relied mostly on smaller 60mm mortars. The heavier 82mm mortars were not a common feature of their arsenal until the later stages of the war when large numbers of Viet-namese troops had been withdrawn from Cambo-dia. Alone, the Cambodian Army (KRAPF) were unable to dominate the countryside as the Viet-namese had done and the resistance were now

able to move about more freely, even utilising bul-lock carts to deploy 82mm mortars for concentrated barrages on enemy positions. One such attack was that mounted by the Armée Nationale Sihanoukist against Treas on 5 December 1989. At the time, Treas was occupied by 400 Cambodian Army troops, supported only by Vietnamese advisors. Over a two-day period the resistance fired 2,000 mortar rounds from nine mortars and launched two assaults before successfully capturing the position.

Supplementing the long-range strike capability of the resistance were 107mm rockets.[8] These appeared only during the last few years of the con-flict and were never available in large numbers. The Vietnamese, on the other hand, had BM-14 multi-barrel rocket launchers (MBRLs). These heavier, 140mm calibre weapons had sixteen launch tubes. Mounted on the back of Russian Zil trucks, they could be used either individually or as part of a battery. They were most effective when used against fixed resistance bases (as in the early phases of the war) or against concentrations of forces building up to attack a base (as in the multi-party resistance effort to capture Svay Chek in 1989).

The Vietnamese were also well furnished with both artillery and tanks. Artillery was used in the classic, Soviet manner of rolling barrages of fire, in advance of ground offensives. It was also available in support of fixed bases or units in the field and for general harassing and interdiction fire into areas thought to contain guerrillas. During the dry sea-

Above: Part of the haul of munitions captured by the ANS when they overran Treas in 1989.

7. This probably occurred at the maxi-mum range of 162 metres.

8.Some with Chinese Type 63-1 twelve-barrel launchers.

son, when the scarcity of water was often a problem, known water-points were shelled spasmodi-
cally to deny their use to the resistance.

Vietnamese tanks (mostly older Russian T-54s
and T-55s) operated in co-ordination with the
infantry during major ground offensives. They also
patrolled the roadways and were a source of
mobile artillery support. In defence of bases they
would fire in direct support, at point-blank range.

For the movement of troops the Vietnamese had
a few eight-wheeled Russian BTR-60 armoured
personnel carriers (APCs), which served side by
side with American M111 tracked APCs left over
from the Vietnam War. Neither type of vehicle was
available in large numbers and troops were routinely left more vulnerable to ambush, sitting in the
back of soft-skinned Zil trucks. The most common
manner of movement for all sides in the active hot-
spots was on foot.

Air strikes were not a common feature of the war
in Cambodia. The Russians had provided Vietnam
with only a limited capability in this field, and
although both Mi-8 and Mi-27 helicopters were
utilised, they were so few in number that the risk of
losing them was enough to ensure that they only
made occasional appearances. Vintage T-28 pro-
peller-driven fighters were more often used for
bombing and strafing, but even these old work-
horses saw little service. Sometimes Antonov
transports were used for 'pallet bombing' (a cargo
of bombs was rolled out of the open tailgate), but
this primitive method of delivery posed little threat
to the guerrillas in the forest below.

The resistance were supplied with a few surface-
to-air missiles (SAMs), but because of the low level
of the air threat most rotted in the humidity long
before they had the opportunity of being used. In
addition, the Khmer Rouge possessed a limited
quantity of anti-aircraft guns and heavier artillery
pieces positioned around their Cardamom mountain
strongholds in south-western Cambodia. After the

Top: A selection of mines.

Above: Even the tropical nights could feel cold. Very rarely, if the area was considered secure enough, guerrillas might stoke up the fire to warm themselves.

Left: An ANS soldier with an RPG.

9. Le Duc Tho, Politburo member of the Vietnamese Communist Party, clandestine meeting in Phnom Phen, 1980. Quoted in *Indochina Report*, July/September 1985, p.2.

10. Le Duc Anh, *'Tap Chi Quan Doi Nhan Dan'* or *'The PAVN and its Lofty International Duty in Friendly Kampuchea'* (the official organ of the PAVN Army), December 1984. Le Duc Anh was also a member of the Central Military Affairs Commission.

11. Le Duc Tho, clandestine seminar held in Phnom Phen in 1980.

Vietnamese pull-out in 1990 they also received a number of T-54 tanks from China. It is doubtful if any of these saw much action other than as mobile artillery support.

The first weapons of Western design began to reach the non-communist resistance in 1988. Among these were various anti-tank weapons — the Swedish 84mm Karl Gustav (a little too heavy for practical daily use in Cambodia's humid climate), West Germany's Amburst (very popular) and French LRACs (rather large and unwieldy in the hands of the slightly-built Khmers). Although primarily designed for use against armour, these weapons were used by the resistance against fixed bases, for 'bunker-busting'. In this context they scored notable successes and did much to boost the morale of the non-communists. Extensive use was also made of American M-79 grenade-launchers, which were reliable and effective weapons. Later, when supplies of M-16s became more widespread, the M203 version (a grenade-launcher slung under the barrel of an M-16) became available, although this did nothing to diminish the popularity of the older M-79. Major Hang Yuth, of the

Armée Nationale Sihanoukist, used one as his preferred choice of personal weapon. The Vietnamese also had M-79s, having captured large stocks after the American withdrawal from Vietnam.

Of the variety of weapons seen in Cambodia, by far the most lethal were land mines. They were available in all manner of types and sizes. Some were designed to lie on the surface, others were buried in the earth. There were simple, wooden box mines, small and sophisticated plastic mines, segmented Pom-Zs perched on top of stakes and dinner-plate size Claymore MON-10s and 100s. They were cheap to produce, light to carry, easy to lay and deadly and as such they appealed to all factions. It has been estimated that as many as 4 million mines were sown in the Cambodian countryside, but the vast majority were laid without the benefit of mapping to enable their safe recovery at a later date. Tragically they are a non-discriminatory weapon, claiming civilian as well as military victims. Long after the withdrawal of Vietnam and the end of the war, many of these mines remain, hidden in the soil, silently waiting to claim their victims.

STRATEGY & TACTICS
In 1980, buoyed by the success of their invasion, the Vietnamese described their presence in Cambodia as the 'sweet phase of a new era'.[9] By 1984, things were no longer so sweet. Vietnam's involvement had, according to the Politburo, entered a new 'hot phase'. The old Vietnamese dream of colonial adventure in Cambodia was becoming a nightmare.

In the beginning, one theme dominated Vietnam's strategic planning. This was described by General Le Duc Anh, the commander of Vietnam's army of occupation, as 'a strategy for irreversibility'[10] (in effect, he had no intention of relinquishing Cambodia at a later date). Le Duc Anh was determined to pursue this course, even when it became apparent that 'irreversibility' was a runaway train, dragging all other strategic considerations behind it.

Naturally, such a strategy called for the long-term presence in Cambodia of a 'Vietnamese army of volunteers and experts'.[11] These battalions of shadow-ministers and political 'advisors' who lurked behind the scenes in Phnom Penh were backed up by a rather more tangible army of 180,000 troops. The exiled Prince of Cambodia, Norodom Sihanouk, was to observe that 'as Lenin's disciples, the Vietnamese communist leadership only respect the language of force.'

The value of force had been hammered home to the Vietnamese during more than forty years of

incessant domestic warfare. They were convinced that their policy of irreversibility could only be achieved on the battlefield. Nothing else mattered. Having embarked on their chosen course, any negotiation on Cambodia, with the United Nations and other interested parties, was merely 'Danh Danh, Dam Dam' ('Talk Talk, Fight Fight').[12]

THE INVASION OF CAMBODIA AND THE ESCALATION OF THE GUERRILLA WAR

During their long wars against France and the United States, the People's Army of Vietnam (PAVN) had been described as the finest light infantry in the world. However, the December 1978 invasion of Cambodia marked a departure from its customary role: this time the PAVN were not the foxes but the huntsmen. Forced into a more conventional role, the supreme exponents of guerrilla warfare were to find the going much harder.

At first, the lightning-strike invasion went well. The Khmer Rouge Army speedily collapsed and by early 1978 had been pushed back to the Thai/Cambodian border. Driven into the forests bordering Thailand, Cambodian resistance to the Vietnamese presence appeared to be largely over. Building on these initial successes, the Vietnamese began a phase of consolidation which was to last until the mid-1980s. Their main objective during this period was to secure the Thai/Cambodian border and to eradicate all permanent guerrilla bases in that region. Despite their best efforts, their problems were multiplied in the early 1980s by the emergence of two new resistance groups, the non-communist ANS and KPNLF. It began to appear as if the flickering torch of Cambodian nationalism was refusing to be extinguished after all.

The constant pin-prick attacks by guerrillas forced Vietnam to take drastic measures. For the dry-season offensive of November 1984-January 1985, 75,000 PAVN troops were mobilised in a concerted effort to eliminate the resistance. This was the climax of the campaign to consolidate the border regions. When it was concluded soon afterwards, in March 1985, it was hailed as another success. However, the destruction of the border bases was to have unforeseen consequences for Vietnam.

The Cambodian resistance realised the pointlessness of expending their efforts in border skirmishes against a more numerous and better equipped enemy and they began to alter their strategy. In order to recruit and expand, they needed to avoid costly confrontations, penetrate more deeply inside Cambodia and win the hearts and minds of the civilian population. While it was important for the guerrillas to demonstrate their muscle, they recognised that this had to be balanced against the need to conserve their limited resources for what was bound to be a long war.

Of the three resistance groups, the KPNLF found it hardest to relinquish conventional tactics for a more fluid, hit-and-run style of warfare. Many of their High Command had served in the old Cam-

Above: KPNLF guerrillas prepare to set off on an ambush in 1987. They carry a very high proportion of RPG rockets, and all wear unit identity scarves, this unit's scarves being grey.

12. 'Danh Danh, Dam Dam' was a classic component of the time-wasting diplomatic strategies employed by North Vietnam in the war against the United States.

13. The Khmer Rouge were trained by the Vietnamese whilst allied to them during Vietnam's war with the United States.

14. Supreme Command Directive of the Democratic Kampuchea National Army (Khmer Rouge): *Voice of DKNA*, 28 February 1985.

15. In the later stages of the war, when the Vietnamese had withdrawn (leaving the army of the Cambodian Heng Samrin regime to go it alone), resistance objectives became more ambitious and included some attacks against targets of more than company size.

16 . Ten of these were combat divisions.

17. There were a few exceptions, such as the Cambodian Army units PSK (688) and PSK (689), attached to Vietnamese units on the volatile Front 479 in north-western Cambodia.

bodian Army under the Lon Nol regime. Their training and previous experience made it difficult for them to adapt to the changing requirements of the new guerrilla war. The Khmer Rouge, on the other hand, benefited from having trained in the past with the supreme masters of guerrilla warfare, the Vietnamese themselves.[13] A Khmer Rouge directive explained that the Cambodian interior, was 'the Achilles' heel of the Vietnamese enemy, [where they] are vulnerable.'[14]

Prince Ranariddh, the son of Prince Sihanouk and the Commander-in-Chief of the ANS, had independently reached the same conclusions. After the reverses of the 1984-85 dry-season offensive he directed his Royalist forces to avoid unnecessary confrontation and concentrate on penetrating deep into the interior.

The Vietnamese were compelled to pull forces away from the border to deal with escalating problems in central Cambodia. This was dangerous as it enabled the flow of guerrillas through the porous border to increase. Once in the interior they were harder to locate and pin down. Having failed to consolidate the success of their initial invasion, the Vietnamese army now faced resistance action simultaneously on two fronts – the Border and the Interior, or Inland Front.

Militarily, the resistance concentrated upon the classic guerrilla stratagy of ambush and harrassment. Small enemy posts were targeted for attack[15] in the hope that they could be overwhelmed as much by surprise as by force. Because of the difficulty of concentrating enough support weapons and the danger of enemy reinforcements arriving to tip the balance, such operations were kept as brief as possible.

It was not in the interests of the resistance to engage in actions not of their choosing. When possible, they tried to avoid being drawn into uneven contacts with Vietnamese patrols, but opposing sides often clashed unexpectedly in the densely wooded terrain. The guerrillas also tried to avoid habitual behaviour such as the frequent use of the same tracks and water-points. If the Vietnamese noticed regular patterns of behaviour, they reacted swiftly: an ambush would be set, or mines laid, or the water poisoned.

Massively outnumbered, and forced to avoid large-scale confrontations, the Cambodian resistance could not be said to be *winning* the war in a military sense, but they *were* successful in tying up huge numbers of PAVN troops. Vietnam's continued presence in Cambodia was rendered ever more costly. While the combined total of resistance forces numbered no more than 50,000 men, the PAVN were forced to keep fourteen infantry divisions[16] (between 140,000 and 180,000 men) permanently inside Cambodia in order to dominate the ground.

PAVN COUNTER-GUERRILLA WARFARE TACTICS

The Vietnamese were firm believers in investing the man-hours required to combat the guerrilla threat. A high proportion of PAVN troops were tied down with routine security tasks guarding potential targets such as roads, bridges, towns and military bases. In areas where the resistance was active, the PAVN established company-size bases, surrounded by platoon-size satellite outposts. Heavy patrolling was carried out between these fixed points. To ease the burden they built up the Cambodian Army of the PRK regime which they had installed in power in Phnom Penh. As these troops took over mundane security duties, Vietnamese manpower was freed for more important tasks. Although the Cambodian forces were sometimes used to supplement PAVN operations, they were, for the most part, ineffectual and could not be relied on for aggressive counter-guerrilla operations.[17]

For this role the Vietnamese employed several dedicated intervention units. These were tasked with more mobile and aggressive patrol patterns, designed to enforce wider-ranging domination of the ground and often involving long periods away from base. At night, they would bed down in the forest and lay ambushes. If an isolated village was to be their overnight stop, the perimeter would be secured and a curfew imposed, to prevent the resistance being notified of their presence.

Military Region 4 (north-western Cambodia) was the most active and dangerous area of operations. This was reflected by the greater density of Vietnamese troop deployment in the region – some

73

Below: Captain Sambat Hov of the ANS lectures new recruits inside Cambodia. The battle for control of the 'Inland Front' was the most strategically important. Whoever was ultimately to control Cambodia had first to win the hearts and minds of the population.

45,000 men. Within Military Region 4, the most sensitive spot was the extreme north-west corner (Front 479). Elite Vietnamese units such as E.117, a *Dak Kong* (Special Action) brigade, were deployed there. Most Dak Kong personnel were seasoned veterans of the war against the United States. Heavily armed, they conducted hunter-killer patrols, seeking contact with the enemy.

As the resistance infiltrated more deeply into Cambodia, it became increasingly important for the Vietnamese to deny them the opportunity of gaining support from the civilian population. To this end, large-scale, dry-season offensives were mounted to drive the guerrillas out of strategic areas and destroy their caches of arms and food. These 'search and destroy' sweeps became an annual feature of the war.

Having no fixed bases inside Cambodia, the guerrillas were able, by moving quickly, to evade these PAVN offensives. Once the activity had ceased, they simply returned to strengthen their ties with the local people. If they won support, the villagers would supply them with food, enabling the resistance to sustain a permanent operational presence on the Inland Front. Relieved of the pressure to ferry food from Thailand, the more dangerous external supply lines could be devoted to vital military supplies.

THE PAVN WITHDRAWAL AND THE CAMBODIAN CIVIL WAR

From the beginning, the Vietnamese made two fatal mistakes in Cambodia. When they stopped short of totally destroying the Khmer Rouge during the first, offensive phase of the war, they were supremely confident that their position in Cambodia was unassailable. This was a serious underestimation of the resilience of the Khmer Rouge.[18] Their second error was in failing to anticipate the emergence of other resistance groups. These factions, untainted by the genocidal policies of the Khmer Rouge, were deemed acceptable recipients of support by the West and by other, regional sponsors.[19] Consequently, the Vietnamese found themselves sinking into an unexpectedly long and costly guerrilla war.

As the 1980s drew to a close, Vietnam was no nearer a solution of its difficulties in Cambodia. However, the world outside was changing. By 1988 the Cold War was ending and the Soviet Union, verging on insolvency, was disengaging from costly foreign involvements. Without the patronage of this powerful ally, Vietnam's army of occupation could not be sustained indefinitely. Furthermore, after a decade of war, international pres-

sure for Vietnam to withdraw her troops from Cambodia was mounting.

Ultimately, the Cambodian resistance prevailed, not by military victory but simply by virtue of having survived for so long to continue the fight. The Vietnamese agreed to a 1990 withdrawal deadline. This ushered in a new phase of political manoeuvring between the resistance and the PRK government, left in power by Vietnam, during which all parties were rapidly building up their forces. Behind the talk of peace lay the reality of continuing war in Cambodia. Although the Vietnamese had reinforced the Cambodian Army before they pulled out, there was little hope that a force of 100,000 Cambodian soldiers could succeed where 180,000 Vietnamese had failed.

As the PAVN released their stranglehold on the countryside, it became easier, and safer, for the guerrillas to manoeuvre and the military strategy of the resistance shifted from infiltration to confrontation. All sides considered it important to show that they were serious contenders for power. Victories in the field would endow them with more weight at the negotiating table. The guerrillas mounted offensives and pushed forward to win a substantial chunk of north-western Cambodia from the forces of the government. There were also serious clashes in the Cambodian interior, in the region of Kompong Thom.

At the negotiating table, the major stumbling block to a settlement was the Khmer Rouge. The PRK Prime Minister, Hun Sen, blamed Prince Sihanouk for insisting that the 'genocidal' Khmer Rouge be included in a transitional Cambodian government (prior to the holding of elections). Sihanouk, who rightly perceived that there was little hope for peace in Cambodia unless the Khmer Rouge participated, retaliated by calling Hun Sen's government 'lackeys of Vietnam'. However, as an

Above: A KPNLF medic treats a guerrilla wounded by an RPG during an ambush.

18. The same criticism can be levelled at the Western alliance during the Gulf War. Having isolated the élite Iraqi Republican Guard, upon which Saddam Hussein's survival depended, the Alliance stopped short of destroying them and allowed them to escape. With most of their armour intact, the Republican Guard were soon in action again, against the Kurds in northern Iraq and the Marsh Arabs in the south.

19. The Association of South-East Asian Nations (ASEAN), a regional political alliance, was concerned by the territorial ambitions of Vietnam and willing to support a resistance to its occupation of Cambodia.

Right: In 1988, Major Hang Yuth briefs subordinate officers during an operation. A Takarov pistol hangs round his neck.

Far right: Major Thlang Chansovanarith. Orphaned by the Khmer Rouge, Thlang was forcibly conscripted into the Cambodian Army created by Vietnam and sent to Russia for training. On his return to Cambodia, he and seventeen colleagues deserted to join the non-Communist resistance, fifteen being killed in the process. Thlang wears wild boar tusks for good luck.

Right: Colonel Prak Sen, commander of an ANS resupply column, in 1986.

Far right: Major Thlang Chansovanarith of the ANS had a sixth sense for detecting mines and often walked in advance of his men. When mines were found they were often left *in situ* and merely marked with a dead leaf. If the resistance lifted them, it betrayed their presence to the Vietnamese, who would lay more. These Russian mines held by Major Chansovanarith were each capable of taking off both of a man's legs.

ex-member of the Khmer Rouge himself, Hun Sen had cause to be nervous: the old Khmer Rouge leadership had not forgotten the 'traitors' who had betrayed them to the Vietnamese.

The path which finally led to the signing of the Paris Peace Accord by all factions in 1991 was a painful one. The talks began, faltered, broke down, and resumed again. In the meantime, much Cambodian blood was shed on the battlefield.

ON THE CAMBODIAN FRONT LINE

When the resistance, reeling from the setbacks of the 1984-85 dry season offensive, were forced back over the Thai border in 1985, the Royalist ANS faction changed their strategy. They were quick to understand the limited value of short, cross-border raids. With the whole of the Cambodian interior denied to them, they would inevitably be marginalised. At issue was not a debate between raiding from Thailand or a more mobile form of guerrilla warfare, but a choice between survival and extinction as a military force.

Prince Ranariddh searched among his ranks for a man with the right credentials to help plan a new strategy. Years of experience with guerrilla warfare made General Toan Chy the ideal choice. Not only had he been actively involved in fighting the Vietnamese but, prior to their invasion, he had led a small resistance against the Khmer Rouge. Between them, Toan Chy and the Prince agreed the foundations of a new strategy of more mobile guerrilla warfare. This began with a plan to infiltrate ANS soldiers into the Tonle Sap region of central Cambodia. The ultimate intention was to use this sparsely populated area as the springboard for future operations into Cambodia's strategic heartland.

Colonel Kreuch Yem, commander of the ANS 2nd Brigade, was selected to lead the vanguard of the move into the interior. His objective was to build up a network of contacts within the civilian population and establish a means of securing internal supplies. Hang Yuth, a young ANS captain who had displayed an aptitude for guerrilla warfare, was chosen by Kreuch Yem as his second-in-command. Together they made a good team and infused enthusiasm and confidence into the 2nd Brigade.

Secrecy and speed were the keys to success. In mid to late 1985 small ANS scouting parties began to infiltrate Cambodia, paving the way for larger numbers following on behind. Over a period of about a month, the 1,553 men from the 2nd Brigade made their way to a rendezvous with Colonel Kreuch Yem close to the great Tonle Sap lake.

The Vietnamese reacted to this new threat by

stepping up aggressive patrolling in the area, which resulted in increased clashes. The size of the resistance came as a rude shock. Moreover, the swampy and heavily forested terrain made coordination between Vietnamese troops extremely difficult and they were forced to commit more manpower to the region in an attempt to trap and overwhelm the guerrillas by force.

While several months of this activity failed to inflict substantial casualties on Colonel Kreuch Yem's 2nd Brigade, the Vietnamese stranglehold began to put a severe strain on his limited supplies. By April 1986 the situation was becoming critical and the ANS dispatched Force *Prak Senn* (a column of 480 men, named after its commander, Colonel Prak Senn) with more supplies. However, manoeuvring such a large number of men past the concentrations of Vietnamese troops near the volatile Thai/Cambodian border and deep into Cambodia was a daunting prospect.

Prak Senn's men travelled in three parallel columns with about half a kilometre between them. The two smaller, outer columns acted as lighter screens to the greater concentration of men in the centre: if one of the columns were to encounter an ambush, the others would still be able to manoeuvre. When they encountered a major obstacle such

Below: 215 Battalion, KPNLF, pass a girl working in a paddy field in 1985, shortly after they had lost their secure border bases in Cambodia. It was essential that they showed the civilian population that they were still a viable resistance force. The guerrillas won widespread support from the civilian population and actively recruited, and obtained food, from the villages. Nevertheless, there were dangers in meeting the local population, as inevitably a sighting would come to the attention of the Vietnamese.

as a river crossing, or a road used by the Vietnamese, the columns converged. This enabled them to pass over quickly and concentrated their strength to punch through any opposition. Once past the obstacle, they split back into three columns.

Knowing the habits of the Vietnamese, Colonel Prak Senn guessed that they would expect him to keep well away from concentrations of Vietnamese troops at bases and that their patrols would make

wide sweeps away from those bases in order to flush him out. He therefore threaded a route close to the bases. After dark, Force Prak Senn would pass silently by, like ghosts, and disappear into the night. The danger increased as they approached the open, cultivated landscape next to Highway Six, a major artery between north-west Cambodia and the capital city of Phnom Penh. Here they were close to the large Vietnamese base at Barai Toek, the regional headquarters of Military District 4.

Picking up the trail of the guerrillas from where they had crossed the highway, the Vietnamese mobilised 8,000 troops to prevent them linking up with Colonel Kreuch Yem's 2nd Brigade. Special Dak Kong units were called in to pursue and pin down Force Prak Senn, or to drive it further south towards larger concentrations of Vietnamese forces waiting to destroy it.

All day Colonel Prak Senn could hear the distant drone of T-28 fighters, flying missions against Kreuch Yem's force further south. At night, Vietnamese artillery shelled the area. Then, inexplicably, the Vietnamese pulled back and opened the way south.

Prak Senn was tempted to risk a dash over the last six kilometres to reach Kreuch Yem. He knew that the 2nd Brigade had run out of food three days previously and were also in urgent need of the munitions which he was bringing. Before he could make a decision, Colonel Kreuch Yem radioed a warning: 2nd Brigade scouts had observed large numbers of Vietnamese troops being ferried into the region by river craft. The way south was a trap. Kreuch Yem advised Prak Senn to abandon the mission and attempt to save his own force from the tightening Vietnamese cordon. Prak Senn immediately dispatched patrols to search for an escape route north. They reported back that the Vietnamese had moved most of their troops southwards, to the anticipated area of battle. This had created a few small gaps between the forces blocking the northern escape route.

The first barrier to Force Prak Senn's escape was the Boeng Veng river, and they raced to cross it before more Vietnamese troops, closing in from east and west, could link up and effectively slam the trapdoor shut. As the guerrillas swam across the river, with their equipment wrapped in plastic sheets, a fire-fight broke out a few hundred metres away. A Vietnamese patrol had collided with a 200-man force belonging to the rival KPNLF resistance faction. As the Vietnamese turned to deal with this force, Prak Senn and his men slipped past unnoticed. The KPNLF unit were not so fortunate. Pushed south, away from the Boeng Veng, they

Left: Colonel Yem Phouan, commander of Colonel Prak Sen's scouting party in central Cambodia, 1986. Yem Phouan had been an army officer during the Lon Nol Government days. When the Khmer Rouge came to power he was rounded up along with other officers, and they were bound hand and foot and driven into the countryside in a truck. When the truck stopped and everyone was being unloaded, Yem Phouan had the presence of mind to worm his way into some bushes, from where he witnessed his fellow officers being shot and bayoneted. The sole survivor, he disguised himself as a peasant farmer and worked on village collectives under the Khmer Rouge before finally escaping to Thailand. Having been granted residential status in the USA, Yem Phouan lived part of each year in California, where he ran a Dunkin' Donuts franchise, but returned annually to participate in deep-penetration operations inside Cambodia.

Left: ANS guerrillas swim across the Boeng Veng river in central Cambodia, 1986.

Above: An ANS medic treats a casualty in 1988.

Above right: Armée Nationale Sihanoukist (ANS) royalist guerrillas among the ruins of an eleventh-century Cambodian temple.

suffered heavy losses over the next few days and only 40 of their 200 men returned to Thailand.

Through the night Prak Senn kept his column moving. It was vital to cross Highway Six before dawn if they were to escape the trap. In the early hours they climbed over the steep earth bank on which the highway rested and dropped into the wet paddy fields on the northern side. Suddenly all hell broke loose as a waiting Vietamese Dak Kong unit sprang into action. In the sudden confusion, with the air full of tracer and the night lit up by exploding RPG rockets, ANS casualties ran into double figures.

A week later, Prak Senn's exhausted men climbed back up the steep Dong Rek escarpment into Thailand. Their break for the border had taken the pressure off Kreuch Yem's 2nd Brigade, which had consequently been able to bypass the Vietnamese in an unexpected dash north. Shortly

afterwards Kreuch Yem rendezvoused with another ANS supply column near Samrong, close to the Thai border. After they had been resupplied, the 2nd Brigade returned to central Cambodia.

In the long haul of guerrilla warfare, victory for the ANS did not lie in winning big battles. It lay in reaching, and surviving in, the strategically important Inland Front. Only there could the resistance hope to expand their organisation and win the hearts and minds of the Cambodian people. This effort was well rewarded nine years later when Prince Ranariddh won a victory at the elections, organised under a UN mandate, which resulted in his becoming Prime Minister of a new Cambodian government.

THE UNITED NATIONS IN CAMBODIA

The Paris Peace Accord constituted an all-party cease-fire and an agreement that an impartial

Far left: In Cambodia, China contributed soldiers to a UN peacekeeping initiative for the first time. This Chinese sentry at the main gate of their base in Kompong Thom wears distruptive-pattern camouflage, a change from their usual plain green uniforms. This may have been to distinguish them from the Khmer Rouge, who still wore the plain green uniforms supplied by China.

Left: A Dutch Marine with a 7.62mm FAL. Note that the muzzle cover on a short line at the end of the barrel is camouflaged white, ready for Arctic training in Norway for which they were preparing when sent to Cambodia at short notice.

United Nations Transitional Authority in Cambodia (UNTAC) would administer the country prior to the holding of free and fair elections in 1993. Involving 22,000 personnel and a budget of $3 billion, UNTAC was at the time the most ambitious and expensive UN operation ever mounted. It was intended to serve as a model for similar future operations – a blueprint for running a country.

UNTAC's mandate in Cambodia was to verify the withdrawal of Vietnamese forces, oversee the hand-over of power from the PRK regime installed by Vietnam, repatriate 320,000 Cambodians from refugee camps in Thailand and register the entire population of the country in preparation for the elections. Most importantly, it was to implement the multi-lateral disarmament which had been the foundation stone of the Accord.

Inevitably, despite the best efforts of the peace-keeping forces, clashes flared between the two rival communist factions, Pol Pot's Khmer Rouge and Hun Sen's former Khmer Rouge. While there was a tendency to perceive the Khmer Rouge as the aggressors, many of these clashes were in fact due to Hun Sen's PRK forces striking at Khmer Rouge areas in a final bid to extend the government's area of influence before the forthcoming elections. The non-communist resistance also suffered clashes and acts of terrorism instigated by the existing government.

Hostility between the Khmer Rouge and the PRK was unwittingly exacerbated by the well-inten-

tioned 'Civil Administration' arm of UNTAC. The UN administrators made a fundamental error which wrecked their chances of complete success in Cambodia. Instead of dismantling the infrastructure of the existing Cambodian government, they worked in tandem with it. This was contrary to the terms of the Paris Peace Accord and was not acceptable to the Khmer Rouge. In their eyes, UNTAC had compromised its neutrality. As a result, the multi-lateral disarmament of all factions collapsed and the Khmer Rouge withdrew from the peace process.

UNTAC implemented the rest of its mandate and elections were held in May 1993, without the participation of the Khmer Rouge. The government which came to power was a Royalist-led coalition, headed by Prince Ranariddh. Members of the previous regime were integrated into the new cabinet, with Hun Sen becoming joint Prime Minister. This was a diplomatic resolution of the power struggle between the widely popular Royalist faction and the militarily more powerful PRK regime.

The elections over, UNTAC had fulfilled its mandate. As the peace-keeping force began to pull out, Prince Sihanouk returned to the yellow palace in Phnom Penh to be reinstalled as head of state. While he received an emotional welcome from the Cambodian people, a shadow hung over these celebrations. Cambodia's future seemed far from assured. Lurking in the jungles like uninvited party

Right: Dutch Marines speaking to Khmer Rouge in the Cardomon mountains.

guests, the Khmer Rouge were still an armed and potent force.

When the feared Khmer Rouge ground offensive did not occur, there was speculation that the Royalist party had made an under-the-table deal to prevent a return to all-out guerrilla warfare. It is possible that the offer of a future government role (perhaps in an 'advisory' capacity) may have been enough to keep the Khmer Rouge in line. It would, after all, give them a vested interest in the survival of Prince Ranariddh's coalition government.

The road ahead was undoubtedly still a rocky one, but there were signs of a new spirit of compromise in Cambodia. UNTAC's presence created a window of opportunity. Whether the various factions chose to step through, to an era of peace and recovery, or slam it shut and return to the old cycle of war and bloodletting, was up to them. At the time of writing (mid-1994), prospects for prolonged peace in Cambodia appear slim. Clashes between the new government and the Khmer Rouge are on the increase.

BIBLIOGRAPHY

John Audric: *Angkor & the Khmers*, Robert Hale, London, 1972

Elizabeth Becker: *When The War Was Over*, Simon & Schuster, New York, 1986

Lawrence Palmer Briggs: *The Ancient Khmer Empire*, The American Philosophical Society, USA, 1974

Nayan Chanda: *Brother Enemy: The War After the War*, Harcourt Brace Jovanovich Publishers, 1986

David Chandler: *A History of Cambodia*, Westview, Boulder, USA, 1983

Kenneth Conboy: *The War in Cambodia 1970–75*, Osprey, London, 1989

Robin Corbett: *Guerrilla Warfare: From 1939 to the Present Day*, Orbis, London, 1986

Michael Freeman & Roger Warner: *Angkor: The Hidden Glories*, Houghton Mifflin, London, 1990

Vo Nguyen Giap: *People's War, People's Army*, Natraj Publishers, Dehra Dun, India, 1974

Martin Herz: *A Short History of Cambodia*, Atlantic Books, London, 1958

Malcolm MacDonald: *Angkor and the Khmers*, Oxford University Press, 1987

M. Henri Mouhot: *Travels in Indo-China: Siam, Cambodia, Laos, Etc*, White Lotus Company, Bangkok, 1986

Henri Stierlin: *The Cultural History of Angkor*, Aurum Press, London, 1984

Chou Ta-Kuan: *The Customs of Cambodia*, The Siam Society, Bangkok, 1987

Michael Vickery: *Cambodia 1975–82*, Allen & Unwin, Australia, 1984

Maslyn Williams: *The Land Between: The Cambodian Dilemma*, Collins, London, 1969

ANTHONY ROGERS

Eritrea

E ritrea borders northern Ethiopia, in north-east Africa. An ancient land – maritime links to Egypt are indicated as early as 3000 BC – it has a tumultuous history of invasions and internal strife. During the second century BC, Semitic immigrants founded a kingdom centred on Aksum, in present-day Tigre. Adulis, today called Zula, served as the main port. The Aksumite Kingdom encompassed northern Tigre, the southern Eritrean Highlands and part of the coast and is believed to have reached across the Red Sea into the Yemen. In the fourth century, the Aksumite King Ezana converted to Christianity. The region continued to prosper until Islamic expansion around the seventh century. In the middle of the eighth century the Aksumites were superseded by the Bejas, who established five independent kingdoms and, for several hundred years, dominated what is today Eritrea, Tigre and north-eastern Sudan. By the fifteenth century, Eritrea was known as *Medri-Bahri* (Land of the Sea) and was constantly at war with invaders from Tigre and Abyssinia (Ethiopia). In the sixteenth century the Ottoman Turks invaded, and by 1557 they had occupied much of the coastal area. The Turks remained until 1865, when they were replaced by the Egyptian Khedevites. Theirs was a short-lived occupation whose withdrawal, some twenty years later, was precipitated by an unsuccessful foray into Ethiopia as well as increased resistance by the Mahdia to Egyptian expansion into the Sudan. Next to arrive were the Italians, who named the region Eritrea. The Italians stayed until their defeat by the British at Keren, in 1941.

Eritrea remained under British administration until September 1952. In the interim, on 2 December 1950, the future of the former Italian colony was decided when the United Nations adopted Resolution 390A(V) that declared Eritrea 'an autonomous unit federated with Ethiopia under the sovereignty of the Ethiopian Crown'. Ethiopia's Emperor Haile Selassie subsequently deployed his forces in Eritrea, ostensibly to protect the federal entity. Soon, however, the government began gradually to dismantle the Eritrean administration. Independent institutions and political parties were subverted and freedom of speech, press and assembly suppressed. Even the local dialects were discouraged in favour of Amharic, the Ethiopian language. Eritrean protests were to no avail.[1]

On 1 September 1961, the Eritrean Liberation Front (ELF) was formed. In

Left: A discarded helmet and a derelict truck at the former Ethiopian tank base near Massawa.

1. Araya Tseggai, *The Long Struggle of Eritrea*, edited by Lionel Cliffe and Basil Davidson (Spokesman), 1988

the face of mounting resistance, Ethiopia's response just over a year later was to abrogate the UN Federal Act and annex Eritrea. That the government could get away with such a move was in no small way attributable to American support for Haile Selassie. In return for being able to safeguard strategic interests in the region, the United States provided Ethiopia with military hardware and training. It was evident that only a forceful and united opposition movement could lead Eritrea to independence. But the potential effectiveness of the ELF was eroded by problems from within. Many felt that it lacked direction and also did little to counter antagonisms brokered by religious and ethnic differences and diverse political opinions.

In April 1970 the continuing discord led to the formation of the Eritrean People's Liberation Forces, subsequently redesignated the Eritrean People's Liberation Front (EPLF). This was an amalgamation of three breakaway groups, one of them headed by Isseyas Aferworki, who would ultimately lead Eritrea in the long struggle to independence.[2] The existence of another Front was seen by the ELF as a potential threat. Consequently, in early 1972 these two organisations turned on each other. And, seizing the opportunity, the Ethiopian government ordered a military offensive in an abortive effort to crush Eritrean resistance once and for all.

Realistically, Emperor Haile Selassie could hardly have expected to succeed in Eritrea when he also faced increasing malcontent in Ethiopia. In September 1974, Selassie was deposed and replaced by the *Dergue* (Committee). The new order lost no time in mobilising thousands of troops in a fresh attempt to defeat the Eritreans. In November the ELF and EPLF, having agreed to a truce, now coordinated their operations and subjected the Ethiopians to a series of humiliating defeats. Towards the end of 1977, the Liberation Fronts controlled most of the Eritrean countryside with government forces reduced to a state of siege in Asmara, Barentu, Adi-Keyih, Senafe, Assab and parts of Massawa. In addition, Ethiopia had to contend with opposition in Tigre as well as an invasion by Somali forces via the Ogaden in June 1977. The *Dergue* might soon have been defeated but for a radical shift in Ethiopia's defence alliance.

By 1977 the Carter administration had decided to suspend further US military aid because of continued human rights violations by Ethiopia. The *Dergue* retaliated by withdrawing a number of facilities while simultaneously turning to the Soviet Union for assistance. Before this, the Russians had been obliged to make do with a base in neighbour-

Left: Ethiopian soldiers proudly show off an AK-47 assault rifle and a 7.62mm PKM light machine-gun.

ing Somalia. Ethiopia, comparatively fertile and altogether more agreeable, was a far better option. The Soviets soon implemented a massive aid programme that included the transfer of Cuban troops from Somalia. Soviet intervention was also instrumental in the continuing rise of a founding figure of the *Dergue* – Mengistu Haile Mariam, who would later become President of Ethiopia.

By 1978 the influx of Soviet armaments and thousands of Cuban soldiers was beginning to take effect. The Somalis were obliged to pull back and, by 1979, the EPLF were forced to conduct a 'strategic withdrawal' to a stronghold base area in the northern Sahel district around Nacfa, a town destined to become a symbol of Eritrean defiance.

Below: When US military support for Ethiopia ended, in 1976, the government turned to the Soviet Union for assistance. This picture, probably taken in the Massawa area in 1989–90, shows what is almost certainly a military advisor during an award-giving ceremony for Ethiopian troops.

84

Right and below: T-54/55
Main Battle Tanks.

In 1980, there was renewed fighting between the Liberation Fronts, which ended in 1981 in defeat for the ELF, leaving the EPLF to concentrate its efforts solely against the *Dergue*.

During the next decade, the war would develop into a series of offensives and counter-offensives. Vast areas were transformed by miles of inter-connecting trench works and bunkers as the warring sides confronted each other in scenes reminiscent of the Western Front in the First World War. Thousands perished.

Following initial successes, the Ethiopians conducted further offensives against the Eritreans but were unable to dislodge them from their defensive positions. A sixth offensive, Operation 'Red Star', was launched on 15 February 1982. As always, the Eritreans refused to confirm their own losses, but it

is known that casualties were heavy on both sides, with some 40,000 government troops reported killed or wounded. A seventh offensive during March–April 1983 resulted in an estimated 7,000 Ethiopian casualties. In January 1984 the EPLF struck back, eventually liberating Tessenai in western Eritrea and a large area of the northern coast, including the port of Mersa Teklay. Government losses are believed to have exceeded 8,000, including 3,100 captured.

In the summer of 1985 the EPLF took Barentu in the south-west. Subsequently an Ethiopian counter-attack on four fronts drove the EPLA from previously won locations, including Tessenai and Barentu. According to EPLF sources, Ethiopian casualties exceeded 11,000. In October 1985, the *Dergue*'s 'Red Sea' offensive pushed the Eritreans back to their defensive positions outside Nacfa. On 19 March 1988, the EPLF won a crucial victory at nearby Afabet, thus relieving the pressure on Nacfa after a decade of fighting.

Of the various rebel groups opposing Mengistu, the EPLF and Tigrean People's Liberation Front (TPLF) were the most dominant. Although divided in their opinions, they managed to reconcile their differences in order to combat a common enemy. In 1988 the TPLF united with three other organisations to form the Ethiopian People's Revolutionary Democratic Front (EPRDF).

The *Dergue* was subjected to further setbacks during 1989 and 1990. In May 1989, there was an unsuccessful *coup* against Mengistu. In February the following year the Eritreans launched an offensive and captured the vital port area of Massawa. It was a major blow for the increasingly demoralised Ethiopians. By mid-1990, Mengistu's demise seemed inevitable. The war continued until May 1991, when the Ethiopian President fled to exile in Zimbabwe. Days later, the EPRDF took control of Addis Ababa while the EPLA received a victorious welcome in the Eritrean capital, Asmara. After 30 years, the war was finally over.

THE ERITREAN PEOPLE'S LIBERATION ARMY (EPLA)

Ever security conscious, the Eritrean People's Liberation Front (EPLF) was never forthcoming in providing details about its armed forces. Neither would the Eritreans discuss their own losses other than to state that the casualty ratio of Eritrean to Ethiopian forces was probably 1:10 in their favour – 'otherwise, we couldn't continue', reasoned one. It isn't much to go on but, assuming that the Eritrean Peo-

ple's Liberation Army (EPLA) numbered at least a tenth of the total Ethiopian figure, by the late 1980s one might expect there to have been some 25–30,000 fighters, probably more. In *Eritrea: Images of War and Peace*, Glenys Kinnock places the figure at 40,000. Andrew Buckoke, in *Fishing in Africa*, believes that there may have been as many as 60,000.

What *is* known is that from humble beginnings the EPLF developed into a well-organised and self-sufficient organisation with a fighting wing that was professional and disciplined and fiercely determined in battle. The success of the EPLA had as much to do with the ideological motivation of each individual as with training standards. Although the Eritreans always insisted that they were 'fighters', never soldiers, the EPLA would develop into precisely what the title implied – Eritrea's army. It would include mechanised forces, infantry, artillery, engineering and commando units, a naval force and People's Militia, the latter comprising Regional,

Right: The plains north and west of Massawa were still littered with battle debris months after the fighting had ended. Seventeen kilometres from the city, on the Massawa-Asmara road, the EPLA had caught an Ethiopian armoured unit, demolishing the T-54/55s with anti-tank missiles. This T-54 appears to have had the turret deliberately removed, probably to facilitate easier access for EPLF salvage crews.

Below: Devastation at Adishrum seen from the approximate position where, in March 1988, the first tank was hit.

Most were provided with an AK-47 and four or five magazines. In action, this was supplemented with an additional 200–300 rounds. Necessities such as side-arms, grenades and canteens were carried in a belt-order with pouches manufactured from Ethiopian army boot leather. Some fighters wore Soviet tropical field hats and Ethiopian combat jackets. Jeans were a popular choice, as were shorts, which might be worn in conjunction with canvas gaiters. The only concessions to uniformity were locally produced black, plastic sandals and a piece of cotton material (*fota*) that served as a wrap-around garment, sun-shield, blanket and carrier.

Equipment was always immaculately maintained. Off-duty personnel seemed to be constantly checking and cleaning their rifles. Other weapons, such as machine-guns and RPGs, were often kept in zip-up carrying bags when not in use to protect them from the dust.

By and large, Eritreans are a paradox: an affable and modest people who are also capable of displaying immense courage and aggression. Only occasionally might one briefly describe another's heroism. Some of those so regaled were incredibly beautiful young women whose apparent frailty belied their prowess in battle. However, the thousands of Ethiopian soldiers held captive in Eritrea testified to the effectiveness of the EPLA – a force that would eventually play a leading role in defeating the largest army in black Africa.

Zonal and Village Militia. Training lasted up to six months for women volunteers and about three months for the men, longer for those who specialised.

Equipment, from small-arms to heavy weapons, from soft-skinned vehicles to main battle tanks, were captured – 'supplied, indirectly, by the Russians', as one Eritrean put it – and used against the former owners. Skills and tactics were learned and improved upon the hard way. If war had become a way of life for those in Eritrea, for many fighters it was the only life they knew.

About a third of the EPLA were female. In a society where clitorectomy and infibulation was widespread, the exigencies of war had liberated women. There appeared not to be any distinction between the sexes in the allocation of tasks. Jobs were given to those capable of doing them, whether it was as part of a gun crew, commanding a tank or leading troops into battle. There was no formal rank structure. A fighter with proven ability was rewarded with a position of authority, and he or she was accepted and respected as such by subordinates.

Generally, EPLA fighters were lightly equipped.

LIFE AT THE FRONT

The only predictable thing about Eritrea's climate is that in the dry season it is certain to be almost unbearably hot, dry and dusty. In the Horn of Africa insufficient rainfall can mean the difference between life and death. Drought leads to crop failure and, eventually, famine. War only exacerbates the plight of those affected. Eritrea can be an unforgiving land. Its people, of necessity, are a hardy race.

Conditions at the front were austere, as might be expected. The Ghinda sector was fairly typical. In September 1990 the front arced in an inverted 'C' shape from west of Keren, east as far as Gheleb, then down past Ghinda and Dongolo (the south-western limits of the February 1990 EPLA offensive) and beyond, skirting Decamere before continuing south-west towards Mendefera. A few kilometres south of Ghinda was a formidable defence system. Protected by EPLA guard posts, the route in followed the disused Massawa–Agordat railway line, a relic of Italy's colonial period. Either side of the track were hills as far as the eye could see. Those immediately on the left concealed the Eritrean front-line. Even in the relatively cooler early hours the long climb was exhausting. It was not until one approached the summit that the first bunkers became apparent. These were built into the hillside for maximum protection against artillery, mortar and air strikes. An attempt had been made to camouflage each entrance using natural cover, this being done in such a way that it also provided the occupants with a lean-to in which to eat and socialise. The staple diet seemed to be a type of bread called *injera*. Water had to be carried in jerrycans from a stream in one of the ravines below the positions.

At the top of the hill were more bunkers together with mortars and machine guns, which formed the headquarters and fire-support line. To the east, and out of sight, sat the artillery. On another range of hills, within a kilometre of the fire-support line, were the forward or 'fighting' positions where Eritrean trenches paralleled those of the Ethiopians just 200 metres away, less in some areas. Below, on the eastern slopes and shielded from enemy observation, the EPLA had built additional bunkers for those not on duty in the forward positions, which were occupied day and night.

The EPLA 1st Battalion had fought in the Battle for Massawa before moving to Ghinda. These young men and women knew it was only a matter of time before they would be required to again go on the offensive. Someone had to take the nearby Ethiopian trenches. There was only one way it could be done, and in some sectors the no man's land between the opposing forces' lines was littered with decomposing corpses of those who had died when called to 'go over the top'.

Until the next action, there was little for the fighters to do. Thanks primarily to the BBC radio World Service the average knowledge of foreign affairs surpassed that of most westerners. So the news was a constant subject for discussion. Otherwise, there were always weapons to be cleaned and equipment to be checked and re-checked. Some of the fighters had even constructed a volley-ball court. For the Eritreans, with the enemy dug in along the next ridge line, it seemed a perfectly ordinary way to pass the time.

EPLA OPERATIONS

In its long struggle for independence, Eritrea was the setting for numerous large-scale military operations, most of which went unnoticed by the West, whose media was usually more concerned with events elsewhere. Today reliable and detailed information about the war is, at best, scarce and often

non-existent unless one is able to spend time in Eritrea in order to conduct one's own interviews and research. Anyone attempting to present an in-depth analysis, therefore, would face a mammoth task. Even if it were possible to compile a chronology of each skirmish and every battle, the material would almost certainly fill several volumes.

What follows, therefore, are brief overviews of just two of the main battles, drawing on what little material is readily available and also based, in part, on personal observations made during subsequent visits to the areas concerned.

THE NACFA FRONT

The Nacfa Front was established after the 'strategic withdrawal' of the Eritrean People's Liberation Front (EPLF) in 1978. It extended for 120 kilometres in a meandering maze of trenches, bunkers, gun emplacements and mortar pits. This formidable defensive position was constructed amongst mountains and valleys from Habero and Rora Habab, on the right flank, to western Afabet and eastern Nacfa. During a decade of bitter contention, the Ethiopians repeatedly attempted to break through to Nacfa and beyond to where the EPLF had established its base areas.

In early December 1987 fighting flared on the left flank of the Nacfa Front. According to the EPLF, some 2,000 government troops were 'put out of action', prompting Colonel Mengistu to order the

Above: Although this particular battlefield had already been partially cleared, corpses still lay *in situ*, their limbs torn apart by hyenas and other desert animals. This unidentified body is almost certainly Ethiopian, as EPLF casualties were quickly dealt with on the spot. Wounded were attended to and then casevaced to the rear; the dead were buried in unmarked graves.

88

execution of the unfortunate head of the regional 'Nadew [Destroy] Command', Brigadier General Tariku Taye. The decisive battle began at dawn on Thursday 17 March 1988. The fate of the Ethiopian forces was decided during the first 48 hours of heavy fighting. Numerous clashes occurred along the Nacfa Front. In a narrow ravine at Adishrum, between Nacfa and Afabet, an Ethiopian armoured column was halted after the Eritrean People's Liberation Army (EPLA) immobilised a tank at the front of the convoy. Then, say the Eritreans, the Ethiopian air force attacked their own men to prevent equipment from falling into EPLF hands. The carnage was terrific. Up to 70 tanks and other vehicles were totally destroyed. For weeks afterwards there remained the charred remains of Ethiopians, some of whom were burnt alive as they tried to escape the inferno. Years later, the rusting remains of the convoy still littered the area.

Another important victory was the liberation of Afabet, from 1979 the headquarters of the Ethiopian regional high command. According to British historian Basil Davidson, who was in Eritrea at the time, Eritrean success was partly due to their 'surprise encirclement' of the enemy who were 'placed in a position in which they simply could not fight. They dropped their weapons and fled.'[3]

Three divisions (14th, 19th, 21st), the 29th Mechanised Brigade and nine battalions of heavy artillery were virtually annihilated. Between 18,000 and 20,000 Ethiopians were killed, wounded or captured. Amongst the casualties was at least one dead Soviet officer and three captives, Colonels Kalistrov Yuri Petrovich and Churayev Yevigniew

Nicolayevich and Lieutenant Covaldin Alexander Victrovich. 'This victory', enthused Basil Davidson, 'is one of the biggest ever scored by any liberation movement anywhere since Dien Bien Phu in 1954.'

MASSAWA
By 1990, Ethiopia's access to the Red Sea was restricted to the ports of Assab and Massawa. In 1990 the latter was divided into four sections. A causeway connected what might be described as a shanty town to the main residential area on Tewalot island. The port itself was on another island, and just to the north was the Ethiopian naval base. At 0100 hours on Thursday 8 February 1990, the Eritreans began an offensive primarily to take Massawa. A coordinated attack was launched along the 200 kilometre Ethiopian defence line that extended from Keren, east towards Ras Kobai, about 40 kilometres north of Massawa. On the right flank (northwest of the port), the Ethiopian army's 6th Divisional Headquarters was overrun and the deputy commander, Lieutenant Colonel Afewerke Tecle captured. The EPLA pushed on to cut the Asmara–Massawa road at Dighdighta before continuing inland towards Dongolo. The road between Dongolo and Massawa was the scene of heavy fighting as the Ethiopians tried in vain to halt the EPLA advance. On the 9th the Eritreans seized the high ground near Dog'ali, which was taken later the same day. Close by, the EPLA captured ten tanks following a major engagement that left the area littered with destroyed armour and Ethiopian corpses. Also on the 9th, the Ethiopian navy lost two vessels in EPLA sea-borne actions off Massawa.

Below: Front line. The Ghinda sector, above the disused Massawa–Agordat railway line, was held by 1st Battalion of the Eritrean People's Liberation Army. Defence positions continued to within three to five kilometres of the Ethiopians in Ghinda. Each side's trenches ran more or less parallel and in one area were just 50 metres apart. Three days after this picture was taken, in September 1990, fighting erupted on each side of this location. EPLF radio reported that 200 Ethiopians were killed and 250 wounded. The picture below shows the Ethiopian trench line as seen from Eritrean positions. The picture provides an indication of the type of terrain that had to be fought over.

90

On the left flank, EPLA mechanised infantry was supported by artillery during the opening stages of the attack. On the sandy plains north of the objective, the Eritreans encountered a vastly superior tank force. Two Ethiopian tanks were destroyed within fifteen minutes, causing panic among the entrenched government troops, who broke and ran. When another tank was hit the Eritreans charged, racing ahead of their own armour in order to come to grips with the enemy. By noon on the 10th, the EPLA had reached the city outskirts. The following day a message was delivered to Ethiopian Brigadier General Teshome Tesema, OC 6th Division, asking that he surrender Massawa or, at least, allow the civilian population to leave. Convinced that reinforcements were en route from Asmara, and clearly unaware or unwilling to accept that a relief force had already been halted on the 9th, Tesema refused both requests. Instead, he gathered his troops at the end of the causeway in Tewalot and awaited the inevitable onslaught.

In desperation, government forces mounted two sea-borne operations to reinforce their comrades besieged in Massawa. Both attempts failed. When the final battle began, the Ethiopians found themselves trapped as EPLA assault troops, deployed by fast patrol boats, closed in from behind, while on the landward side the first EPLA tanks began to cross the causeway. These were fiercely opposed, but as quickly as the first tanks were knocked out they were replaced by others supported by infantry who, in conjunction with those already in Tewalot, now began to crush Ethiopian resistance.

Most of the 3,000 civilians in the city survived the attack. Brigadier General Tesema did not. Subsequently, the air force carried out a number of reprisal raids, inflicting numerous civilian casualties. The battle for Massawa cost Mengistu dearly. In addition to the disruption of Ethiopian supply lines, military losses were placed at one mechanised, three motorised and four infantry brigades. At least 8,000 prisoners were taken. About 75 main

Above left: Massawa, six months after 'liberation', was slowly returning to normality. But the brutalising effects of a protracted war were evident. People seemed remarkably unconcerned that skeletons and mummified corpses still littered the area. Close to the main road just inside the main residential area of Tewalot, a foot protruded from the rubble.

Above right: Ethiopian webbing equipment abandoned at Massawa railway station.

Opposite page, top left: A few kilometres north-west of Massawa was the base of an Ethiopian tank unit, reportedly 4th Tank Brigade. In the shade of a small wood were bunkers, tents and grass huts, all of which contained abandoned equipment. This plaque, bearing the unit emblem and motto 'Always Forward', has been defaced by the Eritreans. The other side bore an inscription which, might be translated as: 'People fear death, but we do not. What we fear for is our reputation.'

Opposite page, top right: On the outskirts of Massawa sheets of corrugated iron surrounding a solitary *mekie* tree, concealed a bizarre and grisly secret: crates full of the remains of Ethiopian soldiers. According to the Eritreans, who discovered the site when Massawa was 'liberated' in February 1990, the bones were those of executed dissidents. Another possibility – not shared by the EPLF – is that they are the remains of government troops killed during previous battles.

Right: About a third of EPLA fighters were women. This bunker was home to two of them. Note the overhead cover, salvaged from the nearby Massawa–Agordat railway line.

4. p. 15, *Adulis*, Vol V, No 9, October, 1988

5. 'Basic Information on Eritrea' supplied by the Government of Eritrea, Mission to the United Kingdom

battle tanks, six BM-21 Multiple Rocket Launchers, six 122mm artillery pieces and ten anti-aircraft guided missiles were captured. Another 24 tanks were destroyed together with nine, possibly twelve, naval vessels. At least two others were seized intact. The EPLA also claimed to have shot down two MiG-23s and a MiG-21.

In January 1991, the port was re-opened, allowing food shipments into drought-stricken Eritrea. Massawa remained in Eritrean hands.

OROTA

As a *de facto* government in areas it controlled, the Eritrean People's Liberation Front (EPLF) had its own ministries, or Departments, conducive to the effective functioning of any country. The system worked, and enabled many people to lead an existence that was superior to other, supposedly civilised, African societies. During the war, virtually every visitor to Eritrea was escorted around Orota. This was the EPLF showpiece, the administrative capital of the 'liberated areas'. It was a splendid example of Eritrean ingenuity and resourcefulness – a citadel concealed in the ground and beneath trees along the valleys of the mountain bowl just inside Eritrea's northern border.

Orota was the location of Zero School with an attendance of thousands, the syllabus including all the usual elementary subjects in addition to more advanced studies. It was also where the EPLF had its Central Hospital, five and a half kilometres of buildings, tents and converted transport containers that housed operating theatres, X-ray facilities, wards, a dental centre and laboratories. A pharmaceutical production plant provided essential drugs in tablet, capsule and infusion form. Quality control, it was maintained, was well up to international standards. Elsewhere, factories produced such basic

essentials as soap and sanitary towels. There were also metal and wood works whose craftsmen, and women, could manufacture a wide range of products. Material salvaged from the battlefields was repaired or re-cycled. Virtually anything, from the engine of a T-54/55 to a wrist-watch, could be taken apart expertly and re-assembled .

The Eritreans were almost entirely self-sufficient. They had to be. However, support, including financial assistance, was provided mainly, it is believed, by Eritreans living abroad. Sympathetic organisations also donated machinery and equipment.

At Orota there were many who had been disfigured in the war. But amputees were assigned essential tasks, which provided them with a dignified place in society and enabled the EPLF to utilise all available manpower. All EPLF members were unpaid volunteers, with food, clothes, medical treatment and other services all provided for. Notwithstanding the lifestyle, the EPLF's Isseyas Aferworki has been quoted as saying, 'It's a misunderstanding when people try to talk about the EPLF as being a totally Marxist organisation.'[4] Certainly, Eritreans were influenced by the principles of socialism, and the Soviet Union had provided political support before deciding to back Ethiopia. But at some point – and probably because of the Soviets' *volte-face* – the EPLF was prompted to reconsider its politics. For two years after the war, Eritrea was administered by a provisional government. In April 1993 a referendum resulted, unsurprisingly, in an overwhelming vote for independence. Presently the country is undergoing a four-year transitional period, 'until a democratic constitution which guarantees the basic rights of citizens and political pluralism, which can also be the basis of all laws is achieved; and an elected constitution government is established'.[5]

Opposite page, top left:
The strain and fatigue of life at the front is portrayed in the expression of this machine-gunner.

Opposite page, top right:
EPLA fighters about to take up night-time positions.

Opposite page, lower left:
A close-up of a fighter's light battle order: AK-47 assault rifle with webbing equipment manufactured from Ethiopian army boot leather and attached to a standard army-issue belt. Included in this set are magazine and grenade pouches, the latter holding a Chinese stick grenade.

Opposite page, lower right:
Carrying a 7.62mm PKM light machine-gun, an EPLA fighter arrives at the 'fighting trench' for his turn at night duty. Note what appears to be a spare barrel slung beneath his left arm. The twisted cloth *fota* serves primarily as a wrap-around garment.

Above right: Another example of EPLA webbing equipment.

Right: An observation post situated on a feature overlooking Ethiopian lines. Note the plastic sandals. These were mass produced locally and worn by virtually all the fighters.

Left and below left: Afabet: a pool for battle-damaged tanks and armoured vehicles and a source of spare parts for the EPLA.

Right: Nacfa, which became a symbol of Eritrean resistance. Once a farm community of 6–7,000, it was destroyed in a succession of artillery and air attacks. One of the only buildings left standing, albeit in a much-damaged state, was the mosque (right of frame).

BIBLIOGRAPHY

Bereket Habte Selassie, *Conflict and Intervention in the Horn of Africa*, Monthly Review Press, 1980.

Basil Davidson, Lionel Cliffe and Bereket Habte Selassie, *Behind the War in Eritrea*, Spokesman, 1980.

David Pool, *Eritrea: Africa's Longest War*, Anti-Slavery Society, 1979 and 1982

James Firebrace and Stuart Holland MP, *Never Kneel Down*, Spokesman, 1984

Eritrea: The Way Forward, United Nations Association of the United Kingdom and Northern Ireland, 1986

John Laffin, *The World in Conflict*, Volumes 1 to 4, Brassey's (UK), 1987, 1988, 1989, 1990

Lionel Cliffe and Basil Davidson, *The Long Struggle of Eritrea for Independence and Constructive Peace,* Spokesman, 1988

Glenys Kinnock and Jenny Matthews, *Eritrea: Images of War and Peace*, Chatto and Windus, 1988

Robert D Kaplan, *Surrender or Starve*, Westview Press, 1988

Bahru Zewde, *A History of Modern Ethiopia 1855–1974*, Addis Ababa University Press, 1991

Andrew Buckoke, *Fishing in Africa: A Guide to War and Corruption,* Picador, 1991

Jeremy Harding, *Small Wars, Small Mercies: Journeys in Africa's Disputed Nations,* Viking, 1993

Adulis, EPLF newsletter

Right: Russian Ural-375 (6 x 6) fuel tanker supplied to the *Dergue* and captured by the Eritreans.

Right: Found at the former location of an Ethiopian tank unit, which clearly had been subjected to aerial bombardment after being taken by the EPLA, was this nose-fuze believed to have come from a napalm canister. The markings are in English but the manufacturer is a mystery.

Below: A typical PLO soldier, with locally produced canvas webbing, an AKM assault rifle and a chequered *kefiyah* (headdress) worn as a scarf.

KEN GUEST

Lebanon

T he area known today as the Lebanon was not conceived as a distinct country in ancient times. In the Middle East, borders were ever-shifting as the region was, in turn, swallowed and disgorged by the parade of conquerors who marched through. The seafaring Phoenicians were among the earliest travellers to arrive, establishing city states along what would one day be the Lebanese coast. These cities lost their independence in the sixth century BC when they were conquered by the Persians. Two hundred years later the Persian Empire fell to Alexander the Great. His Macedonians controlled the region until their empire was, in turn, replaced by the Hellenistic Seleucid Kingdom.

With the coming of the Roman legions in the first century BC the present Lebanese territory became part of the Roman province of Syria. When the Roman power-base was transferred to Christian rulers in their eastern capital of Byzantium[1] in the fourth century AD, Christianity flourished throughout the empire. In AD 641 the Arabs arrived and the last Byzantine troops withdrew from the Lebanon. The new conquerors brought with them a new religion – Islam. From this point forward, the future Lebanon became an Arabic-speaking land, even among the Christian enclaves.

With the Middle Ages the Crusaders appeared, to seize the land for Christianity once more. Richard the Lionheart campaigned through the cedar-clad slopes against his arch-rival Saladin (Sala al-din Yussuf ibn-Ayyub, Sultan of Egypt and Syria). The local Maronite Christians rallied to the Crusader banners, thus sowing the seed of an enmity between themselves and the Moslem population which has endured for almost a thousand years.

In 1379 the pendulum swung back to Islam when the Turks gained control. They hung on to the area tenaciously until after the First World War, when their Ottoman Empire was carved up by the League of Nations. France was awarded the mandate for the Syrian part of the empire and created the present state of Lebanon from Syrian territory. In 1943 the French granted the Lebanon its independence, under the terms of which the constitution of the new state was to reflect its multi-cultural society: the President was to be a Maronite Christian, the Prime Minister a Sunni Moslem and the Chamber of Deputies Shi'a Moslems. By this means it was hoped that the Lebanon would become a sort of neutral 'Switzerland of the Middle East'.

1. Constantinople.

98

The problem was that an inherent power imbalance remained in favour of the Christians. This did not reflect the realities of the demographic situation, as the Moslem population was increasing. However, the Christians were not about to relinquish the political privileges bequeathed to them by the French and a clash became inevitable.

In 1958 a brief civil war erupted over the resistance of the Lebanon's Christian leaders to the pan-Arab unity advocated by President Nasser of Egypt. Although this disruption died down, the fundamental causes of the war had only been put on hold. Nevertheless, a period of increasing prosperity followed, during which the Lebanon emerged as the international banking centre of the Middle East. This was to be the calm before the storm.

Meanwhile, in nearby Jordan, King Hussein was concerned about the rising power and influence of the Palestine Liberation Organisation (PLO), to which he acted as a reluctant host. In 1970, in what came to be known as 'Black September', the Jordanian Army attacked the PLO and pushed them over the border into Syria. Confronted with the unwanted arrival of thousands of PLO fighters, President Hafaz Assad of Syria provided them with arms and moved them on, into the Lebanon. By this means the Syrians hoped to increase their own influence in the neighbouring state, which they considered to be rightfully part of 'Greater Syria'.

The Sunni Moslems of the Lebanon were from the same branch of Islam as the PLO. They were consequently inclined to unite with the Palestinian *fedain* (redeemers), to improve mutual defence. This upset the fragile status quo. By 1975 the Christians felt provoked beyond endurance by the continued presence of the PLO and the slumbering civil war flared into life.

The Syrians saw this as an opportunity to fulfil their territorial aspirations. Within a year their Army had marched into the Lebanese capital city of Beirut under the pretext of unifying the warring factions. The result was inconclusive. The Lebanon splintered into feifdoms under political and religious warlords. Beirut was literally split in two, along a no man's land known as 'The Green Line' which divided the eastern, Christian area from the Moslem west.

It would be simplistic to suggest that *all* divisions in the Lebanon were purely along Christian versus Moslem lines. The factional intricacies and shifting loyalties of the multiple parties could fill volumes. For example, Saad Haddad was a Lebanese-Greek Catholic. Originally a major in the Lebanese Army, he left to form his own 'Southern Lebanese

Above left: A Mourabitoun militia member on the Green Line in Beirut. The Mourabitoun were a leftist Muslim militia whose fortunes were bolstered by the departure of the PLO, as they inherited much of their military hardware.

Above: The PLO forces produced a few home-made armoured cars. This one was seen near the Green Line in Beirut.

Above: A Syrian soldier looks through observation glasses from a building at the Museum crossing, on the Green Line. This building was attacked two days later, and most of the Syrian defenders were killed.

2. A secretive religious sect which has borrowed elements from both Islam and Christianity.

3. What passes for peace in the Lebanon is quantitative. For example, between January and August 1983 alone the IDF was subjected to 260 separate guerrilla attacks and suffered 200 casualties as a result.

Army'. This force was widely represented in the press as a 'Christian right-wing militia', implying that it was also anti-Moslem, but in fact it was composed of a mixture of Druze,[2] Christians and (probably in the majority) Shi'ite Moslems, in opposition to the Sunni Moslem PLO.

Syria's presence in the Lebanon caused ripples of alarm in Israel. The Israelis increased their backing of both the Southern Lebanese Army and the Christian Phalangist militia, while the Syrians nominally supported the PLO and Moslem militias. The steady rise in the number of border incidents between Israel and the PLO finally led to a major Israeli incursion in 1978 (Operation *Litani*). This prompted the United Nations to send a peace-keeping force (UNFIL) to monitor a buffer zone between the two countries.

The presence of UNFIL made little difference. The PLO did not back down and 1981 saw an escalation in border clashes. Israel decided that the growing threat posed by active PLO units in Southern Lebanon and the danger of further Syrian expansionism must be dealt with.

The situation was also becoming dangerous for the Shi'ite Moslems in Lebanon, who were caught between an increasingly belligerent PLO and retaliatory shelling by Israel. With no avenue of escape, they became ever more desperate and looked to Iran, a Shi'ite religious state, for help. Iran was keen to export its own brand of militant Islamic fundamentalism and encouraged the Lebanese Shi'ite leader, Sheikh Fadlallah, to found *Hezbollah* (Party of God). Shi'ites also flocked to join the secular *Afwai al-Muqaamah al-Lubnaniya* ('Battalions of the Lebanese Resistance', better known by its acronym, AMAL).

When the 1982 Israeli invasion finally came, many Lebanese welcomed it. They were convinced that the removal of the Syrians and the PLO was their only hope of salvation from endless civil war. But the Israelis stopped short of expelling the Syrian Army from the Lebanon. After the ejection of the PLO from Beirut, in September 1982, the Israeli Army unexpectedly pulled back to positions in the central Shouf mountains. Except for a flare-up of fighting between the Druze and Christians in early 1983, the Lebanon entered a period of relative calm.[3] This was finally to be shattered when the Israelis withdrew from the Shouf mountains to the Awali river in southern Lebanon, in August 1983, and a civil war of unprecedented ferocity broke out to fill the resultant power-vacuum.

Why Israel stopped short of completely ousting the Syrians as well as the PLO from the Lebanon has never been explained. Perhaps they were swayed by Israeli domestic reaction against their own rising toll of casualties, or perhaps they reasoned that a fragmented Lebanon was less of an economic threat to Israel, or, possibly, they came under diplomatic pressure from the United States. In any event, the tide of civil war dragged on for several more years, until the Syrians once again committed large numbers of troops to impose a semi-ceasefire on the bitterly opposed Lebanese factions. The price of this hostile compromise was the continued presence of a large Syrian force in the Lebanon.

'PEACE FOR GALILEE': ISRAEL'S 1982 INVASION OF THE LEBANON

The 1982 Israeli invasion of the Lebanon was known as Operation *Peace for Galilee*. It was originally planned as a limited incursion of no more than 40 kilometres – enough to keep PLO artillery and Katyushka rockets out of range of Israeli settle-

99

ments in Galilee. The most serious impediment to the plan was posed by the conventional forces of the Syrian Army and Air Force. Every effort was to be made to avoid direct confrontation with them. The PLO were considered a lesser threat. Their ranks, predominantly drawn from local militia forces, were composed of lightly armed infantry, with limited armour-support from outdated tanks.

Israel planned a three-pronged advance: along the narrow coastal plain (only 2km wide in some places) towards Tyre and Sidon; through the central mountains from Beaufort Castle towards the Nabatiyeh Plain; and, in the eastern sector, from Racchaiya and Habsbaiya towards the Bekaa valley. Speed and concentration were the key components of the Israelis' strategy. Any stiff resistance was to be isolated and bypassed, in order to maintain a momentum which allowed the PLO no time to retreat or re-form.

The task of the central Israeli column was to prevent the PLO from escaping eastwards, towards the Bekaa Valley. After reaching Jezzine on the Nabatiyeh Plain, this column was to swing west and link up with the coastal column. The eastern column, heading towards the Bekaa through the mountainous region known as Fatahland, was intended to prevent the Syrians from coming to the aid of the PLO. While the Palestinian High Command were aware that an invasion was pending, no practical steps were taken to implement defence plans. PLO training stressed hardship and sacrifice, not military strategy. When the invasion finally came, the resistance was improvised at a local level, without the benefit of a co-ordinated defence.

The invasion was heralded, on 4 June, by Israeli air strikes and artillery bombardments to soften up the initial objectives. At 11.00 a.m. on 6 June the Israeli Defence Force (IDF) were unleashed and charged forward with great confidence. The PLO on the coastal plain were disorientated by this rapid advance. With little to stop them, the Israelis raced up the open coastal road until they hit the refugee camp of el-Bas, near Tyre. Here pockets of PLO put up an unexpectedly stiff resistance.

This indication of problems to come went unheeded by Israeli Defence Minister General Ariel Sharon and Chief of Staff Rafael Eitan, who were orchestrating the invasion. They had an ambitious, hidden agenda which called for the occupation of Beirut, well beyond the 40km incursion approved by the Israeli cabinet. Sharon and Eitan wanted nothing less than the total destruction of the PLO and the military defeat of Syria.

The central IDF column encountered problems with the terrain as the Shouf Mountains were heav-

Above: An Israeli M-113 enters the outskirts of Beirut.

Top left: Israelis advance through the Shouf Mountains. Infantry, supported by a tank, walk ahead. The rear is brought up by the M113 APC. It was common practice for such units to lay down heavy fire on possible PLO ambush positions, using both small-arms and tank fire.

Lower left: Israeli soldiers, wounded in the battle for Beirut, are tended by medics. The Israelis needed a quick victory in order to avoid a war of attrition, but the PLO had dug in and were prepared for a long siege.

4. *Sayeret Golani* (Golani Brigade): an Israeli reconnaissance commando.

5. They were known as 'Force Bader'. Most of them never made it beyond the Bekaa valley.

6. The commanders of all three PLO brigades (Karameh, Kastel and Yarmuk) fled, along with thirteen (of fourteen) battalion commanders.

7. Israel did lose one A-4 Skyhawk over Nabatiyeh but this was downed by a shoulder-launched SAM-7, fired by a PLO fighter.

ily forested and had few roads. Despite this, they made good headway and reached their initial objective, Beaufort Castle, without encountering significant resistance. In the twelfth century it had taken the Islamic warrior Saladin two years to defeat the Crusader defenders of this castle; in 1982 a platoon-sized Israeli Commando unit[4] stormed and captured it in a matter of hours. Meanwhile the eastern column continued its drive along the narrow mountain roads. Initially the Syrians, believing that the Israeli objective (as in previous incursions) was a punitive strike against the PLO, tried to keep a low profile. They had no wish to be sucked into a war not of their making.

When the PLO appealed to the Arab world for help, they met with little success. Algeria sent three Antonov transports with arms (held up in Damascus), while the Saudis dispatched a few trucks of medical supplies (also delayed in Damascus). Only Jordan actually contributed manpower, allowing a battalion of Palestinian soldiers serving in her Army to leave for Beirut.[5] In desperation the PLO turned to the Lebanese, Druze and Moslem militias (including the Shi'ites) for help. This proved futile as these factions, like Syria, had no wish to be dragged into a war between Israel and the PLO.

By 7 June the IDF had begun seaborne landings north of Sidon at the mouth of the Awali river and the Israeli incursion started to look less like a limited strike. Syria grew concerned that Israel might have greater territorial ambitions: if so, a direct clash was inevitable. The first shots were exchanged later the same day and the Syrians found themselves sliding towards a shooting war.

Most of the PLO Karameh Brigade were trapped on the coastal strip between the IDF's Awali River beach-head and their ground offensive sweeping

up from Tyre and Sidon. The reaction of the PLO command to the worsening situation was panic: several, high-ranking officers fled their posts, abandoning their forces to their fate.[6] Nonetheless, lower-ranking PLO military and militia proved that they were made of sterner stuff and continued to resist against overwhelming odds. Israeli *Golani* units moving into the Ein el Hilweh refugee camp at Sidon unexpectedly encountered an uncoordinated but tenacious local resistance. Finding themselves drawn into a costly urban battle, the IDF called up more firepower, infantry, tanks and air strikes. They would have done well to remember that it was at Sidon in 1976 that the PLO had held off the Syrian army for six days, inflicting heavy casualties in the process.

The fighting around Sidon continued for almost a week. The militia defenders resisted to the last, street by street, house by house. Though courageous, this effort was not to delay the Israeli advance for long. A new road was located, enabling the bulk of the coastal column to bypass Sidon, link up with the IDF beach-head at the mouth of the Awali river and push on towards Damour.

In the central sector IDF armour pushed north in an attempt to bisect the Beirut-Damascus highway (never a part of the original objective). On the way they clashed heavily with a Syrian force (which included some PLO) at the important Jezzine crossroads. The Syrians were forced to retire, losing eight tanks in the process. The situation was reversed during the night of 8 June when the IDF ran into a brigade-size Syrian ambush on the outskirts of Ain Zehalta. In the ensuing fight the Israelis sustained serious casualties and were forced to pull back, thereby losing their first opportunity to cut the Beirut-Damascus highway.

The original Israeli plan had stressed the need to avoid direct confrontation with Syria. Now, urged on by Defence Minister Sharon and Chief of Staff Eitan, the ground war developed its own momentum. Clearing the way ahead required substantial air strikes by the Israeli Air Force, which in turn necessitated the destruction of Syrian surface-to-air missiles in the Bekaa Valley. In the resulting battle for control of the skies Syria lost 91 aircraft without shooting down a single Israeli jet.[7] The ground war expanded correspondingly, as the IDF eastern column clashed head-on with the Syrian 1st Armoured Division in the Bekaa.

By the fifth day of the war lead elements of the IDF coastal advance had reached Kfar Sil on the outskirts of southern Beirut. Here they encountered a spirited defence by commando units of the Syrian

85th and 62nd Infantry Brigades, supported by units of the PLO. However, in the central mountains the Syrians had been driven back from around Ain Dara, from where the IDF could see the coveted Beirut-Damascus highway.

The first of many cease-fires was agreed between Syria and Israel on 11 June. With most of the PLO forced back to Beirut, the IDF began to close the trap. Christian Phalange forces controlled the east of the city while the IDF edged forward into the southern suburbs. As West Beirut was bounded by the Mediterranean Sea, the only remaining escape route lay along the Beirut-Damascus highway. The cease-fire of the 11th was extended on the 12th to include the PLO but collapsed again on the 13th. This was a cycle which was to be repeated many times over the next few weeks.

To consolidate their position south of the city, the IDF attacked Khaldi, defended by Syrians and PLO. As the battle for Khaldi raged other IDF units penetrated East Beirut to link up with the Christian Phalange militia at a checkpoint near Basaba. Meanwhile a third Israeli force swept around the city, to cut off any escape along the Beirut-Damascus highway. With all exits effectively sealed, both the Syrian 85th Brigade and the PLO were now trapped inside West Beirut. The Syrians moved up reinforcements from the Bekaa and prepared for a larger action, to contest control of the Beirut-Damascus highway.

Over the next few days localised fighting flared up and died down while the IDF consolidated and manoeuvred into position, ready to strike at the Syrians outside Beirut. On 22 July they were ready,

and the 48-hour battle for control of the Beirut-Damascus highway began. After intense fighting the Syrians were gradually pushed back towards the Bekaa Valley.

With the IDF occupied by the battle for the highway, the PLO were granted a brief reprieve to improvise a defence of West Beirut. Frantically reorganising their forces, they scattered mines in likely avenues of approach[8] and used bulldozers to create earth ramparts on roads leading into the city. By this means they hoped to channel any Israeli advance into predetermined killing grounds.

Other PLO groups, still scattered in the mountains outside Beirut, continued to oppose the IDF. In this terrain, ideally suited for guerrilla actions, the Israelis were fortunate that a lack of effective central command prevented the PLO from making the best use of their resources. Even so, the tenacity of their resistance had not been anticipated.

Standing at the very gates of Beirut, the IDF were badly let down by the Christian Phalangists. Israel had expected them to join the battle to eject the PLO from West Beirut. Instead, the Phalange leader Beshir Gemayle decided to conserve his forces for the power struggle which would inevitably follow the removal of the PLO. Left to go it alone, the IDF kept up the pressure through air and artillery bombardment and made adjustments to their line. On 4 June they attempted a triple assault on West Beirut. The plan was to punch through the 'Green Line', at both the 'Museum' and 'Port' crossings while simultaneously pushing up the southern coastal road into the Embassy enclave at Ouzai. For Israel this was to prove the

Right: A Lebanese Army soldier. United States support for the Lebanese Army stemmed from a fundamental misconception. Far from being an impartial force which could enforce peace on the Lebanon, the Lebanese Army was predominantly Christian-controlled. Once the USA began training and equipping them, the US-backed forces were no longer perceived by the Muslim community as a neutral presence in the escalating civil war. The ultimate consequences for the US Marines were catastrophic, 245 being killed when a bomb, hidden in a truck, was driven into their base.

Far right: A Druze in traditional costume, armed with a Russian SKS carbine.

Below left: An Israeli soldier, minus helmet, at one of the hastily-improvised PLO street barricades consisting of earth mounds. This basic defence slowed down the Israeli advances and channelled them into more suitable 'killing grounds'.

Left: An M-113 after driving over a mine. As the Israeli Army, trained for fast, mobile warfare, began to engage in urban warfare, their casualties began to mount.

8. The PLO's minelaying was not very systematic and often left gaps in their defences.

9. On this day nineteen Israeli soldiers were killed and 64 wounded – an unheard of level of casualties for the IDF.

single most costly day of the entire war. Against the determined and entrenched Syrian and PLO defences, all three attacks failed; at the Port crossing the IDF were hard-pushed to advance 500 metres.[9]

This was the IDF's last attempt at a major thrust. Afterwards the level of conflict generally subsided to localised skirmishing, although heavy Israeli air strikes were mounted to subdue particularly troublesome PLO defence-points. There were also retaliatory strikes for casualties inflicted by PLO guerrillas in the mountains.

The Palestinians had nowhere to go, nothing to lose and everything to gain from a negotiated settlement. The IDF, having trapped the PLO inside West Beirut, were unwilling to suffer the casualties involved in a major urban battle. A political resolution was clearly the only way out. Clashes continued while Israel and the PLO thrashed out an agreement.

The cease-fire had already been agreed when, on 12 June, the entire peace process was threatened by the Israeli Defence Minister, Sharon. Without consulting the cabinet he ordered massive, day-long air strikes and artillery bombardment. The war had already escalated far beyond the limited incursion agreed by Israel's government. Unsatisfied with Sharon's justifications, they revoked his emergency powers and, at the eleventh hour, the peace agreement was saved.

Lead elements from a multi-national peacekeeping force arrived in Beirut on 21 August. Their job was to guarantee the security of the PLO during their departure to exile in various Arab states. By 3 September 14,398 Palestinians had been evacuated by sea. The Syrian 85th Brigade and their Palestinian Liberation Army auxiliaries left for Syria along the Beirut-Damascus highway. The 1982 Lebanon war was over.

WEAPONS AND TACTICAL LESSONS OF THE 1982 WAR

The Israeli Defence Force which invaded the Lebanon in 1982 was one of the most experienced modern armies in the world. In the recent past, pitched against the armies of neighbouring Arab countries, it had won a string of spectacular victories. The key lay in superior training and rapid movement, enabling the IDF to concentrate force in the right place and at the right time.

Unlike previous Arab-Israeli conflicts, Israel fought the 1982 war on only one front. It was also a limited conflict, in which the PLO never achieved full deployment owing to a lack of cohesive command and the Syrians committed only a portion of their available forces. Consequently, while Israel's deployment was also limited, the IDF invasion force enjoyed the advantage of larger numbers than the PLO and Syrians combined.[10]

In some regions this advantage was offset by difficult terrain, more suited to guerrilla action than to a conventional conflict. In the eastern Fatahland region the IDF were forced to advance in a linear formation along the narrow mountain roads. Here they presented an ideal target for the lightly equipped PLO. The Palestinians were able to confront limited numbers of IDF forces at the tip of the column whilst the bulk of the force waited impotently behind. Concentrating on the regular forces which opposed them, the Israelis failed to allow for the attrition that could be caused by improvised PLO militia and irregular guerrilla units well away from Beirut. It is revealing that 60 per cent of IDF casualties were inflicted after Beirut had been encircled.

Once drawn into the war, the Syrian forces performed better than expected (although they suffered disproportionately high losses). They made little attempt to compete in the type of warfare at which Israel excelled – fast, mobile, tank-dominated actions. Instead, they made good use of the available terrain and opted for a strategy of brief blocking actions designed to blunt the IDF advance and inflict casualties. When sufficient force was brought to bear by the IDF, the Syrians simply pulled back to a new defensive position. Thus, while the IDF advance was steady, it did not produce the easy victory that had been anticipated.

As the Syrians defended positions only a short distance in advance of the IDF, it was often difficult for the Israeli Air Force to strike at them without hitting their own forces. In the confusion of battle, some Israeli units were bombed by their own aircraft.[11] The Israeli Air Force also attempted to wipe out the PLO leadership by the use of precision guided munitions (PGM). Although at least two Beirut buildings suspected of harbouring the PLO headquarters were destroyed, PLO leaders survived intact by constantly changing their locations.

Both the Syrians and the Israelis used the 1982 war as a testing ground for weapons new to the Middle East. Among them were Israel's new Merkava tanks. The Merkava was slower than Syrian tanks and there had been some concern that its standard 105mm gun might not have much impact on the Syrian Army's newly acquired T-72s (which had improved armour and a 125mm gun). However, the Merkava fired fin-stabilised, armour-piercing rounds which proved effective even against thick frontal armour. Ultimately the T-72 proved as prone to burn as other Soviet-designed tanks whereas the Merkava had an excellent fire suppressant which dramatically reduced injuries to the crew.

The Syrians also deployed new technology. Their helicopters, armed with HOT anti-tank missiles, achieved a notable success rate by contour-flying and 'pop-up' shooting tactics. In addition the large-scale use of 'Sagger' anti-tank weapons by the Syrians also resulted in many tank kills. Even with the extra protection of add-

Above: A PLO fighter fires an 82mm mortar, which remains one of the most dangerous weapons on the modern battlefield. It is particularly effective if the target is caught in the open.

Right: Druze M-46 130mm heavy artillery in the Shouf mountains.

10. PLO 17,000, Syria 30,000 and Israel 76,000.

11. Accidental clashes between Israeli ground forces also occurred.

on armour and armoured skirts, IDF vehicles remained vulnerable. The PLO and Syrians also fired RPGs at such close range that they caused great damage, albeit often at the cost of the life of the RPG operator.

Although the standard M-113 armoured personnel carrier used by the IDF had previously been deployed to good effect in mobile, desert-warfare scenarios, it was not ideal for the Lebanon. In mountain and urban environments its high profile was vulnerable to enemy infantry armed with RPGs or even small-arms. The IDF attempted to compensate by adding a heavy machine gun, but this left the gunner sitting on top, exposed to enemy fire. Some M-113s also had composite and reactive armour added. Although this improved survivability,

basic design faults remained: M-113s had a reputation for burning fiercely when hit. It is hardly surprising that Israeli infantry often preferred to walk when approaching enemy positions.

The mobile desert warfare which it had encountered in previous conflicts had led the IDF to favour armour over infantry. In the Lebanon it consequently suffered high losses of armour owing to insufficient infantry support. One IDF colonel was ordered to attack Jezzine with no infantry support at all and suffered accordingly. Israeli armour in Ain Zehalta endured a similar mauling for much the same reason. This failure to support armour with infantry (particularly with the proliferation of modern shoulder-fired anti-tank rockets) was the Achilles' heel of the IDF's tactical deployment.

Far left: The French Foreign Legion clearing mines in Beirut after the PLO departure.

Near left: Druze soldiers with a SAM-7 missile in the Shouf mountains.

Right: 'Spyglass' was the codename for the US Marine sniper sections. This is Bravo Company's Spyglass section in action with the Remington M40A1 sniper rifle.

Lower, far left: A US Marine wounded by mortar fragmentation. The flag behind flies at half-mast in commemoration of another marine killed in action.

Lower, near left: The PLO went to ground in the urban landscape and dug in. They defended positions until the pressure was too great or they were in danger of being outflanked, and then simply fell back to other prepared positions. This made it very difficult for the Israeli Defence Force to get to grips with the PLO without sustaining higher-than-usual casualties.

Right: Taps being sounded as the US flag is lowered over Bravo Company's position in Beirut.

Far right: A US Marine door-gunner on a Huey helicopter overflying Beirut.

The IDF also failed to maximise on the weaknesses of the Palestinians, who lacked experience of large conventional operations. PLO training was concentrated on small infantry units, rarely larger than platoon-size. While they were reasonably proficient at this level, command and control grew weaker as the scale of operations grew larger. Regardless of these factors, the IDF forced a situation where they faced the bulk of the PLO in an urban landscape ideally suited to small-unit actions.

In this environment the Israeli advantages of superior numbers, mobility and firepower were minimized. In order to get at the Palestinians, they were reliant on squad-level action. At this level, PLO training came into its own: even small groups of men, defending buildings, were able to hold off much larger IDF forces. Despite the hundreds of air strikes and constant shelling which the PLO suffered inside Beirut, their casualties remained relatively light.[12] Conversely, forced into house-to-house fighting in order to winkle out the Palestinians, the IDF suffered higher casualties than they were used to.

Had the Israelis stopped after the first three days, when their original 40km objective had been achieved, they would have suffered only 25 men killed in action. The costs of the more protracted war on which they embarked were significantly higher – 368 men killed and 2,383 wounded by mid-August 1982. As the IDF remained in occupation well after the 1982 departure of the bulk of the PLO, it continued to suffer casualties.[13]

Although the 1982 war had destroyed the PLO as a viable military threat on Israel's border, it was not an unqualified victory for the Israelis. The symbolic resistance of the Palestinians in Beirut won them wider sympathy in the outside world than they had ever enjoyed before. Outnumbered, outgunned and cornered, the PLO had fought on longer than any other Arab force in all the Arab-Israeli wars to date.

THE UNITED STATES' ADVENTURE IN THE LEBANON

The United States was involved in behind-the-scenes negotiations for the withdrawal of the PLO and Syrians from Beirut. It was agreed that a Multi-National Force would be deployed to guarantee security during the departure phase. The troops would comprise contingents from the USA,[14] Italy, France and Great Britain. Under the terms of the agreement, Israel undertook not to enter West Beirut after the PLO withdrawal. The Multi-National Force was also to ensure that the Christian militias

kept out of West Beirut. President Reagan promised that the peace-keeping force would remain *in situ* for at least a month after the PLO departures to ensure the safety of Palestinian civilians left behind.

The French contingent (Foreign Legion and paratroopers) were the first to arrive, stepping ashore in the port area of Beirut on 21 August. On the same day they supervised the departure of the first PLO units. Even as this was happening, the Lebanese were busy with elections. Just two days after the PLO departures began, Beshir Gemayel, the leader of the Christian Phalange militia, was elected President of the Lebanon.

On 25 August 800 United States Marines came ashore and, over the course of the following week, the remainder of the PLO withdrew to exile in various Arab countries. The Syrians and their Palestinian Liberation Army (PLA) auxiliaries left by road for the Bekaa. They were all gone by 3 September. Just a week later, contrary to all their guarantees to the Palestinians, the Multi-National Force proceeded to pull out. On 14 September the newly elected Lebanese President, Beshir Gemayel, was assassinated by a command-detonated bomb. The outraged Christian Phalangists blamed the Moslems and were determined to exact a bloody revenge. Within hours Israel had activated plans for Operation *Iron Mind*, the occupation of West Beirut. This was in direct violation of the peace agreement. However, since the Multi-National Force had left, many Moslems in West Beirut thought that this was

Above: As the Marines were sucked into the conflict they became increasingly subject to hostile fire and were effectively under seige. This view of their helipad was taken through a shell hole in the building occupied by Bravo Company.

12. Approximately 1,500 by the end of the war.

13. Up to 1985 Israeli casualties totalled 650 killed and almost 4,000 wounded.

14. It was not the first time that the United States had acted as peace-keepers in the Lebanon. In 1958 US Marines had landed on the beaches south of Beirut as part of Operation 'Bluebat'. They were there to restore order after simmering resentment between rival Lebanese factions had boiled over into a brief civil war.

15. The Syrian National Party was a radical splinter faction of Christian Phalangists sponsored by Syria.

Above: US Marines of 2nd Platoon Bravo Company on foot patrol in Beirut. They march tactically deployed and well spaced, having already come under fire.

their only chance of protection from the vengeance of the Christians. What they could not have anticipated was that Israel would sanction the hostile Christian Phalange militia to enter the Palestinian civilian refugee camps, ostensibly to locate any remaining PLO fighters. Between 18 and 20 September, while Israeli forces blocked all avenues of escape from the camps, the Christian Phalangists embarked on an orgy of bloodshed. More than 600 Palestinians, of all ages and both sexes, were massacred. Afterwards evidence came to light to prove that President Beshir Gemayel had not been assassinated by the Moslems but by rival Christian forces in the Syrian National Party.[15]

The assassinated president was replaced by his brother, Amin Gemayel, at whose request the Multi-National Force returned to Beirut. This time the United States deployed 1,200 Marines from the 32nd Marine Amphibious Unit (MAU). Right from the start, the objectives of this second deployment were unclear.

Each of the regional players interpreted this redeployment differently: Israel saw it as a demonstration of US political support; the Moslem Shi'ites thought that the Americans were there to protect them from further Christian vengeance; and to the Christian militias it implied American support for their bid to regain military dominance over the Moslems. In the hot-house politics of the Middle East, this jumble of contradictions seriously jeopardised the security of the peace-keeping force.

The commander of the US Marines' 32nd MAU,

Colonel James Mead, was ordered to take control of Beirut International Airport. This may have been considered a politically symbolic objective, but to Colonel Mead's trained military eye it was also militarily untenable. The airport was located on flat ground backing on to the sea in the west and overlooked by higher ground. It was perhaps the least defensible position in the Lebanon. Mead's recommendations, that the Marines should hold higher ground further east and employ only a token force at the airport itself, were overruled by the White House.

Next, the United States Defense Department dispatched a military team to conduct an assessment of the Lebanese Army, with a view to training and re-equipping it. The Department chose to overlook the fact that the Lebanese Army was *not* a national defence force which would impartially protect the interests of all factions – it was almost wholly controlled by the Christians. By the end of 1982, the first shipments of US arms had arrived and American Special Forces advisors were supervising Lebanese Army training. By authorising these actions, US politicians undermined the neutrality essential to the security of their Marines in the Lebanon.

Any remaining doubts harboured by the Moslems about which side the Americans were on, were dispelled when Amin Gemayel, the Christian President, was favoured with an invitation to Washington. Gemayel also believed that the US was demonstrating a clear preference for the Christian cause. Confident of US support, he avoided implementing the political reforms to which (having effectively won the upper hand during the 1982 civil war) the Moslem militias felt entitled.

US 'neutrality' was further eroded when the United States announced that talks were to take place to resolve border differences between Israel and the Lebanon. The fact that this announcement was made by the United States was, in the subtle nuances of Middle Eastern politics, interpreted as a pro-Israeli stance. Concluding that the US was firmly behind Israel in the Middle East power struggle and, additionally, supported Christian interests over Moslem ones in the Lebanon, the Moslems felt both threatened and marginalised.

Rightly or wrongly, Israel remained sufficiently confident of US support to sanction IDF reconnaissance patrols along the Sidon road, which ran past the US Marine positions at Beirut Airport. As no objections were voiced by the Marines, these patrols were stepped up to include 'reconnaissance by fire', in which targets which might harbour a guerrilla ambush were fired upon without warning.

On at least five occasions rounds fired by the IDF patrols landed inside the US Marine compound. When no steps were taken to prevent this happening, it was perceived as yet more evidence of American support for the Israeli occupation of the Lebanon. The Moslems grew increasingly afraid that the Multi-National Force could not, or would not, protect them.

On 2 February 1983 Israeli tanks attempted to enter the US Marine compound. They were only prevented from doing so when Captain Charles Johnson of the Marine Corps jumped aboard the lead tank and ordered it to withdraw. He reinforced this order by pointing a loaded pistol at the head of the tank commander. With US Cobra helicopter gunships flying overhead armed with TOW missiles, the IDF tanks pulled back. Although this demonstration of American resolve went some way towards easing the tension in the Moslem community, it was too little too late. Moreover, the incident was played down in order to protect diplomatic sensibilities between Israel and the US.

United States support was also seen as a major factor behind the severe terms imposed by the Israelis in the Israel-Lebanon border talks. By this time Moslem alarm was widespread. Almost 1,000 Moslems had been kidnapped by the Lebanese Army (still being trained by the United States); none was heard of again.

The Lebanon was now a time-bomb waiting to explode.

On 15 March an Italian patrol from the Multi-National Force was ambushed. The next day five American Marines were wounded by a grenade thrown at a US patrol in Moslem-controlled Ouzai. As the month progressed, open warfare broke out once more among rival Lebanese factions. In April the US Embassy in Beirut was the target of a bomb left in a parked truck. Seventeen American citizens were killed in the blast. Responsibility for the bombing was claimed by a group calling itself *Jihad-al-Islami* (Islamic Holy War).

Seemingly oblivious to the deteriorating situation, the United States did nothing to demonstrate its neutrality. In June, rather than cancelling or de-scaling the training and arming of the Lebanese Army, the US Marines began joint patrols with them. On 22 July Druze artillery in the Shouf Mountains overlooking Beirut Airport shelled the US Marine compound for the first time, wounding three Marines. At the same time the Lebanese President was assured that more US arms would be hastened to the Lebanese Army.

The Marine compound came under further Druze shell-fire on 28 August, this time killing two Marines. US Marine gunners used 'Firefinder' to locate the artillery responsible. 'Charlie Battery' then retaliated with a warning salvo of para-illumination rounds. Mystified by the sudden arrival of three para-illumination flares over their position in daylight, the Druze continued to fire their artillery. The next salvos from the Marine's 155mm howitzers were high-explosive rounds. This marked the beginning of the shooting war for the United States forces in the Lebanon.

During the summer of 1983 the situation quickly degenerated into a ferocious battle between rival Lebanese factions, with the Multi-National Force caught in the middle. The Druze and Lebanese Army hammered away at each other around Bhamdoun, Alley and Souk El Gharb. When the Lebanese Army were forced to pull back, in order to strengthen their key position around Souk El Gharb, the Druze quickly moved forward to fill the gap. This allowed their artillery point-blank line of sight to the US Marine position at Beirut Airport Colonel Mead's earlier assessment, that the airport was a poor choice for deployment, was vindicated; but this was little comfort to the Marines, bunkered down under mortar and shell-fire.

With Souk El Gharb under pressure and in danger of falling to the Druze, the United States announced, on 12 September, that the town's survival in the hands of the Lebanese Army was vital for the safety of US Marines at the airport. In fact, as an argument for the escalation of US military involvement in support of the Lebanese Army, this was rather tenuous. Beirut Airport was, as Colonel

Below: US Marines search for mines on the Beirut beachhead.

Mead had rightly pointed out, overlooked by mountains on three sides, not just from Souk El Gharb.

Nevertheless, political pressure was brought to bear and the Marines were authorised to use their guns to support the Lebanese Army. Their new Commanding Officer, Colonel Timothy Geraghty, protested that this would be a mistake: the only possible outcome would be to increase the danger for the Marines. Like Colonel Mead before him, his military judgement as the man on the ground was overruled in favour of political posturing. Although the Marine guns held off, air strikes and naval gunfire from the battleship *New Jersey* were sanctioned and used instead. In addition, further emergency shipments of arms were dispatched for the beleaguered Lebanese Army on 14 September.

When the American Ambassador's house was hit by shell-fire on 29 September, Colonel Geraghty finally gave way to pressure to use his guns in support of the Lebanese Army. Then, on 1 October, yet another huge shipment of arms was delivered to the Lebanese Army, including M-48 tanks and long-range artillery. For many Moslems this was last straw. Up to this time the Marines had suffered only light casualties, more often the consequence of occupying a poorly chosen site between warring factions than the result of deliberate targeting. Now any illusion of American neutrality was over and the Marines were fair game.

The use of car-bombs as weapons of terror was widespread in the Lebanon: they had devastated buildings and claimed hundreds of lives in both Christian East and Moslem West Beirut. On 18 October four Marines on convoy duty were wounded by a small car-bomb. The warning went unheeded. Five days later, at around 6.20 a.m., a yellow Mercedes truck drove into the airport car park next to the US Marine compound. Unknown to the American sentries who watched it, the truck was loaded with 12,000lb of explosive, wrapped around butane gas canisters. It turned towards the Battalion Landing Team (BLT) building. Inside, there were over 300 sleeping Marines, about 25 per cent of the US contingent. The Marine sentries had been issued with live rounds but were not allowed to have them chambered. When the truck turned into the BLT gateway and drove straight through the single strand of concertina wire blocking the way, at least two sentries tried to load and fire at the driver. Neither was able to do so in time. The truck hurtled through the hangar-like open doors of the BLT building, stopped in the cavernous centre and a few seconds later, at 06.22, the driver detonated the explosives. The resultant blast vaporised the truck and its driver, flattened the building and killed 241 American Marines. Minutes later, a similar bomb detonated at the main French base, killing 58 French paratroopers.

In retrospect, it seems clear that there was a basic incompatibility between the political and the military objectives of the United States during its adventure in the Lebanon. The Multi-National Force left Beirut in February 1984. In the 533 days of its deployment nearly 250 American servicemen had been killed. Why they were there and what they achieved is still a subject for debate.

BIBLIOGRAPHY:

Colonel Abu Attayib, *Flash Back, Beirut 1982*, Sabah Press, Nicosia, 1982

Robert Brenton Betts, *The Druze*, Yale University Press, London 1988

John Bulloch, *Final Conflict, the War in the Lebanon*, Century Publishing, London 1983

Anthony Cordesman and A. Wagner, *The Lessons of Modern War, Vol. 1, Arab Israeli Conflicts 1973–89*, West View Press, Boulder, USA, 1991

Trevor Dupuy and Paul Martell, *Flawed Victory: the Arab-Israeli Conflict and The 1982 War in Lebanon*, Hero Books, Fairfax, USA, 1986

Yair Evron, *War and Intervention in Lebanon: the Israeli-Syrian Deterrence Dialogue*, Croom Helm, London 1987

Richard A. Gabriel, *Military Incompetence: Why the American Military Doesn't Win*, Hill & Wang, New York, 1985

Richard A. Gabriel, *Operation Peace for Galilee, the Israeli-PLO War in Lebanon*, Hill & Wang, New York, 1984

Eric Hammel, *The Root: the Marines in Beirut*, Harcourt Jovanovich Publishers, London, 1984

Rashid Khaldi, *Under Siege: P.L.O. Decision-making During the 1982 War*, Columbia University Press, New York, 1986

Samuel Katz and L. Russel, *Armies in the Lebanon 1982–84*, Osprey, London, 1991

Samuel Katz, *Arab Armies of the Middle East Wars*, Osprey, London, 1988

Michael Petit, *Peacekeepers at War: a Marine's Account of the Beirut Catastrophe*, Faber & Faber, Boston, USA 1986

Johnathan Randell, *The Tragedy of Lebanon – Christian Warlords, Israeli Adventurers and American Bunglers*, Chatto & Windus, London, 1983

Kamal Salibi, *A House of Many Mansions: the History of Lebanon Reconsidered*, I.B. Tauris & Co Ltd, London, 1988

Ze'ev Schiff and Ehud Ya'ari, *Israel's Lebanon War*, Counterpoint, London, 1986

Roger Scruton, *A Land Held Hostage: Lebanon and the West*, The Claridge Press, London 1987

Left: Preparing for a week's deployment in the bush of north-central Namibia, this young Koevoet constable carries a belt of 0.50-calibre ammunition to the Casspir APC to which he is assigned. The minimum age for recruitment into Koevoet was 17. Because of the élite nature of the unit and the relatively high pay, there were always more applicants than openings.

JIM HOOPER

Namibia

I n 1989 Namibia entered the history books as the last African colony to gain independence. Since Diogo Cão first planted his cross on the barren Skeleton Coast in 1484, parts of this vast and sparsely populated land had seen Portuguese, Dutch, British, German and South African explorers, colonisers and administrators. Over the centuries they were allied with, occasionally at war against, or often simply ignored by the indigenous Ovambos, Kavangos, Hereros, Caprivians, Tswanas, Namas and San (bushmen).

Although the country was virtually ignored for three centuries following its discovery by the Portuguese, by 1795 the British had unofficially annexed the entire coastline in response to Dutch interest. Shortly thereafter, German businessman Adolf Luderitz established a trading post on the bay of Angra Pequena. In 1884 Bismarck, the German Chancellor, impressed with the commercial success of Luderitz, declared that all of 'Luderitz land' was under the protection of Germany. With the raising of the German flag at Angra Pequena, the formal colonisation of the future Namibia began. It was the luck of the draw: shortly after the turn of the century the discovery of copper and the richest diamond fields in the world greatly enhanced Germany's coffers.

Facing the Atlantic Ocean, with Angola to the north and South Africa below, Namibia was hacked into its present shape by nineteenth-century politicians with little knowledge of its topography and even less interest in its ethnic configurations. An agreement between Imperial Germany and Portugal dictated that its border with Angola should be drawn east from Epupa Falls on the northernmost hook of the Cunene River, but a German land surveyor mistook Ruacana Falls, 50 miles farther south, for his point of departure, thereby placing five sub-tribes of the Ovambos in Portuguese Angola and the remaining seven in German South West Africa.

German administration was severe even by the standards of the time, leading to the Herero and Nama uprising of 1904-6. Hopelessly outgunned and outmanoeuvred by German forces, who realised the strategic importance of potable water and threw cordons around the few springs in the arid south, the Herero retreated into the Kalahari desert to die in their thousands. Their Nama allies turned to low-intensity guerrilla warfare, but they, too, were soon defeated. An Ovambo uprising four years later was suppressed with equal brutality.

114

Less than a year after the outbreak of the First World War, South African forces captured German South West Africa and proclaimed it the South West Africa (SWA) Protectorate. In 1920 the League of Nations formally confirmed the territory as a 'C' Mandate to be governed as an integral part of the Union of South Africa, then part of the British Commonwealth.

Following the Second World War, the new United Nations charter ended the mandate system and established an international trusteeship on a voluntary basis. Loath to lose the mineral wealth of its *de facto* colony, South Africa declined to surrender SWA to the United Nations. The issue was submitted to the International Court of Justice (ICJ), which ruled that South Africa should continue its administration of the territory under the terms of the original mandate.

In 1960 Ethiopia and Liberia instituted proceedings against South Africa over the South West Africa issue at the ICJ. In 1966 the ICJ judged that neither country had the necessary legal right or interest in the matter, and rejected their claims. As a result of the rising Afro-Asian majority in the United Nations, however, the General Assembly revoked South Africa's mandate of SWA; in 1968 the Assembly renamed it Namibia and called for its independence. In 1971 a reconstituted ICJ reflected the mood of the day by deciding that South Africa was illegally occupying the country. This was rejected by South Africa as being both illegal and illogical.

WINDS OF CHANGE

The liberation movement that was the catalyst for these later events was one of many that sprang up throughout Africa in the 1950s. Based on the most populous tribe in Namibia, it began life as the Ovambo People's Organisation 1958. Two years later, in an attempt to imply a broader base, it was renamed the South West Africa People's Organisation (SWAPO). By 1962 SWAPO, under the leadership of Sam Nujoma, had set up headquarters in Tanzania and begun recruiting Ovambos for guerrilla warfare and sabotage. Recruits were sent to various Eastern Bloc countries for training as cadre members of the People's Liberation Army of Namibia (PLAN), the military wing of SWAPO. The first of these infiltrated into Ovamboland in late 1965. Their first base camp, established near Umgulumbashe, was reported to the South African Police (SAP) by Ovambos loyal to the government. The ensuing attack on 26 August 1966, code-named Operation *Blou Wildebeest*, killed two insurgents and captured eight. SWAPO claimed that the skirmish was the opening of the 'final phase' of its liberation struggle.

Nujoma's assessment of the opening shots of a bush war that would last for the next 23 years was somewhat optimistic. The training his few hundred insurgents had received was minimal, and poorly suited to the terrain and the technological superiority of the South African security forces. The arid conditions of most of Namibia's 824,000 sq km

Above left: A soldier from the South West Africa Territory Force (SWATF) 701 Battalion, wounded by a Soviet-manufactured POM-Z anti-personnel mine, is carried to a waiting Alouette III helicopter of the South African Air Force at Nkongo. He was flown to the SADF base at Eenhana, and from there by C-47 Dakota to the primary trauma centre at Ondangwa Air Force Base.

Above: Although little insurgent activity occurred in the Kaokoveld owing to the lack of water and the distances involved, regular patrols were undertaken by the South African security forces. This view over the twin 0.30 Brownings of a Wolf Turbo APC shows the desert conditions regularly encountered in the far northwestern corner of Namibia.

made it ideal for aerial surveillance. And because any guerrilla force can only move as far as the limit of the water it carries, the guarding or patrolling of water points by counterinsurgency (COIN) units prevented replenishment and thus restricted the insurgents' radius of action.

The exception to this was the heavily-bushed Ovamboland in the north-central part of the country, as well as the Kavango and the Caprivi Strip to the east. But, even in Ovamboland, the scene of most of the infiltrations owing to the close tribal affiliation with the predominantly Ovambo SWAPO, the rains are seasonal, generally lasting for the summer months of December, January and February. During the dry winter months the guerrillas were not only reliant on the few year-round water holes, but were subject to aerial surveillance owing to lack of cover.

Another limiting factor at the beginning of SWAPO's bush war was the difficulty of logistics. Given the efficiency of the South African security forces (which had penetrated SWAPO at a very early stage), it was virtually impossible to move men and weapons through Namibia. SWAPO did manage to transport small amounts of arms by foot from Zambia through southern Angola, but it was a long and hazardous route. The Portuguese colonial administration in Angola was fighting its own guer-

rilla war against the MPLA, UNITA and FNLA,[1] and had every reason to help South Africa by sharing intelligence with the SAP.

The Caprivi Strip was also used for infiltration by SWAPO, but this was even more dangerous because of the number of police and army bases scattered along its length. Even when the insurgents did reach Ovamboland, the risk of being killed or captured was high owing to the efficiency of the security forces, whose primary sources of information came from a local population less sympathetic to the guerrilla movement than SWAPO seemed to realise, or was prepared to admit.

Encouraged and assisted by the Soviet Union and other Eastern Bloc states, SWAPO's war of liberation sputtered on inconclusively over the next eight years. Although SWAPO made extravagant claims of military successes, up to 1974 only eleven security force members had been killed, most of them in land-mine incidents.

SOUTH AFRICAN RESPONSE

The South African Government's response was to give the SAP, rather than the South African Defence Force (SADF), primary responsibility for halting SWAPO incursions. The SAP already had a long presence in Namibia, understood the nature of the conflict, and employed local tribesmen as policemen. These black constables spoke the languages, enjoyed the trust of the local population from which they came and were intimately familiar with the terrain. As a result of specialised counterinsurgency training and experience gained by SAP members during South Africa's support of the white government in Rhodesia, the SAP was better equipped than the SADF to deal with the low-intensity conflict. There was also a legal consideration: the terms of the old UN Mandate precluded the use of troops in Namibia. This was playing to the gallery, of course, in that the South African Government shrank from dignifying the conflict by committing the SADF, preferring to present it as one between cops and robbers, rather than between trained combatants.

The SAP, using classic police investigation techniques bolstered by regular foot and armoured car patrols, plus boat patrols along the River Zambezi between the Caprivi Strip and Zambia, coupled with aerial reconnaissance, effectively checked armed infiltration into the country. By exercising the new Terrorism Act of June 1967, passed by the South African Government and made retroactive to June 1962, those suspected of 'terrorist' activity could be arrested and detained incommunicado for indefinite periods. SWAPO activists inside Namibia, where

115

Right: This Koevoet policeman has just thrown a white phosphorus grenade to pinpoint his position for an inbound helicopter. Because of the almost featureless terrain, navigation was often a problem for aircrews. The resulting plume of white smoke rising above the trees could easily be spotted by the helicopter crews.

1. *Movimento Popular de Libertacao de Angola* (Popular Movement for the Liberation of Angola), *Uniao Nacional para a Independencia Total de Angola* (National Union for the total Liberation of Angola) and the *Frente Nacional de Libertacao de Angola* (National Front for the Liberation of Angola).

the organisation was never banned by the South Africans, could likewise be arrested and detained. Thus, with only a minimal expenditure in men and *matériel*, South Africa was able to contain the best efforts of SWAPO to destabilise the country.

The 1974 *coup d'état* in Portugal by a communist junta led to a decision to grant Angola Independence. Although elections were to be held between the MPLA, FNLA and UNITA, the new Portuguese government, in collusion with the Soviet Union, facilitated the arrival of thousands of Cuban troops to support the MPLA before elections.[2] The unanticipated appearance of the Cuban army sent shock waves not only through Pretoria and Washington, which had just lost the war in Vietnam, but through a number of black African states, fearful of Soviet expansionism.

At the behest of the USA, Zambia, Zaire, Ivory Coast and Kenya, the South African Government launched Operation *Savannah*, an invasion of Angola. The objective was the destruction of Communist Bloc forces and the capture of the Angolan capital of Luanda. After the SADF had fought its way to within 60km of Luanda, the USA suddenly withdrew its political support and forced Pretoria to recall the invasion force. This pusillanimous behaviour by Washington guaranteed the MPLA's military victory over the FNLA and UNITA. It also opened Namibia's 1,600km northern border to SWAPO infiltration from Angola.

By late 1976 SWAPO, with the open backing of the new Marxist government in Luanda, had begun to establish permanent training and logistics bases in southern Angola. Taking advantage of Cuban, Soviet and East German instructors and virtually unlimited supplies of Eastern Bloc weapons, SWAPO began preparations for larger-scale operations.

Reacting to this new threat, which had hitherto been contained by relatively small numbers of SAP personnel, the South African Government began deploying units of the South African Defence Force to Namibia. In conjunction with the straightforward military efforts of interdiction, the SADF invested heavily in Communications Operations (COMOPS), a hearts and minds approach designed to draw the local population away from SWAPO. Schools and hospitals were built, agricultural and animal husbandry programmes instituted, and irrigation and infrastructure projects undertaken.

By late 1977 it was estimated that up to 300 insurgents were active in the operational area extending from Ovamboland to the Caprivi Strip. The intelligence assessment was that another 2,000 were based in Angola, and 1,400 more in

Zambia. Contacts between small SWAPO units and the security forces were by now averaging 100 per month. Still, as late as October 1977, the SADF was referring to it as the 'corporal's war', a reference to the highest-ranking member of the standard ten-man patrol. On October 27, however, the situation changed dramatically when a 100-man SWAPO unit crossed the border. Contact was soon made, and in a three-day running fight 61 insurgents were killed for the loss of six members of the SADF. Although this would not warrant more than a footnote to accounts of larger conflicts, to the security forces the implications were clear: SWAPO

Above: The driver of a Koevoet Casspir APC, hit in the leg by a Soviet-manufactured M-60 anti-armour rifle grenade, is carried to an Alouette III helicopter. The Alouettes, which provided fire support and aerial reconnaissance for South African security forces pursuing SWAPO insurgents, were always available to casevac the wounded to the nearest base for treatment.

Left: These police trackers have marked the spoor of SWAPO insurgents with a smoke grenade for a following combat group. Once back on board this Wolf Turbo APC, they will race forward to search for fresher spoor. Known as *voorsny* (cutting ahead), this leap-frogging tactic, developed by Koevoet and copied by the SADF and SWATF, was extremely effective in rapidly closing the distance between the insurgents and their pursuers.

Top right: Although the armoured personnel carriers used by the South African security forces provided reasonable protection against most small-arms fire, nothing could stop or deflect the

high-explosive anti-tank (HEAT) weapons used by the insurgents. The most common were the RPG-7, the M-60 anti-armour rifle grenade, and, to a lesser extent, the RPG-75. The 40mm laminated glass armour on this Casspir APC was hit by an RPG-7, which killed the white car commander standing behind the twin 0.30 Browning GPMGs.

Right: Owing to the threat of SA-7 surface-to-air missiles occasionally carried by the insurgents, flight operations were flown at low altitude. This prevented the missile operator getting a 'lock' before the helicopter had flown past the position and was once more hidden from view by the trees.

2. With the threat of Soviet expansionism central to the US policy of containment, the CIA moved quickly to provide covert aid to the FNLA in the form of money and weapons. When it was clear that the openly Marxist MPLA was the beneficiary of increasing Soviet support, the CIA's efforts spread to Jonas Savimbi's UNITA, which had received its training and few weapons from Red China.

was preparing to escalate the bush war.

The following year the United Nations passed Security Council Resolution (UNSCR) 435, which called for UN-supervised elections in Namibia When the UN Security Council refused to allow observer status to any party other than SWAPO during proceedings on the Namibia question, South Africa refused to accept the conditions of the resolution. The UN's insistence on recognising only SWAPO, which it described as 'the sole and authentic representative of the Namibian people', and none of the other parties in Namibia, convinced Pretoria that there was little probability of free and fair elections

ever occurring under UN supervision.

Despite the steady increase in SWAPO infiltrations from Angola, the security forces had been limited to interdiction patrols on the Namibian side of the border. It was a time-consuming and frustrating process that did little more than preserve a shaky status quo. The SADF, which had been casting about for an alternative course of action for months, eventually looked at the Israeli model of pre-emptive and punitive raids. Rather than waiting for the insurgents to cross the border, the South Africans would hit them where they trained for and planned their infiltrations.

The target chosen was Cassinga, a former Portuguese mining town 250km north of the border, used by SWAPO as its main operational headquarters for southern Angola. Aerial reconnaissance revealed a camp large enough to house up to 1,200 insurgents, consisting of a vehicle park, various headquarters buildings and extensive surrounding trenchworks. Given its distance from the border, the only way to maintain the crucial element of surprise would be to use airborne troops. The problems involved were glaring, however. Extraction would have to be by the South African Air Force's (SAAF) preciously few Super Frelon and Puma helicopters, which were highly vulnerable not only to ground fire but to Cuban-piloted MiGs. It was also known that a FAPLA (Angolan army) armoured unit with Cuban advisers was at Tetchamutete, 16km to the south. Although it operated obsolete T-34 tanks and BTR-152 armoured personnel carriers, lightly-armed airborne troops would be at severe risk if FAPLA came to the aid of its SWAPO allies.

None the less, Operation *Reindeer*, a surgical airborne assault against Cassinga in conjunction with a mechanised infantry sweep of smaller SWAPO bases in the vicinity of Chetequera, was approved by the South African Government. Command of the airborne force was given to the legendary Colonel Jan Breytenbach, founder of the SADF's parachute battalion, as well as the Reconnaissance Commandos (special forces) and 32 Battalion. Comprising barely 300 men, the majority of whom were Citizen Force reservists, the force lifted off from Grootfontein Air Force Base in Namibia early on 4 May. They were preceded by Buccaneer and Canberra light bombers, which rocketed, strafed and bombed the Cassinga complex. Smoke from the bombardment was still rising when the formation of Lockheed C-130 Hercules and Transall C.160s, approaching the target at treetop level, popped up to 600ft and began dropping the paratroopers.

Four hours later the paratroopers were mopping

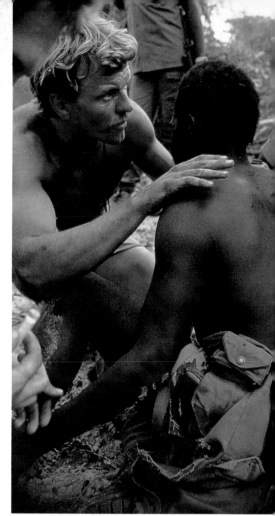

Above left: Following a contact with SWAPO insurgents, a combat group leader talks to the pilot of an inbound Alouette III helicopter after throwing a smoke grenade to mark his position. Helicopter landing zones were cleared by the simple expedient of using APCs to knock down the bush.

Above: An Ovambo warrant officer wounded by shrapnel from an RPG-7 that struck his car is treated immediately after the contact, in which four insurgents were killed. Although apartheid existed in South Africa throughout the Namibian border war, the comradeship between white South Africans and black Namibians was extremely close.

Far left: Following a night attack on the SAP Security Branch base at Ohangwena, a

wounded constable is carried to a waiting Puma helicopter. Night operations by the SAAF were rare because the enhanced heat signature of the helicopters' turbine engines made them easier targets for SA-7 missiles. In this case, the critical nature of some of the wounded made immediate casualty evacuation imperative.

Opposite page, bottom right: During a night mortar attack against the SAP Security Branch base at Ohangwena, an 82mm mortar bomb landed inside this Casspir APC, setting off white phosphorus smoke grenades and rupturing the fuel tank.

Right: Before leaving their Casspir APCs for a 'silent follow up' foot patrol, these Ovambo constables with Koevoet prepare their weapons. This man has screwed the propellant charge to the base of the RPG-7 warhead and is sliding it into the launcher. Although never faced with the threat of SWAPO armoured vehicles, the security forces regularly carried RPG-7s, which were effective against ambush positions.

up the last pockets of resistance and destroying captured ammunition stores. The evacuation helicopters, five Super Frelons and twelve Pumas, were inbound when a column of Cuban T-34s and BTR-152s arrived on the outskirts of Cassinga. They were initially halted by Breytenbach's men, who quickly destroyed at least five BTRs. Already low on ammunition, the South African force was conducting a fighting withdrawal when the Buccaneers, Mirages and Canberras returned to strafe the attacking armour with air-to-ground missiles and 30mm cannon fire. Another twelve to fifteen BTRs and at least two T-34s were destroyed before the aircraft ran out of ammunition. When they turned for home, tanks entered Cassinga and opened fire as the helicopters were landing. A single Buccaneer, out of ammunition and low on fuel, remained on station to make repeated mock attacks on the T-34s at turret level, stopping them long enough for the last of the paratroopers to board the helicopters and escape.

For the loss of five dead and eleven wounded, the airborne force killed upwards of 600 insurgents and wounded another 300 to 400, many of them highly experienced. Known Cuban losses amounted to 16 dead and 63 wounded. Humiliated by the savaging, SWAPO would later claim that Cassinga was a refugee camp, and that the dead were all non-combatants. The Chetequera side of *Reindeer* killed another 250 insurgents and captured over 200 more, while losing two dead and 16 wounded. It was a spectacularly successful operation that confirmed the SADF's planning and fighting superiority. Although the South Africans would not mount another airborne attack during the war, there were many cross-border operations to come.

At the end of 1978, South Africa startled outsiders and further complicated the situation in Namibia by holding its own internally-supervised elections without UN involvement. In spite of South Africa's invitation to SWAPO to participate, its leader, Sam Nujoma, chose to boycott the elections. The UN, still backing SWAPO, refused to recognise the legitimacy of either the elections or the new government.

THE WAR ESCALATES

Concurrent with its political efforts, South Africa continued raising the stakes in the military arena. By the early 1980s the pre-1974 force level of some 3,000 SAP personnel had been increased to approximately 20,000 with the deployment of SADF units. Non-white SADF units, among them the Cape (Coloured) Corps and the black 21 Infantry Battalion, were also sent to 'the border'. The South

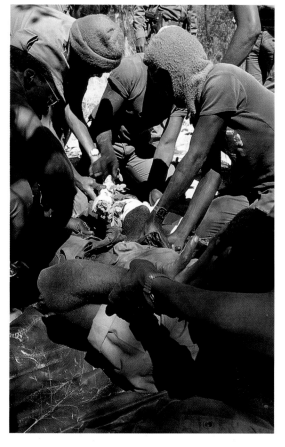

Left: A Koevoet car commander, wounded in an ambush with SWAPO insurgents 15km east of Eenhana, is told by the group's ops medic that he is to be casevacked on an Alouette III helicopter that has just landed. The Ovambo constable supports and attempts to shield the wounded man's face from the sand and downwash of the helicopter's blades.

Lower left: The driver of a Casspir APC is treated for the traumatic amputation of his lower leg after the front of his car was struck by a Soviet-manufactured M-60 anti-armour rifle grenade.

Top right: An Ovambo constable with Koevoet loads a belt of 7.62mm ammunition into the co-axially-mounted GPMG atop a Casspir APC, before heading into the bush of north-central Namibia for a week of hunting SWAPO insurgents.

Right: Members of a black SADF unit debus from a Buffel APC in the operational area. Many Western observers were surprised by the numbers of non-whites who served in the South African security forces.

African Air Force deployed helicopter (Puma and Alouette III), ground support (Impala), fighter and fighter-bomber (Mirage) and bomber (Canberra) squadrons to Namibia. At the same time there was a move to 'Namibianise' the war by conscripting white 'Southwesters' into Area Force Units, and by recruiting Ovambos, Kavangos and East Caprivians into ethnically exclusive volunteer units. These formed the basis of the new South West Africa Territory Force (SWATF), 90 per cent of which was black.

A parallel effort was undertaken to build a multi-racial police force, leading to the South West Africa Police (SWAPOL). Although designed to operate in tandem with, and remove part of the burden from, the SADF and SAP, in reality the leadership of these new structures remained white South Africans seconded from the SADF and SAP.

UNCONVENTIONAL AND PROXY FORCES

Low-intensity conflicts are tailor-made for novel approaches, and the South Africans, drawing on their own history during the Zulu wars, the Anglo-Boer wars and their experience in Rhodesia, were quick to incorporate unconventional and proxy forces in their defence of Namibia.

At the end of the Angolan War for Independence, both UNITA and the FNLA had scattered in the face of the communist MPLA forces backed by Cuban infantry, armour and air support. UNITA withdrew into southeastern Angola, where, with South African support in training and equipment, it slowly began to reassert itself as a viable guerrilla army. Pretoria's logic in this was twofold: first, to help UNITA establish a controlled area that reached part of the southern border, a *cordon sanitaire* that denied SWAPO access; second, to keep the Cubans involved with seeking out UNITA, rather than threatening the Namibian border west of UNITA's area of control.

By the early 1980s, UNITA's self-styled 'liberated zone' abutted all of the Caprivi Strip bordering Angola and most of Kavango, allowing the South Africans to concentrate their counter-insurgency efforts in Ovamboland. An unanticipated benefit of UNITA's success was the Angolan government's demand that SWAPO, as a *quid pro quo* for basing itself in Angola, dedicate substantial numbers of its insurgents to fighting UNITA directly or guarding various key points, thus freeing government soldiers to seek out UNITA. By the mid-1980s up to 3,000 SWAPO insurgents, more than a third of its total combatants, were so engaged.

Unlike UNITA's Jonas Savimbi, the FNLA's leadership went into exile outside Angola, abandoning

121

its soldiers to their fate. When a few hundred of the ill-trained and demoralised fighters arrived on the Namibian border in 1975, they were turned over to SADF Colonel Jan Breytenbach, who led them on a madcap and daring drive against FAPLA and its Cuban advisors during Operation *Savannah*. Later incorporated into the SADF as 32 Battalion, the unit evolved into a deep-penetration force that operated on both sides of the border, but principally in Angola. Led by white, Portuguese-speaking SADF officers and senior NCOs (though a number of outstanding Angolans were commissioned), it wrought great destruction against SWAPO and its FAPLA allies. It would end the war with almost 7,500 kills against the two organisations, suffering 156 dead of its own.

The SAP also began to examine the concept of unconventional forces. In 1978 Colonel Johannes 'Sterk Hans' Dreyer was sent to Ovamboland to determine what role the SAP could play against SWAPO. In interviews with the author he explained that, based on experience gained from his time in Rhodesia and in Mozambique with the Portuguese-trained *Flechas* (Arrows), he at first envisioned a Selous Scout-type unit, employing local Ovambos as pseudo-SWAPO. Dreyer was allocated six officers and granted permission to recruit 60 Ovambos

skilled in tracking and weapons handling. Among the founding officers was Captain E. A. de Kock, who not only set standards the unit would try to emulate for the next ten years, but went on to become one of the legendary figures in southern African COIN operations. Officially designated the South West Africa Police Counterinsurgency unit (SWAPOLCOIN), it was known internally as Operation Koevoet (Crowbar). Initially operating on foot in section- to platoon-size units under the leadership of white South African officers, Koevoet regularly began engaging SWAPO units of 80 to 100 men and emerging victorious.

Its successes against SWAPO earned Koevoet a fearsome reputation and a greatly expanded budget, which was invested in more Ovambo recruits, newer weapons and Casspir armoured personnel carriers. With the acquisition of APCs, Capt De Kock discarded the Selous Scout concept and developed unique tactics to pursue, find and destroy infiltrating SWAPO units. Organised by De Kock into combat groups of 40 Ovambos, four whites, and four heavily armed Casspirs accompanied by a Blesbok supply vehicle, they would move from kraal to kraal in the Ovamboland bush, questioning the local population about the presence of insurgents. When information eventually led them

Above: Three Wolf Turbo APCs and a Casspir APC at far left pause on the southern edge of the 'cutline' before crossing the cleared strip into Angola on search and destroy operations against SWAPO insurgents.

Opposite page: This interior shot of a Casspir APC shows only part of the firepower carried by one of the four vehicles in a combat group. Visible are the Armscor 5.56mm R5 assault rifles with 50-round magazines carried by the Ovambo constables, plus two Soviet-made PKM GPMGs and two Armscor copies of the FN GPMG. In the pintle mount on top of the Casspir are co-axially-mounted 0.30 and 0.50 machine-guns operated by the car commander, plus a single GPMG operated from

inside by the co-driver. Some group commanders' vehicles carried an Armscor 20mm cannon in place of the 0.50 Browning.

3. The policy of hot pursuit was generally interpreted by the security forces to mean that they could cross the border at will, and both Koevoet and the SWATF 101 Bn did so, operating with impunity inside Angola for days at a time.

to the spoor of a SWAPO unit, the trackers would debus to follow it. Once the general direction was determined, half of the group (*voorsny* – literally 'cutting ahead') would sweep forward one or two kilometres in their APCs to locate fresher spoor. As soon as this was found, the trailing half would race forward to take it again, while the *voorsny* half would cut ahead once more.

When the trackers determined that the spoor was no more than 15min old, helicopter gunships (Alouette IIIs with door-mounted 20mm cannon) were scrambled from Ruacana, Ondangwa or Een-hana. These flew orbits ahead of the Koevoet group, forcing the insurgents to seek cover each time they came overhead and thus slowing their escape. This leapfrogging tactic in concert with gunship support inevitably led to a contact in which the exhausted, outnumbered and outgunned insurgents always lost. If the insurgents were able to escape back into Angola, a policy of hot pursuit allowed Koevoet to follow them.[3]

Although Koevoet comprised no more than 15 per cent of the security force presence in the operational area, it often accounted for up to 90 per cent of the annual kills against SWAPO. (This statistic does not take into account those killed by 32 Bn during deep-penetration covert operations, or by conventional SADF troops during cross-border operations in Angola.) Koevoet shared 32 Bn's reputation for such ruthless efficiency that SWAPO and the UN mounted an extensive propaganda campaign in the hope that the international community would bring enough pressure to bear to force

the South African Government to disband them. This did not happen until the lead-up to elections in early 1989, with almost disastrous results.

CROSS-BORDER OPERATIONS AS POLICY

Still smarting from its defeat at Cassinga, SWAPO took more than a year to plan Operation *Revenge*, a stand-off mortar and rocket attack against the SADF base at Katima Mulilo at the eastern end of the Caprivi Strip, to be followed by a ground assault. On August 23 1979 ten South African soldiers died when a barrack was struck by a 122mm rocket fired from Zambia. The 600 SWAPO fighters who had been assembled for the ground assault scattered under South African counter-fire. The SADF responded with a mechanised infantry strike into Zambia that killed dozens of PLAN insurgents and destroyed a number of bases for no losses to themselves.

By late 1980, SWAPO's strength in southern Angola had risen to 8,000, leading to a sudden upsurge in infiltrations and the SADF's decision to launch another major operation. The objective of Operation *Sceptic*, the most ambitious cross-border attack up to that time, was the destruction of SWAPO's command and control centre for southern Angola and northern Namibia. Located at Chifufua, code-named 'Smokeshell' by the South Africans, it lay 260km north of the border. Aerial reconnaissance revealed a sprawling, camouflaged complex of sub-bases spread over 45 sq km and surrounded by well-positioned gun emplacements and an extensive trench system – evidence that Cassinga had taught

SWAPO a valuable, if expensive, lesson.

On May 25 three mechanised infantry battle groups crossed the border at last light, driving flat-out through the night to hit 'Smokeshell' at 1430 the next day, and achieving total surprise. When the battle groups withdrew they had lost 17 of their own for the deaths of 360 SWAPO insurgents. (Another 500 would die before the end of the year in COIN operations along the border.) Equally damaging to SWAPO was the destruction or capture by the SADF of over 300 tons of food and Soviet-supplied equipment.

The following year saw much the same pattern: an escalation of small unit infiltrations by green SWAPO insurgents who entered Namibia convinced that the South African security forces were being badly beaten. This cynical propaganda fed to the inexperienced youngsters by SWAPO and Cuban cadres was designed to maintain pressure on the South African Government, regardless of casualties. According to SWAPO insurgents captured by the security forces, those who survived missions and returned to Angola were segregated from new recruits to prevent their telling how deadly efficient the South Africans were.

By late August 1981 SWAPO had lost more than 700 insurgents in contacts on both sides of the border. Knowing the pattern would continue, the SADF responded in its own predictable fashion and launched Operation *Protea*. Preceded by a wave of strike aircraft that struck the Angolan air defence radar installations at Cahama, a two-pronged SADF and SWATF mechanised infantry force crossed the border on 23 August to capture and destroy the SWAPO, FAPLA and Cuban base at Xangongo. Mongua and Ongiva fell next to the South Africans. A 32 Bn blocker group north of Ongiva killed two Soviet lieutenant-colonels in a sharp encounter with fleeing FAPLA forces, and captured a Soviet warrant officer. SWAPO, FAPLA, Cuban and Soviet losses amounted to some 1,000 dead, against 10 for the attackers. SWAPO's arsenal, replenished since *Sceptic* by the Soviet Union, was captured once more and either destroyed *in situ* or driven back to Namibia. Between 3,000 and 4,000 tons of Eastern Bloc equipment belonging to SWAPO and FAPLA, including tanks, armoured personnel carriers, anti-aircraft weapons, surface-to-air missiles, multiple-barrel rocket launchers, mortars, machine-guns and literally millions of rounds of ammunition were passed on to South Africa's UNITA allies.

For minimal losses, the South Africans had overwhelmed the Angolan air defence systems with their ageing Mirages, brushed aside the Cubans

and Angolan army and inflicted another major defeat on SWAPO. The operation also provided a clear message to SWAPO's supporters. If they were in the way when a fight started, their noses would be bloodied as well. Rather than give up their gains and withdraw to Namibia as they had in the past, the South Africans remained in Xangongo, Mongua and Ongiva to provide in-depth defence against further incursions from southwestern Angola.

Daisy, a follow-up operation in November, attacked SWAPO bases at Bambi and Chetequera in south-central Angola, killing an additional 70 insurgents for three security force dead. Though hardly spectacular compared with *Protea*, it seriously damaged SWAPO's logistical infrastructure and re-emphasised the South African ability to attack deep into Angola with relative impunity. Whereas the Angolan army stayed well clear of the fight, the Angolan air force did not, prompting the first aerial combat of the war when a South African Air Force Mirage destroyed a Cuban-flown MiG-21.[4] The end of 1981 saw the deaths of at least 2,500 SWAPO, FAPLA, Cuban and Soviet soldiers at the hands of the SADF, SWATF and Koevoet in Namibia and Angola. Incredibly, security force losses for the same period amounted to no more than 56, a kill ratio of almost 45:1. The results left no doubt as to the South Africans' military professionalism, or their determination to defend Namibia.

The border war continued unabated into 1982, with regular infiltrations by freshly-trained insurgents and their near-annihilation by the security forces. A new SWAPO logistics base was discovered in the mountainous region of southwestern Angola. In the hastily mounted Operation *Super*, 45 members of 32 Bn helicoptered in to kill 201 for the loss of three of their own. By the end of June almost 600 insurgents had died, while security

Above: After a contact with SWAPO insurgents by a Koevoet combat group, an Alouette III gunship lands to casevac a wounded constable. Morale among all of the South African security forces was bolstered by the willingness of the SAAF pilots to land anywhere to pick up the injured.

Top right: A Koevoet combat group, on the alert for SWAPO insurgents, approaches an Ovambo kraal. The red star and epaulets worn by the one special constable were taken from a dead insurgent. Among the Ovambo the colour red ensured luck and protection.

Right: Members of an SADF Citizen Force (reserve) artillery unit on their annual deployment to the operational area go through a training exercise with their 140mm piece near Katima Mulilo in the Caprivi Strip.

4. A senior South African Navy officer in the pay of the USSR had passed on details of the upcoming attack to his KGB controller. The intelligence was passed on to SWAPO, which was already in the process of shifting bases when Operation *Daisy* (dubbed 'Oops-a-Daisy' by a few wags in the SADF) struck.

force losses totalled 47.

With mounting international pressure for a South African withdrawal from Angola and elections in Namibia, Pretoria stated that it was prepared to accede – provided the Cubans withdrew from Angola. Early cease-fire talks brokered by the USA began between South Africa, Angola and SWAPO, but were strained by the announcement of yet another SADF pre-emptive raid. *Mebos*, a covert operation involving heliborne paratroopers and Reconnaissance Commandos (the equivalent of Britain's SAS), was the response to intelligence that SWAPO was preparing to attack the SADF bases at Xangongo and Ongiva. In the course of the fighting, which cost SWAPO almost 350 lives, a Puma helicopter was shot down, killing 15. The total losses to the South Africans of 29 raised questions in Parliament. The normal wall of secrecy surrounding 'Recce' operations was lifted, and the SADF were forced into admitting the raid.

Angola angrily rejected the linkage between elections in Namibia and a Cuban withdrawal. The reason was clear: without the Cubans, Angolan government forces stood little chance against Jonas Savimbi's increasingly powerful UNITA guerrilla army. From Pretoria's side, if it granted independence to Namibia and SWAPO won the elections, South Africa's northwestern border would be facing a hostile government supported by Cuban and Soviet forces. For the South Africans it was an unacceptable situation, in spite of the economic strain the war was placing on their economy and the opprobrium from the West. Although basic groundwork had been prepared for future talks, the war went on, and 1982 ended with SWAPO losses of 1,288 compared with 77 for the security forces.

Negotiations continued, however, and various proposals were mooted. An interim measure that held out hope for a cessation of hostilities was the creation of a demilitarised zone north of the Namibian border. An early solution seemed imminent until SWAPO launched a major rainy-season infiltration into the Kaokoveld, Ovamboland and Kavango in February. Operation *Phoenix*, an intensive SWATF internal counter-insurgency effort heavily supported by Koevoet, cost 27 security force members but killed more than 300 insurgents of SWAPO's Cuban- and Soviet-trained 'Volcano' unit. The talks foundered as the diplomats on all sides returned to their respective capitals.

In December, despite a thinly disguised warning from the Soviet Union that South Africa's presence in Angola was intolerable, the SADF embarked on Operation *Askari*. With the 'Volcano' infiltration still fresh in their minds, the objective was to neutralise

SWAPO before the onset of the seasonal rains. The SADF and SWATF swept through the Angolan bush to destroy a number of insurgent bases. In early January 1984 one mechanised element of the operation near Cuvelei was attacked by a numerically superior force comprising a FAPLA armoured brigade supported by two Cuban mechanised infantry battalions. When the dust settled, the hastily retreating attackers had sacrificed a dozen T-55 tanks and a 'body count' of 324 in exchange for seven South African dead.

Progress on a cease-fire and the creation of a demilitarised zone (DMZ) continued in direct talks between Angola and South Africa, with the USA acting as an intermediary and a defiant SWAPO issuing contradictory statements from the sidelines. An agreement was finally hammered out. The Angolans guaranteed that Cuban and SWAPO forces would remain outside the designated DMZ, which would be scoured by a joint monitoring team from FAPLA and the SADF. Once this was declared 'clean', South Africa would withdraw and the Angolan army would remain to prevent the DMZ being used by SWAPO to infiltrate into Namibia.

In exchange, the South African Government would accelerate the implementation of UNSCR 435, allowing free elections. It was a sincere effort by the South Africans to mollify the West and head off sanctions, but in retrospect it was a naive effort

at compromise. Angolan assurances of compliance to the contrary, the heavy military pressure being exerted by UNITA, which was being supplied by the SADF through Kavango and the Caprivi Strip, meant that Angola simply could not risk the election of a non-SWAPO government in Namibia.

Even as the Joint Monitoring Commission (JMC) was being set up at the end of February 1984, SWAPO was intensifying its efforts. South African protests met with stonewalling by the Angolans and a statement from SWAPO that all SWAPO fighters had already left Angola and were in Namibia. Intelligence gleaned from captured insurgents showed that, far from preventing movement through the area, FAPLA was actively supporting SWAPO. By the year's end, however, South Africa not only remained at the negotiating table, but was actually completing its withdrawal ahead of schedule.

The first month of 1985 saw no diminution in SWAPO activity. By the middle of February, in fact, there was a major increase as hundreds of insurgents took advantage of the Angolan army's deliberate blind eye to enter the country. As the fighting escalated, the SADF declared that their withdrawal had stopped 40km north of the border because of the Angolans' inability to halt SWAPO movements through the DMZ. Pressure from the West, however, prompted the final stage of the withdrawal a month after the dissolution of the Joint Monitoring Commission in mid-May.

Far left: A SWATF lieutenant, wounded in the legs by a POM-Z anti-personnel mine, radios for a casevac helicopter.

Left: Before setting out from an overnight stay near the Eenhana fire support base, these Koevoet NCOs and special constables co-ordinate the day's search patterns.

Within days of the last South African soldier leaving Angolan soil, FAPLA had already opened its bases to SWAPO. But the years of war had seriously eroded SWAPO's numbers and left few surviving cadres of any experience. Nonetheless, the organisation continued to send new recruits against the hardened South African security forces in what amounted to suicide missions. In September, combat groups from Koevoet and the SWATF 101 Bn discovered the spoor of a large group of insurgents in Ovamboland and followed it to the Angolan border. Permission was received to engage in 'hot pursuit', and Operation *Egret* crossed the border in the first external raid since *Askari*. Fifteen insurgents were killed and more than 100 captured, and large caches of land mines and ammunition were discovered. A document found on the body of one insurgent, who was identified as the intelligence secretary of the Central Region, underscored just how desperate the morale within SWAPO had become:

'TO ALL DET COMMISAR

Dear Comrades,
Our liberation struggle is now approaching...
another stage of criticality which [is] of course created by the powerful forces of occupation with the sole purpose of [preventing] the independence of our country Namibia.

The RHQs [Regional headquarters] has critically tried to analyse the situation in Namibia and in our operational sector in particular and drawing examples from our many setbacks and the work of our political department in regard with the political mobilisation of the masses and political work among our Combatants were reassessed. Viewing the facts of the past we concluded that drastic measures should be taken to regain the support of the masses. The RHQ put emphasis on our organisation standing through these difficult times. The following guides should be followed during the Political Mobilisation among the masses and own troops.
– Try to make the masses understand the critical situation for SWAPO and they must stay in high morale for the future.
– The use of force is allowed on those who do not want to support the organisation.
– Enemy propaganda should be countered as soon as heard or dropped in an area of our jurisdiction because we cannot allow a further drop in morale.
– Meetings should be conducted to individual persons or collectively whenever applicable but always remain vigilant of the large number of puppets and agents of [the South African] regime in our midst.
– Murder should be limited only to suspected enemy agents and supporters.
– Large numbers of children if possible a whole

Below: A Koevoet combat group leader co-ordinates the other Wolf Turbo APCs of his group during operations in the harsh Kaokoveld west of Ovamboland. In the latter stages of the border war, 20mm guns were received by Koevoet and used with impressive results. The 60mm mortar on the swivel base plate was a personal modification.

village or school must be captured to rebuild our organisation.

– A revolutionary has always a goal to achieve. To be cruel in the struggle is to do good for the future.

– We must [not] expose the atrocities committed by our own troops, but side them to the enemy. Therefore atrocities should not be committed in front of masses.

– The firing squad will be re-implemented for cases of desertion among own troops ...

– The revolutionary movement which is separated from the people will not in any way win Victory, or its victory cannot last long.'

The year 1986 saw a continuing deterioration in the quality of SWAPO combatants. Part of this was explained by a major Soviet-and Cuban-led offensive against UNITA. Commanded by Russian General Konstantin Shagnovitch, a highly decorated officer from the Soviet Union's war in Afghanistan, it was a do-or-die effort to destroy the guerrilla army, and SWAPO's more experienced units were pulled from the southern border to reinforce conventional FAPLA units. Thus, in Ovamboland, the only area of Namibia still accessible to them, the odds were so stacked against the new and ill-trained insurgents that the security forces began grimly to refer to the wet-season infiltrations as 'the summer games'. At least 640 SWAPO fighters had been killed by the end of the year, 399 by Koevoet and most of the balance by 32 Bn and SWATF 101 Bn.

In late 1987 the Soviet-led offensive against UNITA in Angola, though badly mauled and forced to withdraw by UNITA and the SADF, shook its head and, like an old fighter, stepped back into the ring. Again, SWAPO was called on to contribute, meaning that the quality of insurgents entering Namibia remained low. The numbers were still there, however, and by the end of the year 745 had died at the hands of Koevoet and the SWATF.

To the fury and frustration of the Soviet Union, the much-vaunted offensive ended in yet another humiliating defeat. Billions of dollars-worth of equipment had been destroyed or captured by either the SADF or UNITA, and close to 5,000 FAPLA, SWAPO, Cuban and Soviet soldiers killed. Shagnovitch was recalled to Moscow in disgrace. Soviet Premier Mikhail Gorbachev weighed the advantages of continued support for Angola against *realpolitik*: the Cold War was ending, the Soviet treasury was approaching bankruptcy, and Western economic support would be crucial to the future of the USSR. It was time to disengage.

Negotiations were accelerated, this time with the

involvement of the Soviet Union, which put pressure on its Cuban surrogates to reach an acceptable compromise with the South Africans. By August an agreement had been reached whereby the Cubans would withdraw north as the SADF moved south. Meanwhile, Cuba and Angola would guarantee that SWAPO retreated from the border area as well. In a scheme reminiscent of 1984, a Joint Military Monitoring Commission (JMMC) composed of Cuban, Angolan army and South African personnel would ensure compliance. Once the South Africans had withdrawn completely and embarked on implementing UNSCR 435, Cuban and South African forces would begin staged withdrawals from Angola and Namibia respectively.

As the initial stages of the agreement proceeded, however, it became clear that SWAPO was continuing to operate with the collusion of their long-time allies. South African protests to the Cuban and Angolan army side of the JMMC were ignored. In spite of the violations, however, the SADF's withdrawal was completed ahead of schedule on 1 August 1988. Much blustering continued to come from the Cuban and Angolan governments,

Above: After a long pursuit across the border into Angola, this SWAPO insurgent and five others died in a contact with a Koevoet combat group.

Right: Following a contact with SWAPO insurgents south-east of Eenhana, a Koevoet car commander stands in his position behind the pintle-mounted twin 0.30 Browning GPMGs and points to where an AK-47 round struck. Another struck the windscreen in front of the driver.

which threatened to derail the process, but this was seen as mainly face-saving rhetoric for failing to defeat the SADF militarily. A final peace treaty was signed in New York on 22 December. At the head of the list of agreements setting out the phased withdrawal schedules of Cuban and South Africa forces was the date for initiating implementation of UNSCR 435: April 1 1989. Sam Nujoma, president of SWAPO, formally undertook to cease all hostilities on the same date.

One of the first acts of goodwill on the part of Pretoria was to disband Koevoet, something

SWAPO had been demanding for almost ten years. This ferociously efficient counter-insurgency unit was relieved of its heavy weapons (light and heavy machine guns, 20mm cannon and mortars) and incorporated into the South West Africa Police command structure. Units of the SWATF, including 101 Bn, were stood down or confined to base, and SADF units began redeployment to South Africa. Intelligence showed that SWAPO insurgents were still crossing the border to establish arms caches and intimidate the local population, but it was such a low-level activity that Pretoria did little more than

Left: Riding in the back of a Casspir APC, these Koevoet special constables scan the surrounding bush as they close on a group of running SWAPO insurgents. Although Koevoet regularly suffered casualties, the insurgents always lost to the heavily armed and experienced Koevoet.

Right: Koevoet's success in the counter-insurgency war along the Namibian-Angolan border was in part due to the co-operation of a local population that was generally unsympathetic to SWAPO. These constables question an Ovambo woman about the presence of insurgents in the area.

February, however, a deserter revealed that SWAPO was establishing command and logistics headquarters well inside the neutral area in Angola. A formal protest was made, but, true to form, this was ignored by the Cubans and Angolans.

The United Nations Transitional Assistance Group (UNTAG), a 4,500-man multinational UN military mission to take over security as the SADF withdrew, began to trickle in. Few had ever seen Africa or heard a shot fired in anger. For the seasoned South Africans they were poor imitations of real soldiers.

On the night of 31 March / 1 April 1989, upwards of 1,500 heavily armed SWAPO insur-gents slipped across the border on a 300km front. Barely three hours after the official cease-fire between the South Africans and SWAPO had taken effect, a lightly armed police patrol manned by for-mer Koevoet members discovered the spoor of a large group of insurgents. Urgent radio messages were initially dismissed as an April Fool joke – until contact was made and a fierce fire-fight ensued in which 31 insurgents died for the loss of two police-men. Within hours, contacts had broken out across the operational area. The UNTAG units already in Ovamboland scrambled for safety. Meanwhile, Koevoet, which had remained a cohesive unit within SWAPOL, frantically rearmed their APCs and raced forward to engage the invaders head-on.

Left: Flanked by Casspir APCs, a Koevoet group leader carrying a tactical radio accompanies the track-ers as they follow the faint spoor left by SWAPO insur-gents. The ability of the Ovambo trackers was con-sidered far superior to that of the Bushman 202 Battalion, whose members were employed by various units of the SADF and SWATF.

Once it had been confirmed by UNTAG that SWAPO had violated the truce, Martti Ahtisaari, the UN's special representative in Namibia, released SWATF and SADF units to support the police. By April 2, as the reactivated units headed into the bush, almost 150 insurgents were dead, along with ten members of the vastly outnumbered police. The South African Air Force re-mounted cannon in their Alouette III gunships and made ready the Impala fighter-bombers.

The death toll mounted steadily, with contacts occurring almost hourly. As one six-year Koevoet veteran of the bush war told the author, 'Compared to the April incursion, all the contacts I'd been in up to that point were just "shooting incidents". This was war.' For the first time in the 23-year history of the bush war, Impalas flew ground-attack missions south of the border when more than 350 insurgents dug in near Eenhana.

On 9 April, under pressure from Russia, Cuba and Angola, SWAPO began retreating to its UN-protected sanctuary in Angola. By then, 23 Koevoet members and four from 101 Bn had died. Officially, 305 insurgents had been killed. Unofficially, it was estimated that at least twice that number fell under the guns of the security forces in nine days, most of them to Koevoet. So ended the shooting war.

In the subsequent run-up to elections, UNTAG and other UN observers ignored blatant intimidation of the local population by SWAPO. On 9 November 1989, SWAPO won the elections by a narrow margin.

Below: 'Mister Duro', a serious and taciturn member of HOS, during an excursion to within about 200 metres of 'Četnik' positions. The weapon choice is unusual in that it appears to be a 5.45mm AKS-74 assault rifle.

ANTHONY ROGERS

Yugoslavia

Those in the former Yugoslavia never tire of explaining how the present stems from the past, referring in particular to the mixed origins of the main ethnic and religious groups – the Orthodox Serbs, Bosnian Muslims and, predominantly, Roman Catholic Croats and Slovenes. If one is to have any chance of comprehending events in what was Yugoslavia, it is necessary to understand something about its long and complex past; and while this is neither a history nor a political analysis, what follows should help in explaining something of the background to the first protracted European war since 1945.

Yugoslavia was once also part of the Roman Empire. The decline of the Empire left it divided between Rome, in the west, and Byzantium, in the east, with a corresponding split in the Christian Church – Roman Catholic in the west, the Orthodox Christian in the east. In the Balkans, the dividing line more or less followed the river Drina, which today marks much of Serbia's border with Bosnia and explains, in part, why the religion is mainly Orthodox Christian east and south of the Drina, and largely Roman Catholic farther north and along the coast. But how did Islam come to what is today Bosnia-Herzegovina?

The centuries following the collapse of the Roman Empire saw the emergence of various Balkan states out of which evolved today's Serbia, Croatia and Bulgaria. Subsequently the Slovenes, Macedonians, Montenegrins, Bosnians and people of Herzegovina would also develop their specific regional and national identities. By the thirteenth century the region of Bosnia was populated by Roman Catholics, Orthodox Christians and followers of the persecuted dualist Church of Bosnia. The mainly Orthodox Christian Herzegovina was added to Bosnia in the early fourteenth century.

Muslim expansionism led to the crucial Battle of Kosovo in 1389. There the Ottoman Turks defeated the Serbs, who were eventually driven north to the Danube. The advancing Turks also succeeded in pushing the Croats north towards what is now Zagreb – Croatia's capital. Those who remained in Bosnia and Herzegovina were compelled to convert to Islam, and by the time the Ottoman thrust had been halted, at the end of the seventeenth century, the majority of those in the region were Muslim. Later, as the Ottomans were forced back, many Muslims sought to escape persecution by seeking refuge in Bosnia and Herzegovina.

133

The region was taken over by the Austro-Hungarian Empire following the Russo-Turkish War of 1877–8, which also led to the independence of most of Bulgaria. An emergence of nationalist fervour culminated in the early twentieth century with Serbia, Montenegro, Bulgaria and Greece uniting in a brief war against Turkey. The Turks were defeated. Another conflict, between the victors this time, resulted in a substantial increase in Serbia's borders. Relations between Serbia and the government of Austria and Hungary dissolved altogether when, on 28 June 1914, the Habsburg Archduke Franz Ferdinand was assassinated by a Bosnian Serb in Sarajevo – thereby initiating events that would lead to the First World War and to the demise of the central and east European empires.

The post-war period witnessed the rise of the Serbian-dominated Kingdom of the Serbs, Croats and Slovenes. In 1929 the Serbian King Aleksandar Karađorđević declared direct rule by decree in an unsuccessful attempt to curb continuing dissent amongst the member states. In 1934, King Aleksandar was assassinated. It was not until 1939 that home rule was bestowed on Croatia by Aleksandar's successor, the Prince Regent Pavle. The move did nothing to pacify the Serbs, however.

After Hitler invaded, in April 1941, the pro-Nazi *Ustaša* (Insurgents), composed of Croats and Muslims, proceeded to eliminate Serbs, Jews, Gypsies and any non-fascists. The situation spawned two other organisations: Serbian Colonel Draža Mihailović's *Četniks* (from *ceta*, meaning battalion) and the partisans under Croatian Josip Broz Tito, the general secretary of the Communist Party. By the end of 1943, Tito's multi-ethnic partisans had emerged as the dominant force. In the autumn of

1944 the intervention of the Red Army led to the defeat of the Germans in Yugoslavia. Following the liberation of Belgrade, on 20 October, the Russians departed and Yugoslavia was transformed into its post-war state.

Following the death of Tito in 1980, Yugoslavia was again threatened with civil unrest. In 1987, Serbian Slobodan Milošević became President. The post-Communist elections of 1990 saw the rise to power of the Croatian Democratic Union (HDZ) under Franjo Tuđman, and Bosnia's President Alija Izetbegović.

COUNTDOWN TO WAR
Slovenia

At 0500 hours on 27 June 1991, tanks and armoured vehicles of the Yugoslav People's Army (JNA) were deployed in response to Slovenia's Declaration of Independence. Opposing forces consisted of lightly-armed but well organized and determined Territorials. There followed a series of clashes. The JNA, whose troops often seemed confused and uncertain about their role, put up only a token resistance. Tanks and other equipment were seized and added to the Territorials' rapidly-growing arsenal. During the confusion, Slovenian conscripts deserted. The JNA faced imminent defeat. It was all over within ten days. According to the Slovenian Red Cross, 60 people had been killed. In accordance with the Brioni Accord negotiated by the European Community (EC), which acknowledged Slovenia's liberation from the control of Belgrade, the JNA would subsequently withdraw from Slovenia. Meanwhile across the border the Croats had been closely monitoring events, which were soon to be re-enacted on their own soil – but

Above left: 'Batman', from Nustar. His helmet was adorned with a peace emblem on one side, 'Born to Kill' on the other. On the front was a *Ustaša* badge – 'Just a joke', according to 'Batman'.

Above: 'Batman' entertains his mates in their farmhouse cellar 'bunker' at Nustar.

Above: As shots are fired, these Croats attempt to spot the Serbian fire position(s) estimated to be 500 metres away, in Mirkovci. During the opening stages of the war many Croats, desperately short of weapons, had to make do with hunting rifles.

on a far greater scale than anybody could have imagined.

Croatia

On 25 July 1990, the Serbian Democratic Party issued a declaration proclaiming the sovereignty of the Serbian people in Croatia. The Serbian Autonomous Region Krajina was proclaimed nine weeks later. On 16 March 1991, the Executive Council of Krajina decided on partition from Croatia.[1] Political tension now combined with an alarming increase in internecine incidents, and in eastern Croatia's Slavonia region a culmination of events resulted in twelve policemen being killed while attempting to rescue colleagues abducted by Serbs at Borovo Selo, a suburb of Vukovar.

When Croatia declared independence on 25 June 1991, conditions in Slavonia rapidly deteriorated into daily gun battles between Croats and Serbs, the latter supported by the predominantly Serb-led JNA. Throughout the country, the newly-formed Croatian National Guard (ZNG) began to lay siege to Federal barracks. The so-called 'Barracks War', which lasted all summer, ended with the Croats in possession of a large quantity of captured equipment, including tanks and heavy weapons. The fighting escalated. Serbian militia, in conjunction with Federal Forces, now engaged the Croats in open warfare. Towns and villages were devastated and thousands made homeless in a seemingly endless series of mortar and artillery barrages, bombings, tank assaults and infantry attacks and counter-attacks. Both sides dug in as they attempted to consolidate what had been won. By autumn, the front extended from Vukovar west to the Papuk mountains and south-west to Novska.

1. p. 10, *Review of International Affairs* (Belgrade), Vol XLIV, 1014.

2. Ibid, p. 11.

3. Ibid, p. 11.

4. p. 73, *Seasons in Hell* by Ed Vulliamy (Simon & Schuster), 1994.

It continued along the River Sava to Sisak and beyond, along the River Kupa to Karlovac. There was also fighting up and down the coast, particularly around Zadar, Šibenik and Dubrovnik.

On 27 November, the United Nations Security Council agreed to send a peace-keeping force to former Yugoslavia on condition that the latest cease-fire prevailed and that the Croatians lifted their siege of military installations, thereby enabling the JNA to withdraw. Two days later, the Federal Army began to pull out of Zagreb. Elsewhere, the war went on. It was not until 21 February 1992 that the UN Security Council finally approved Resolution 743 allowing the deployment of a United Nations Protection Force (UNPROFOR) in what had been Yugoslavia. Six weeks later the first UNPROFOR units landed in Croatia. For a while hostilities continued. In June, the Croats succeeded in relieving Dubrovnik. Thereafter, events in Croatia were largely overshadowed by the war spreading to Bosnia-Herzegovina.

Bosnia-Herzegovina

During late 1991, the Serbs in Bosnia-Herzegovina had made clear their support for a 'Serbian Republic... within the framework of Yugoslavia'.[2] But at the end of February 1992, within weeks of European Community recognition of Slovenia and Croatia, a referendum resulted in a majority vote in favour of autonomy for Bosnia-Herzegovina. The Bosnian Serbs, most of whom had boycotted the referendum, responded by erecting barricades in the capital, Sarajevo, ostensibly in protest against an incident on 1 March during a wedding procession in front of Sarajevo's Serbian Orthodox Church that left one man dead and the officiating clergyman wounded.[3] Within weeks, the situation had seriously deteriorated. In scenes reminiscent of those in Slovenia and Croatia, Sarajevo's army barracks were besieged and looted. The first mortar bombs landed in the city on 6 April.[4] In May, an escalation in hostilities prompted the UN to withdraw its headquarters from the city.

Sarajevo became a focal point for journalists, but Muslims, Croats and Serbs were battling for control throughout Bosnia-Herzegovina – at Bosanski Brod and Brcko, in the north-east, and around Bihać, in the north-west, and at Bugojno, Mostar, Foča, Goražde, Višegrad, Bratunac... Frequently, the war went unreported, as in the vast Majevica and Ozren regions, simply because western journalists hardly ever ventured to these and other places. In the early stages, the superior firepower of the Serbs enabled them to achieve significant gains in spite of a united Muslim-Croat effort. Later, the alliance would collapse as everybody disputed territorial claims. Consequently, the Bosnian Muslim *Armija* would have to contend with both the Bosnian Serbs and Croats – each reinforced by their compatriots from across the border.

In August there was international outrage and condemnation after the media announced the existence of Serbian detention camps in Bosnia.

With the onset of winter the situation in Sarajevo worsened. Water and electricity services were severely disrupted, and there was a desperate shortage of food and medicines. From the hills around the city, Serbian gunners kept up a constant barrage, and in many areas snipers added to the misery and mayhem. Elsewhere, all three sides fought to retain what each considered to be their territory. In areas that were untenable, the inhabitants were killed or forced to flee and their property destroyed. The place then became a sort of no man's land with a vigilant enemy quick to shoot at anybody risking entry.

In January 1993, fighting again erupted in Croatia when the Croats launched an offensive to recapture key positions around Zadar. In Bosnia-Herzegovina, the Serbs took Kamenica in February and Cerska the following month. In April continuing actions in the Drina valley resulted in the UN evacuating Muslim civilians from Srebrenica. Ironically, the operation attracted adverse criticism from the Bosnian Muslim government, with the UN accused of 'ethnic cleansing'.[5] Also in April, Croats and Muslims clashed at Kiseljak and, between April and May, at Jablanica and Konjic on the Mostar–Sarajevo road. In May fighting intensified in and around Mostar. May also witnessed the collapse of the much-publicized Vance–Owen plan.

Under continued international pressure, and faced with the alarming prospect of a military alliance between Bosnian Serbs and Croats, President Alija Izetbegović conditionally agreed, on 7 June, to establish six 'safe areas' for Muslims in Bosnia.[6] Simultaneously, renewed fighting around Travnik culminated in Croats fleeing their Muslim erstwhile allies to seek refuge with the Serbs.

Hostilities continued through the summer and autumn of 1993. North-east of Sarajevo, Žuč was subjected to a devastating artillery barrage. Southwest of the city, Muslims and Serbs also battled for possession of Mounts Igman and Bjelašnića, from which, the victorious Serbs would later be forced to withdraw in order to fend off the threat of NATO air strikes. Elsewhere, the Muslims achieved considerable success, taking control of several important towns including Gornji Vakuf, Fojnica, Busovača and Vareš.

Above: A Croatian BOV-3 self-propelled anti-aircraft vehicle armed with triple 20mm cannon. Croats, Serbs and, later, Bosnians often displayed a bizarre 'Hollywood' mentality in their approach to the war. The title on this vehicle near Karlovac says it all.

As Bosnia-Herzegovina entered its second winter of the war, the fighting showed little sign of abating until the renewed threat of NATO intervention persuaded the Serbs to begin pulling back their guns from around Sarajevo.

By the end of February 1994, after having been under attack for 22 months, the capital was finally able to enjoy its first real chance of a return to some semblance of normality.

In April 1993, Operation *Deny Flight* was launched to enforce a UN 'no-fly zone' over Bosnia. On 28 February 1994, NATO carried out its first offensive action in its 45-year history when American F-16 fighters destroyed four Serbian aircraft operating in defiance of the ban.

During March, a tentative peace was negotiated between Bosnian Croats and Muslims subsequent to forging a joint federation. On 19 March the Bosnian Serbs besieging Maglaj suddenly pulled back – a move that allowed the UN to send in their first aid convoy in five months. There was a comparative lull until the end of March when there were reports of 'fierce fighting' between Muslim and Serbian forces in central Bosnia. In eastern Bosnia, the UN-designated 'safe area' of Goražde also continued to come under attack by the Serbs. On 10 and 11 April, Serbian positions around the embattled Muslim pocket

5. *The Independent*, 2 April, 1993.

6. *The Independent*, 8 June, 1993. The 'safe areas' were Bihac, Tuzla, Sarajevo, Srebrenica, Zepa and Gorazde.

7. *The Times*, 29 June 1994.

8. Information provided by the International Institute for Strategic Studies. Ten countries had both larger armed forces and armies. These were: United States (in Europe), Russia (west of the Urals), France, Germany, Italy, Spain, Turkey, Great Britain, Poland and Romania.

were bombed by NATO aircraft in their first ground attack since the war began. The situation worsened as UN personnel were temporarily abducted in a retaliatory move by the Serbs. By the 24th, following the death of a British 'joint commission observer' and the loss of a British Sea Harrier – from which the pilot ejected to safety – the threat of further air strikes had persuaded the Serbs to halt their offensive. The fragile peace lasted a week. Elsewhere, the fighting continued.

Talks aimed at securing a cease-fire throughout Bosnia-Herzegovina commenced in Geneva on 6 June 1994. On the 8th, the warring factions agreed to a one-month cease-fire. Within days, however, fighting was reported in the north-west Bihać enclave and between Zenica and Tuzla, around Brčko and in the area of Vozuća in the Ozren region. Commander of the UN forces in south-west Bosnia, Brigadier Andrew Ridgway, was quoted as stating on 28 June: 'There is no peace in Bosnia and no cease-fire, not even a cessation of hostilities...' Pessimistically, he continued, 'There will be at least twenty years of war.[7]

THE VANCE-OWEN PLAN
In January 1993 Lord David Owen and Cyrus Vance presented their solution to peace in Bosnia. The Vance-Owen plan called for Bosnia to be divided into ten autonomous regions dominated by Bosnia's Muslims, Croats or Serbs. It more than appeased the Croats, who were provided with considerably more territory than they might otherwise have expected. Although it negated any prospect of maintaining a unitary multi-ethnic state, the plan was reluctantly accepted by the Muslims, partly

because it represented the best hope for intervention in the peace process by the new US administration. The Serbs, however, objected. They pointed out that Serbian communities would remain in areas dominated by Muslims and Croats (an argument that also applied to the Muslims and Croats in areas not under their control). The Serbs were also denied a corridor linking the Serb-inhabited region in the north-west to Serbia itself, until a last-ditch concession provided for a six-mile-wide UN corridor across north Bosnia.

Finally, under pressure from Serbian President Slobodan Milošević, the Bosnian Serb leader Radavan Karadžić provisionally agreed to the proposal on 2 May. This should have resulted in a cessation of hostilities and separation of opposing forces, the restoration of Bosnia's shattered infrastructure, the opening of routes between and within provinces, and the demilitarization of Sarajevo. Instead, in mid-May, a Serb referendum overwhelmingly rejected the deal, causing uncertainty and confusion in Washington and Europe. In June the reluctance of the United States to commit ground forces to Bosnia raised doubts as to whether there would even be sufficient troops and resources to make the plan work. Despite the long efforts of the principals, the plan was never implemented and, eventually, abandoned.

OPPOSING FORCES
In June 1991, the Yugoslav People's Army (JNA) was reported to be the eleventh largest in Europe.[8] Consisting of ground, sea and air forces, the JNA was also responsible for the Frontier Guard and Territorial Defence Force (TO). Total strength was

Right: Serbian militiaman in his bunker at Majevica. The machine-gun is either a Second World War German MG42 or, most likely, 7.92mm M53, the Yugoslav variant.

estimated at around 169,000, including 95,000 conscripts. The Frontier Guard comprised another 14,000, while 885,000 could be mobilised for service with the TO. The JNA was created by Marshal Tito primarily as a deterrent against possible Soviet aggression but also, ironically, as a symbol of national unity. In time of conflict, the JNA was to be assisted by the Territorials, whose task was to safeguard key points and to employ guerrilla tactics to harass the enemy. Volunteers and conscripts came from throughout Yugoslavia, with Serbs constituting the largest ethnic component – a fact reflected in JNA leadership. The TO, along with former members of the JNA, would subsequently form the nucleus of the armies of Slovenia, Croatia and Bosnia-Herzegovina.

On 28 May 1991, the newly-formed Croatian National Guard (ZNG) paraded for the first time in Zagreb. Prior to President Franjo Tuđman's call for mobilisation, the ZNG comprised male and female volunteers who were equipped mainly with small-arms and a number of armoured vehicles. Additional transport, heavy weapons and tanks were subsequently acquired, in much the same way as the Slovenian Territorials had done, during clashes with the JNA. Serbs in the Republic of Krajina and Bosnia-Herzegovina also formed militias, with arms and equipment freely provided by a largely sympathetic JNA.

Most who joined the fledgling forces were sufficiently experienced to at least recognise one end of an assault rifle from the other. Many, particularly those in rural areas, were also hunters whose affinity with the Balkans' often-rugged terrain combined with shooting skills to produce ideal guerrilla material. Before long, they were joined by patriots from as far afield as the United States and Australia, to where their parents had emigrated from Yugoslavia in the years following the Second World War. Frequently, the new arrivals were fluent in the languages of both their adopted land and the old country and instilled with such a sense of nationalistic pride that they had little trouble in adjusting to what should have been an alien situation. In addition, there were numerous other foreign volunteers, many of whom were employed as instructors. Virtually anyone was welcome, particularly by the Croats, who were keen to learn western military skills and tactics.

The brief conflict in Slovenia did nothing for the credibility of the JNA. In Croatia there was further humiliation as the Croats besieged barracks and installations and captured vast amounts of arms and equipment. Serb commanders struggled to retain control over their dwindling forces as more and more Croats continued to desert. Ultimately the JNA would consist primarily of Serbs. Following purges

Above: The remains of an M-84, the Yugoslav version of the Soviet T-72. This was the only Serbian MBT to penetrate Croatian defences at Nustar.

Above: Serbian defenders of Mount Majevica during a lull in the fighting that flared here early in September 1992.

9. Many of the facts and figures derive from *Jane's Sentinel: The Unfair Advantage*, published by Jane's Information Group, 1993. The Editor, Paul Beaver, believes the information, compiled up to November 1993, is 'eighty per cent accurate'.

amongst general and senior staff, there would be no doubt about the loyalty of those who remained.

Inevitably, the war in the former Yugoslavia has shaped and reshaped the armed forces of the various republics. Subsequent to the withdrawal of the JNA from Slovenia, the Slovenian Territorial Defence Force (STO) commenced a major restructuring programme that includes the establishment of its own military institutions.

At the time of the cease-fire in Croatia in January 1992, the Croatian army (HV) is said to have been 200,000 strong.[9] There followed plans to reorganize the force into an army of both regulars and conscripts. A home defence force would also defend the border with the disputed Serb-held territories. In the event of mobilization, numbers would be dramatically increased by a massive call-up of reservists. Economic problems and a UN arms embargo have affected the development of Croatia's army, navy and air force, all of which are still largely dependent on arms and equipment captured during the war.

The army of the Republic of Serbian Krajina is also reliant on weaponry acquired, albeit freely, via the JNA. Reliable statistics are unavailable, but it is widely assumed that militarily Croatia and Krajina are fairly evenly matched. However, the continued existence of the latter very much depends upon further clashes with Croatia, as well as the level of support provided by Belgrade.

In Bosnia-Herzegovina the three main adversaries are the Bosnian Serb Army (BSA), the predominantly Muslim Army (commonly referred to as the *Armija*) and the Croatian Defence Council (HVO).

In May 1992, Belgrade ordered the withdrawal of Federal forces from Bosnia-Herzegovina. Although it is generally accepted that about 15,000

military personnel actually did leave, the remainder promptly transferred to the BSA, along with their tanks, heavy weapons and other arms and equipment. Active support is also provided by irregulars from Serbia/Vojrodina.

The *Armija* was created by combining the Patriotic League with other formations and originally also included Bosnian Croats and Bosnian Serbs. Although the *Armija* continued to retain a mixed-ethnic component, events would eventually lead to partition in most areas.

Formed from local communities, the Croatian Defence Council is supported and assisted by the Croatian Army (HV). Initially, the HVO force and the *Armija* were united against the Bosnian Serbs. Friction between Bosnian Croats and Muslims then led to the HVO forming a localized alliance with their former enemy. Subsequently, the Bosnian Croats and Muslims managed to settle their differences, and by mid-1994 they were brought even closer by the formation of a joint federation.

Foreign volunteers serve throughout Bosnia. The BSA is bolstered by an undisclosed number of, mainly Russian, mercenaries. The *Armija* and HVO both include fighters from all over the western world. Reports also indicate the presence with the *Armija* of Algerian, Turkish, Iranian and other Mujahideen – whose fundamentalism is not always appreciated by the generally more liberal-minded Bosnian Muslims.

In addition to the three main adversaries in Bosnia-Herzegovina, there exist private armies – effectively bandits – apparently with no allegiance to anyone but themselves.

Since being withdrawn from Croatia and Bosnia, the JNA has continued to undergo drastic changes. Events have significantly reduced the once-formidable inventory of the army, navy and air force. The future of the new JNA depends on such factors as a possible confrontation with Croatia, particularly in regard to oil reserves in the contested region of eastern Slavonia. Continuing international sanctions have also had an effect. Add to this an increased sense of dissatisfaction among the people of Serbia/Vojvodina and Montenegro, especially the Muslims of the Sandžak region and the mainly Muslim Albanians of Kosovo.

For what is left of the old JNA, and the government it serves, recovery is likely to be a lengthy and difficult process.

WEAPONS AND EQUIPMENT

It is practically impossible to provide a detailed assessment of the composition and holdings of the armed forces that have arisen since the collapse of

139

the Federal Republic. For one thing, the situation is ever changing. For another, the opinions of noted and respected defence analysts often differ on even the most basic issues. For example, one eminent source recently stated that throughout the former Yugoslavia the number of main battle tanks (MBTs) was 2,400. Yet the generally accepted figure for all MBTs in Yugoslavia *before* the war was a comparatively modest 1,850.

Much of what was included in the JNA inventory in mid-1991 was taken over by the opposing forces so that each tends to use more or less identical weapons systems and equipment. Tanks and heavy weapons have played a prominent role since the war in Croatia. Of the former, the T-54/55 is the most common. The Yugoslav-built version of the more modern Soviet T-72, the M-84A, as well as the outdated T-34/85 are also widely used. To combat the ever-present tank threat, there exist a variety of anti-tank (AT) weapons – tank destroyers, AT guns, recoilless rifles, rocket launchers and wire-guided missiles. Mines are also often used against tanks and vehicles generally. It is not unusual for several AT mines to be left in the open across known routes as a simple, but often effective, deterrent.

Artillery and mortars are numerous and vary considerably in type and calibre, up to 262mm M-87 'Orkan' multiple rocket launchers.

There is a seemingly inexhaustible supply of infantry weapons, from the obsolete to the latest issue. A First World War Lewis gun was seen near Bjelovar, in Croatia.[10] It is also still possible to come across the Second World War German MG42, from which derived the Yugoslav 7.92mm M53, which, along with the 7.62mm M84, are two of the more widely used GPMGs. Amongst the light machine-guns (LMGs), the 7.62mm M72B1 is a popular choice. Heavy machine-guns (HMGs) are likely to be the .50 calibre Browning and 12.7mm NSV. Of the many different types of rifle, the most common are the 7.62mm Yugoslav M59/66A1 – which is similar to the Soviet SKS – and variants of the Soviet AK (Kalashnikov), particularly the M70B1 and the M70AB2, the latter being the folding-stock version and preferred choice of many. Sniping has always been a feature of the fighting in Croatia and Bosnia. The 7.62mm M76 is the standard Yugoslav sniping rifle, although any suitable rifle fitted with an appropriate telescopic sight will suffice. The 9mm Uzi, .45 calibre Thompson and 7.62mm M56 are just a few of the types of submachine-gun (SMG) likely to be seen. Machine pistols and handguns are also very popular.

Slovenia, Croatia and Serbia each have their own navy and air force. In Bosnia, the Croats, Mus-

lims and Serbs also maintain various aircraft. Since the enforcement of a 'no-fly zone' over Bosnia, there is a reduced risk of air attack, discounting the threat from NATO. Anti-aircraft (AA) guns are now deployed almost exclusively in the ground-fire role. Often they are mounted on vehicles – such as the BOV-3, which is fitted with triple 20mm cannon. Only when considered absolutely necessary are surface-to-air missiles (SAMs) likely to be brought into action, as on 16 April 1994, when a British Sea Harrier was destroyed by Serbs over Goražde.

VUKOVAR

Up to the end of 1991, the town of Vukovar was situated in Croatian eastern Slavonia, a region bordering Serbian Vojvodina. Violence had resulted in a number of deaths in the area even before the war began in Croatia. By July 1991 the situation had deteriorated into major fire-fights as Croats and Serbs laid claim to surrounding villages and suburbs. In August the Federal Army launched an offensive with Vukovar as the main objective. For the Serbs the town was the lynch-pin needed to consolidate their hold on eastern Slavonia. In taking the territory west of the River Danube, the Serbs would extend their own border and, in the process, take possession of the oilfields at Privlaka

Left: The Croats, Serbs and, later, Bosnians loved to create 'Special Forces' units. These are some of 'Đuro's Men', a Croatian 'Special Police Anti-Terrorist' group said to total some 150 men when this picture was taken in February 1992. Seen at their base, a former holiday camp at Nin, near Zadar, personnel clean rifles during weapons training. The man in the foreground holds a stripped-down 7.62mm Yugoslav M76 sniping rifle. A Romanian AKM lies close by.

10. p. 38, *War in the Balkans*, by Eric Micheletti and Yves Debay (Histoire and Collections), 1993.

11. p. 167, *Fear, Death and Resistance*, edited by Lada Cale Feldman (et al), Zagreb Institute of Ethnology and Folklore Research (etc), 1993.

12. Ibid, p. 185–6

13. Ibid, p. 186

14. Ibid, p. 199

Top: Start of a patrol, by Serbian 'Silver Wolf Brigade', into Vozuca suburb destroyed by Muslims.

Above: No one side is really any better, or worse, than the others. Atrocities continue to be perpetrated by Croats, Serbs and Muslims. This Serbian ambulance was ambushed allegedly after the Muslims had given it clearance to pass. Four wounded are reported to have died in the attack.

and Srijemske Laze, south of Vukovar.

On 24 August 1991, the Serbs commenced heavy bombardment against those in and around Vukovar.[11] Artillery, mortars and tanks, assisted by the Serbian air force and by gunboats on the Danube, concentrated a tremendous amount of firepower against the little town. The strategy was effectively simple: cut off Vukovar's energy, water and food supplies, disrupt communications, and turn the place into one deadly killing zone. In order to survive, the population – Croats and Serbs and others – took to living in cellars. Anyone who dared show themselves above ground risked terrible injury or death. Nobody knew where or when the next salvo would impact. There would be the dreadful, rushing 'whoosh' of another incoming round followed a second or two later by a tremendous 'bang' – like a huge door slamming shut.

Sometimes there would be no warning whatsoever: only the explosion. Occasionally the shelling would lessen as the Serbs tried to take an area with tanks or infantry or both. Nenad, who lived through the siege, remembered how the Croats tried, in vain, to fend off the inevitable. He described how a four-man crew would move 'a small gun' from one fire position to another in order to make it appear that there were more weapons than actually existed.[12]

For 87 days a heroic defence was conducted by a vastly outnumbered force consisting of Croatian National Guard (ZNG), police and Croatian Defence Alliance (HOS). At 1728 hours on 18 November 1991 it was reported by *Tanjug* (the Yugoslav news agency) that, 'The majority of the Croatian guardsmen and policemen who are encircled in Vukovar surrendered at about 1500 hours local time to Yugoslav People's Army units... Military sources said that the entire central part of Vukovar was this afternoon under the army's control, but that all houses and cellars had not yet been searched...' There were occasional shots as the Serbs continued to mop up isolated pockets of resistance, but by the following day the battle was effectively over.

As the victors took over what remained of the devastated town, the dazed and bewildered inhabitants began to emerge from their shelters. Nenad recalled how he was threatened with summary execution but was saved by the intervention of a neighbour – a Serb.[13] Others were not so fortunate. Those suspected of being combatants were detained. According to the Croats, thousands are still missing, 'about whom no one knows anything...'[14] On 21 November the Serbs showed off their prize to representatives of the press who were treated to lunch at the battered Hotel Dunav. 'Not one window pane remained,' recalled Sabina Gazić, a photographer. 'They had been replaced with white sheets. Major Veselin Šljivančanin (Commander of Group South) told a subordinate to remove the sheets – so that we could see the *Dunav* (Danube) and landscape, he said. Maybe it was meant as a joke...'

Vukovar cost the Serbs dearly and almost certainly contributed to a cease-fire agreement two months later – thereby suspending, if not quite ending, the war in Croatia. Vukovar is now a Serbian town in the Republic of Krajina.

'INTERNATIONALS'

As the war spread, foreign volunteers, attracted by rumours of a non-existent 'International Brigade', began to arrive both singly and in small groups. They came from all over the world. Some turned up

Opposite page:

Top left: Devastation in Nustar.

Top right: Vinkovci, only fourteen kilometres southwest of Vukovar, was terribly damaged by Serbian artillery, mortar and tank fire. In the opening stages of the conflict, Serbs at nearby Mirkovci maintained that a Croatian machine-gun post was located in the hospital, pictured here. At the time, the Croats would neither confirm nor deny the allegations. Whatever the reason, the hospital became a prime target, in spite of which it continued to function with staff, patients and medical facilities all crammed in the basement.

Lower left: A member of HOS at Mala Bosna. The Ministry of Interior (MUP) patch on his left jacket pocket indicates that the man is probably a former policeman. Note, too, the rosary and crucifixes. The green canister contains gamma globulin.

Lower right: This member of the ZNG, pictured at Borovo Naselje, carries a 7.62mm Romanian AKM and has what is possibly a Yugoslav Model M70 or M70(k) tucked in his belt.

This page, top & bottom: At the front-line at Privlaka. Armed with an M70AB2 assault rifle, this member of the ZNG opens fire from a trench before sending a couple of *tromblon* (rifle grenades) across the River Bosut. The target: five tanks approximately 500 metres away! Provoked, no doubt, by this show of bravado, the Serbian tanks later used their main armament to return fire.

with little more than the clothes they wore. Others brought their own uniforms and equipment, and a few, notably the Americans, their own weapons. Many stayed for only a few days or weeks before disillusion or the frightening reality of the situation prompted their departure. A minority remained.

Kaj, a Dane, arrived as a tourist in what was then Yugoslavia. When Croatia declared independence he decided to stay and assist the Croats, putting to use the experience acquired during service with the Danish army. Kaj was soon to be involved in a number of operations including intelligence-gathering missions in Serbian dominated areas. His *modus operandi* was simple. Driving a Danish registered van, Kaj told anybody who stopped him that he was a tourist visiting Serbian friends – a ploy not without risks. Kaj recalled how, at a Serbian road-block, he had watched as a driver was dragged from his vehicle and beaten to death. The Dane felt certain that he, too, would be killed. His passport saved him. The harrowing experience did not put a stop to such excursions. Ironically, the 'tourist' eventually compromised himself – by appearing, in uniform, in an interview on Croatian television.

Kaj may well have been the first International. Nobody will ever know how many followed – hundreds, certainly. Among the first British volunteers was Dave Fersen, who admitted to being absent without leave from the French Foreign Legion, which he claimed to have joined after serving as a radio operator in the Royal Navy. Dave arrived in Zagreb in August 1991. After enquiring as to where the fighting was, he boarded a train for Sisak and from there took a bus to nearby Petrinja. He joined the forces of the Croatian Interior Ministry (MUP) a few days later. Dave recounted his involvement in various tasks including a series of attacks culminating in the seizure of a Yugoslav People's Army (JNA) radar installation. After six weeks he returned to Zagreb, where he encountered an ex-Legion SNCO, now an officer in the Croatian forces, who offered him the opportunity to serve as a sniper with a 'special unit' at Kumrovec. Dave accepted and was subsequently promoted to lieutenant. However, it quickly become apparent that, even as an officer, he could hardly expect to make a fortune. As a lieutenant, Dave could expect 16,000 dinars (about £140.00) a month. Ordinary soldiers' earnings equated to just £100.00 'beer and cigarette money'. Dissatisfied with the financial situation, the Briton returned home in November 1991.[15]

What was the attraction of serving as an International in Croatia? Certainly not the money.

When questioned, most foreign volunteers claimed they were ideologically motivated. They had seen the television and newspaper reports which, from the very beginning, portrayed the Serbs as 'the bad guys' and the Croats as the all but defenceless underdogs. The message was simple: Croatia needed help. What Croatia received was a handful of professional soldiers and an influx of pseudo-mercenaries with little or no formal military training. Among the former were those who had seen active service and, whether or not they cared to admit it, saw in Croatia a convenient opportunity to experience again the adrenaline rush that only combat provided. The latter category included impressionable youngsters whose notion of war owed much to Hollywood. They also considered the whole thing as an adventure, albeit for different reasons. Many looked on Croatia as some kind of romantic crusade. All of them enjoyed the macho 'merc' image. But anybody could *look* the part. Most left when the action started.

An exception was nineteen-year-old Neil Valentine, from London. He claimed to have temporarily

Left: Brian, a 51-year-old Englishman, claimed to have served with both the British and Australian armies. In early December 1991, he was the only British volunteer with HOS at Mala Bosna. 'I'll stay as long as they want me,' he said at the time. 'I've got nothing else to do – nothing to do and the rest of my life to do it in...' He is carrying what appears to be an M72B1 LMG with grenade launcher attached.

15. By November 1991 the dinar had been greatly devalued. Although the official exchange rate for £1.00 was about 38 dinars, the local currency was worthless outside the former Yugoslavia. Many people went by the black market rate, which at the time fluctuated at about 114 dinars

Right: Twenty three year old Karl Whitburn, a former electrician and pizza delivery man from Birmingham, on his last patrol about a kilometre from Serbian lines. Later the same day he discarded his rifle and uniform and took up residence with his girlfriend in Zagreb.

Below: Karl Whitburn in a fire position alongside a knocked-out T-34/85. His weapon is a 7.62mm

served as a boy soldier 'in the Guards'. Sympathy for the Croats and 'a dislike for communists' led to his departure to *Belgrade*, where amused officials redirected the politically naïve teenager to Croatia! Treated just like any other volunteer, Neil was assigned to a unit in Vinkovci where, for several weeks, he had ample time to learn to recognise the difference between incoming artillery, mortar and tank fire. Neil was fairly philosophical about the situation. The brutality of war, he admitted, 'does get you down sometimes, but you can't do anything about it'.

Some could though. The sudden realisation that they were now in a situation where injury or death was an occupational hazard was often too much. Karl Whitburn had been an electrician and pizza delivery man in Birmingham before concluding that there had to be more to life. Croatia seemed like a good choice, and soon after arriving in Zagreb the 23-year-old was accepted into the Croatian National Guard (ZNG) and sent to Vinkovci. A few weeks later, and now with 110 Brigade at Karlovac, south of the capital, Karl decided that he had had enough. Clearly disturbed by horror stories from the front-line, he seemed particularly concerned about what he could expect if captured by the dreaded Četniks. After returning from patrol one day, he left his assault rifle with colleagues in their farmhouse cellar 'bunker', changed into civilian clothes and returned to Zagreb and his Croatian girlfriend. Nobody tried to stop him.

Initially, the Internationals were welcomed. Unfortunately, there were those who lied unashamedly about their background, and generally the trusting Croats believed them. Those from Britain often claimed to be former members of the SAS or the Parachute Regiment or the Royal Marines. It seemed as though all the Americans had served in Special Forces and the Australians in the Special Air Service Regiment. All kinds claimed to have been in the French Foreign Legion. A few even had the berets to 'prove' it. While some simply made up the whole thing, others actually did belong to the Territorial Army and a few really did serve as regulars – before going AWOL. The Walter Mittys tended to attract media attention and did nothing for the reputation of the genuine professionals who, for the most part, avoided publicity. Those who agreed to be interviewed tended to be paranoid and not very cooperative, a dislike for the press being a common trait among servicemen.

Keith Phillips agreed to talk only because he knew this journalist from time spent together in the Royal Marines. After leaving the Corps, Keith had worked in airport security. He did not enjoy civilian life. Boredom drove him to take advantage of a voluntary redundancy scheme at a time when he was already considering Croatia. He was approaching 40. It would probably be his last opportunity to do again what he felt most suited to. Soon after, Keith took a train to Zagreb and introduced himself to an official at the Ministry of Defence. Satisfied with his credentials, the Croats assigned him to an anti-aircraft unit on the island of Pag. But, with little happening there, Keith again grew bored and transferred to the MUP. Subsequently, he was accepted into a 'Special Police Anti-Terrorist' group known, after their commanding officer, as 'Đuro's Men'. According to Keith, the unit had seen 'a lot of action' since its formation a year previously. During this time, not a single man had been lost. The ex-Royal Marine believed this was partly due to the attitude of the CO. 'We've got a real good boss,' Keith explained, 'He's an incredible man. He won't send his men out on anything that he considers is unsafe.'

Keith maintained that his role was that of an instructor and was reluctant to discuss his own involvement in any fighting, preferring instead to highlight the actions of his colleagues. They, in turn, spoke of how, in between training, Keith accompanied the men into battle. One episode, in particular, did much to enhance his reputation. Over open sights, Keith had used an FN rifle to shoot a Serb standing on a tank some 700–800 metres distant. The Croats were suitably impressed with such marksmanship. So was Keith, who in fact had been aiming at the tank itself, merely hoping that the round hitting the armour would be enough to discourage the enemy. By January 1994, Keith Phillips had left the police to join the army. A major now, he has settled in Zadar and has no plans to leave.

What of those whose pasts cannot be so easily verified? When someone goes under a pseudonym or refuses to provide his surname, checking up on that person can be a lengthy and often inconclusive process. Adrian, an Australian-Croat, hinted of previous service, perhaps as an officer with the Royal Australian Regiment. Brian, a portly Californian, claimed he was a former captain in the United States Marine Corps and 'still part of the military organisation' where his 'boss is a one-star in the navy'. Another Brian, British this time, allegedly served 'in Sarawak with the Green Jackets and Aden...' and in Vietnam with the Australian SAS. William, a Frenchman, said he was nineteen-years-old and had served two years in the French infantry. Nothing special about that. But, according to a colleague, William was later apprehended by the side he professed to be serving after being

Left: Instructors included a number of foreign personnel, the longest serving of whom was Keith Phillips, a former Royal Marines Commando.

Lower left: Another instructor was 22-year-old ex-Scots Guards, Bryn Hankin, seen here wearing British DPM camouflage.

observed returning from Serbian line at the time. He was wearing Croatian uniform at the time and claimed to be on a quest for his older brother who was fighting for the Serbs! The story is so fantastic that it may even be true. Later it was reported that William had become 'a liaison officer between the Croats and the mainly French UNPROFOR' around Zadar.[16]

When the war spilled into Bosnia-Herzegovina, a number of Internationals continued to fight there for the Bosnian Croats. Newcomers often elected to side with the Bosnian Muslims. A few are believed to have volunteered to serve with the Bosnian Serbs, whose forces also include Russian volunteers.

The effectiveness of these men is debatable. At best, some may well offer professional advice and leadership. At worse, they are simply cannon-fodder or even a hindrance. One thing is certain: their presence will hardly affect the outcome of this particularly brutal and protracted war.

THE SERBIAN GUARD AND MAJEVICA

Ninety kilometres north-east of Sarajevo, and overlooking Tuzla to the south-west, is the mountainous

region of Majevica. During the summer of 1992, Serbs and Muslims were engaged in a savage battle for control of the area. Much of the fighting was centred around a television and radio relay station high above the village of Priboj. From their bunkers and dug-outs, Serbian militiamen and irregulars maintained a tenuous hold in the face of infantry assaults, mortar and, judging by the size of some craters, artillery fire. Possession of Majevica means ownership of a vast area of rich agricultural land. The Serbs maintained that an ongoing Muslim offensive was also part of an overall plan to open a corridor linking Croatia with the country's south coast. In order to achieve their objective, the Muslims would need to seize Priboj, thereby providing a link north via Čelić and Brcko, to Croatia. However, the veracity of information depends very much on its source – at the same time, the BBC was reporting that the Muslims were accusing the *Serbs* of attempting to cut Bosnia in two!

Attempting to keep some kind of control in an ever-deteriorating situation was Major Ranko Lainović of 1st (Majevica) Battalion, the Serbian Guard. In existence since 1 May 1991, the Serbian Guard was commanded in the field by the major's brother, Branko 'Dugi' Lainović. Volunteers followed a sim-

Right: While moving through the ruins, a gunner, armed with a 7.62mm Yugoslav M84 General Purpose Machine Gun, keeps a watchful eye on the Muslim-occupied side of Vozuca

16. *Evening Standard*, 26 January 1993

148

ple doctrine that did not tolerate either deserters or traitors and supposedly disallowed any political affiliation. Allegiance was only to the Serbian people. (In fact, the Serbian Guard has been linked with the anti-Milošević Serbian Renewal Movement whose leader, Vuk Drašković, is a personal friend of Major Lainović.)

Major Lainović maintained that he was responsible for 680 personnel, including 104 'special operations' troops. In common with many other units, the Serbian Guard included volunteers from various ethnic groups, including Muslims who, for whatever reasons, had chosen to fight against their own kind. According to the major, his battalion held 72 kilometres of front-line in conjunction with local forces. Throughout the area, the war was conducted with customary ruthlessness. The Serbs related how two officers were captured while attempting to reach the bodies of two of their men, killed when Muslims overran their positions. Later, the bodies of all four were recovered. The officers were all but unrecognisable, having suffered horrific head and facial injuries caused, it was said, by

sledge-hammers. On another occasion, four wounded Serbs died when their ambulance was ambushed, allegedly after the Muslims had given it clearance to proceed. The Serbs described how the Muslims subsequently contacted them by radio and taunted them about the incident. Neither were civilians spared as villages and hamlets frequently became the front-line. Others were singled out for destruction simply because they happened to belong to the wrong side. 'Ethnic Cleansing' was practised by Serb, Croat and Muslim.

Majevica was typical in that opposing factions were totally convinced that only they were fighting for a just cause. Notwithstanding the fact that he came from Novi Sad, Major Ranko Lainović had no doubt whatsoever about his motives. As a Serb, he was helping the Bosnian Serbs to retain what was rightfully theirs. Just as he had helped the Serbs in Croatia.[17]

A VERY COMPLICATED SITUATION

Slovenia's war was over before the West could really grasp what was happening. Croatia was different. What began as a few internecine incidents quickly escalated into widespread violence before erupting into a full-scale war. It kept the media busy up to and beyond the January 1992 cease-fire – until events in neighbouring Bosnia-Herzegovina degenerated into an even bloodier affair.

Due primarily to its location, the Balkans has received considerably more news coverage than other, less accessible, conflicts of recent times. Nevertheless, some reports and statements have at times resulted in an over-simplification of a very complicated situation. In Croatia, a precedent was

Left: Shortly before this picture was taken, several mortar rounds, or possibly rifle grenades, landed close by. The tension clearly shows in the face of this member of the 'Silver Wolf Brigade'. Soon after, the area was declared clear and the patrol withdrew.

Above: Members of HOS at Vinkovci in December, 1991. The effect of continuous shelling was clearly evident in the expressions and mannerisms of some of these troops. Others seemed remarkably unaffected. Twenty-one-year-old Brankica Bukovski (far right) appeared to be more concerned about her appearance. 'I was on duty last night and slept late this morning', she explained when her picture was taken, 'so I haven't had time to brush my hair.'

17. The author was provided with an opportunity to spend time with the Serbian Guard. This portrait provides an example of just one of the many fighting formations in the region.

Below: Many foreigners have fought for the Croats, Serbs and Bosnians. This is 'Cliff', alias Ian Thorburn, with his T-54/55 at Nustar. Thorburn, who claimed to be AWOL from the British Army, maintained that he was in Croatia purely for ideological reasons.

established as the Serb-dominated Yugoslav People's Army deployed against the Croatian National Guard and police units. It was all too tempting then for the West to view the confrontation as one in which the Croats were simply defending their right to self-determination. This was something to which the general public could easily relate, but in fact it represented only part of the problem. The opinions of the Serbian community in Croatia were less publicized, and sometimes ignored altogether.

Listening to the arguments of all concerned does not necessarily provide one with a clear idea as to what is happening, but it does present a better understanding as to why a once-united people are now at war with themselves. Yet, paradoxically, such insight can also serve to confuse the issue further, for if the antagonists are to be believed it would appear that *everybody* is fighting for a just cause. Irrespective of whether or not this is actually so, journalists are expected to remain impartial. But how objective is news coverage? Before the war, about 1.9 million, or 44%, of those in Bosnia were registered as Muslim; 31% were Serb and 17%

Left: People must learn to adjust in areas subjected to mortar, artillery, tank and sniper fire. In many parts of the former Yugoslavia it can be fatal to remain on the streets for longer than is absolutely necessary. Motorists, taking advantage of lulls in the firing, will drive as fast as possible, hoping that they will be a more difficult target if the shooting starts up again. This lady was involved in an accident when two cars collided, apparently after a shell landed close. A young man in one of the vehicles was killed outright and a young woman with him critically injured. Two journalists in the other vehicle were slightly hurt. As this picture was taken, more shells were impacting less than 100 metres away.

Left: Croatian National Guard (ZNG) observing the Serbian village of Mirkovci. This area would soon be the scene of heavy fighting between former friends and neighbours.

Below: ZNG wearing East German helmet and camouflage suit near Privlaka during the winter of 1991.

Croat; but for a long time the media referred to Bosnian Serbs and Bosnian Croats as Serbs and Croats, and only to Bosnian Muslims as Bosnians. The inference is obvious and certainly contributed to influencing public opinion in the west.

The media has a responsibility to report all relevant facts, but in Bosnia major events are sometimes given little or no coverage.

In September and October 1992, the British media was offered controversial material acquired by three Western freelance journalists in Bosnia. Evidence was provided that supported Serbian allegations of a Muslim offensive in which the Serbs were suffering 'ethnic cleansing' and other atrocities. It was also disclosed that ammunition, supplied to the United Nations, was finding its way to those doing the fighting. At the time, not one television station and none of the national newspapers would even consider any of the stories.

In Bosnia there really is no right or wrong side, and as long as the West remains involved this fundamental fact must be taken into account, especially when considering any kind of solution in the region.

In February 1993 the United States proposed an alternative policy of arming the Muslims and bombing the Serbs. But America had not committed any ground troops to Bosnia, where those serving with UNPROFOR were better situated to foresee the potential hazards of such a move. No action was taken, but the possibility remained. In January 1994, when the matter of air strikes again became the subject of debate, the Bosnian Prime Minister, Haris Silajdžić, urged NATO to attack Serbian gun positions around Sarajevo. The following month there was international outrage when 68 people were reported killed and nearly 200 wounded, apparently by a single mortar bomb detonating in a crowded marketplace in the Bosnian capital. Although nobody was able to ascertain who was responsible, the Serbs were subsequently given ten days to withdraw their heavy weapons from around the city or face the consequences. Simultaneously NATO called upon the Muslims to place their heavy weapons under UN control. In another diplomatic move, apparently to dispel any accusations of prejudice, particularly from Moscow, US President Bill Clinton also announced that NATO would strike at *anybody* who continued to shell Sarajevo. The Serbs, no doubt realising who was likely to stand accused in the event of any such violation, prudently decided to comply with the ultimatum.

By June 1994 the pressure had increased for a lifting of the arms embargo on the Bosnian Muslims. Of course, with the ratification of the Muslim-Croat federation, the Bosnian Croats would also now benefit from the ending of such sanctions, leaving the Bosnian Serbs in an unenviable, and probably untenable, position. In the circumstances, the Serbs might relent and acquiesce to an internationally brokered settlement that would leave them with considerably less of Bosnia than they have at present. Or, they could continue fighting – and risk losing anyway, but at a far heavier cost – land secured in previous battles.

In any event, there can be no victors, only victims.

Far Left: Life returns to Vukovar, 15 May 1993. Once part of Croatia, now a city in the Republic of Serbian Krajina.

Lower far left: Remains of a chandelier still hanging in the ruins of the Serbian Orthodox Church at Vukovar.

Left: Members of the 1st Battalion The Prince of Wales's Own Regiment of Yorkshire during a quiet moment near Prozor.

Below left: This railway bridge on the River Bosut once linked Privlaka to Vinkovci, five kilometres to the north.

Left: Serb with locally manufactured grenade-launcher.

Left: Major Ranko Lainovic, commander of 1st (Majevica) Battalion, the Serbian Guard. By all accounts an extremely brave individual, the effects of a bitter war were nevertheless clearly evident in the nervous mannerisms displayed by this officer. Like all those involved in the fighting in Bosnia-Herzegovina, Major Lainovic firmly believed that his was a just cause. 'We are just saving our homes,' he maintained. 'Because of this, God has to be on our side...'

Right: Nineteen-year-old Neil Valentine, from London, after several weeks in Vinkovci in December 1991.

Far right: Nineteen-year-old Goca Borenovic was the only woman serving with the Serbian Guard at Lopare. In April 1992 she decided to visit her brother, a soldier then serving at Sremska Mitrovica. While there, recalled Goca, 'The borders were closed and I was unable to return to Sanski Most.' She remained at Sremska Mitrovica for three and a half months before volunteering to fight. Goca had heard nothing from her parents for more than four months. Her brother, she knew, was at the front near Banja Luka. For Goca, Lopare was now home. 'I'm very happy,' she maintained. 'I don't see any reason why I shouldn't be.'

Right: Milorad Jovic, a veteran of the fighting in Croatia, recalled that initially the unit refused to allow Goca into battle. 'She used to cry, because we wouldn't let her go with us, because she's too young. But, in the end, because of the tears, we took her.' She had quickly proven herself. 'She is excellent,' said Milorad, proudly. 'Better than a lot of men.'

155

156

Opposite page, top and bottom: 1 September 1992: While covering a patrol forward of the Serbian lines, a camera team from Television Novi Sad is forced to take cover after coming under fire from nearby Muslim positions. There followed a deadly game of cat and mouse, during which both sides taunted the other with shouted threats and insults and sporadic bursts of rifle fire. Eventually, all the Serbs managed to return to their own lines.

Right: Member of the Serbian Guard outside Battalion Headquarters at Lopare. He is armed with a 7.62mm Yugoslav M72B1 LMG.

158

Left: The war coined a new phrase: 'Ethnic Cleansing'. At Prozor, the Muslim community lived in a state of terror in anticipation of the time when the Croats might order them to leave – or worse. Two Croatian commandos, en route back to their unit, found themselves in the Muslim suburb after their vehicle took a wrong turn. Trembling and crying with fear, a woman approached and offered a bottle of *rakija* (local 'brandy') to the men who, she thought, had come to kill her.

Above: The commandos, however, expressed their sympathy. Visibly upset, the senior of the pair, an officer named Rudolf, promised to send some of his men to safeguard the Muslims against possible attack by the Croats. Here 'Joe', one of the commandos, jokes with Dino, a little Muslim boy. A few months after these pictures were taken, the Croats *did* 'cleanse' Prozor of its Muslim population. Early in 1994 Rudolf was reported killed at Gornji Vakuf. The fate of 'Joe' and the villagers is unknown.

Left: Muslim prisoners near Lopare, on 2 September 1992. All claimed to be civilians forcibly removed from their homes – 'Muslim places on Serbian territory', according to Television Novi Sad's Darko Kamarit, seen interviewing one of the men. None knew the fate of their families. In contrast to other, much publicised Western reports about the maltreatment of Muslim captives, this particular group appeared to be well-treated and on good terms with their guards.

BIBLIOGRAPHY

Paul Harris, *Somebody Else's* War: *Frontline Reports from the Balkan Wars*, Spa Books, 1992.

Misha Glenny, *The Fall of Yugoslavia: The Third Balkan War*, Penguin Books, 1992.

Edgar O'Ballance, *Civil War in Yugoslavia*, Galago, 1993.

Lada Čale Feldman, (*et al*), *Fear, Death and Resistance: An Ethnography of War: Croatia 1991–1992,* Zagreb Institute of Ethnology and Folklore Research (etc.), 1993.

Rabia Ali and Lawrence Lifschultz, *Why Bosnia? Writings on the Balkan War*, The Pamphleteer's Press Inc, 1993.

Colonel Bob Stewart, *Broken Lives: A Personal View of the Bosnian Conflict*, Harper Collins Publishers, 1993.

Eric Micheletti and Yves Debay, *War in the Balkans: 600 Days of Conflict in War-torn Yugoslavia*, Histoire and Collections, 1993.

Bloody Bosnia: A European Tragedy, The Guardian and Channel 4 Television, 1993.

Paul Beaver, *Jane's Sentinel: The Unfair Advantage: The Balkans*, Jane's Information Group, 1993.

Lee Bryant, *The Betrayal of Bosnia*, University of Westminster Press, 1993.

Ed Vulliamy, *Seasons in Hell: Understanding Bosnia's War,* Simon and Schuster, 1994.

Mihailo Crnobrnja, *The Yugoslav Drama*, I. B. Tauris, 1994.

Mark Almond, *Europe's Backyard War: The War in the Balkans*, William Heinemann, 1994.